William C. Magee

The Gospel and the Age

sermons on special occasions

William C. Magee

The Gospel and the Age
sermons on special occasions

ISBN/EAN: 9783337285562

Printed in Europe, USA, Canada, Australia, Japan

Cover: Foto ©Lupo / pixelio.de

More available books at **www.hansebooks.com**

THE GOSPEL AND THE AGE

THE GOSPEL AND THE AGE

Sermons on Special Occasions

By W. C. MAGEE, D.D.
LORD BISHOP OF PETERBOROUGH

SECOND THOUSAND

LONDON
WM. ISBISTER, Limited
56, LUDGATE HILL
1884

LONDON:
PRINTED BY J. S. VIRTUE AND CO., LIMITED,
CITY ROAD.

PREFACE.

The sermons contained in this volume were preached, as their title states, on special occasions. They were selected for publication not as possessing, for that reason, any special merit, but because they were the only ones the publication of which was possible for their author.

The preacher of what are called extempore sermons—that is to say, sermons not read from manuscript, but delivered from brief notes—cannot reproduce them in print unless they happen to have been taken down at the time by a reporter. Such reports can hardly ever be verbatim, and are for the most part more or less imperfect and inaccurate. The process of revising them and of supplying their omissions, with a view to publication, is not an easy one, even when attempted after the lapse of a few days—still less so after that of years; and its results are rarely quite satisfactory either to the author or the reader. A sermon thus patched and mended has neither the freshness and point of the extempore nor the smoothness and sustained thought of the written composition. It is neither a religious speech, which the extempore sermon ought to be—nor a religious essay, which the written sermon ought to be; and it runs the risk of uniting the defects of both styles with the merits of neither. Such as it is, however, this method was the only one available for me, when, in compliance with many and repeated requests, I employed the enforced leisure of a long convalescence in preparing for the press those few sermons of mine which have been reported with sufficient accuracy to allow of the attempt to reproduce them in somewhat better form.

Their dates and occasions have been given in order to explain expressions and allusions in most of them which would otherwise have been unmeaning. Their title was chosen because, when put together, they seemed mainly pervaded by the thought—which should indeed never be absent from the mind of a preacher—of the antagonisms between the Gospel which he preaches and the spirit of the Age in which he lives, and by the desire to find, if possible, some reconcilements of these, or, where this is not possible, some clearer conception of them and of the reasons for them.

Most deeply thankful shall I be if any word in these sermons shall have proved helpful, in this respect, to any earnest thinker or doubter. I would ask of such an one, if such there be, that he would, in return, give the preacher a place in his prayers, and that he would ask for him that he may be enabled more and more to realize in his heart and set forth in his life whatever of truth there may be in the thoughts he has thus endeavoured, however imperfectly, to convey to others.

BEACH HOUSE, WORTHING,
April 30*th*, 1884.

CONTENTS.

I.
THE SEEKER AFTER A SIGN AND THE SEEKER AFTER
    WISDOM 1
    An Ordination Sermon preached in Whitehall Chapel, London,
    December 23rd, 1860.

II.
THE FINAL OVERTHROW OF EVIL . 31
    Oxford Lent Sermons, 1866.

III.
THE MISSIONARY TRIALS OF THE CHURCH . . . 55
    Anniversary of the Church Missionary Society, St. Bride's
    Church, Fleet Street, London, April 30th, 1866.

IV.
REBUILDING THE WALL IN TROUBLOUS TIMES . . 87
    Preached at St. Andrew's Church, Dublin, November 30th,
    1866.

V.
THE VICTOR, MANIFEST IN THE FLESH . 113
    Oxford Lent Sermons, 1867.

VI.
SPEAKING PARABLES 137
    St. Paul's Cathedral, 1867.

VII.
THE CHRISTIAN THEORY OF THE ORIGIN OF THE
    CHRISTIAN LIFE 153
    Preached before the British Association, Norwich Cathedral,
    August 23rd, 1868.

VIII.

THE BREAKING NET 179
 Preached before the Dublin Church Congress, St. Patrick's Cathedral, September 29th, 1868.

IX.

CHRISTIANITY, A GOSPEL FOR THE POOR . . . 203
 St. Paul's Cathedral, 1876.

X.

THE GATHERING OF THE VULTURES 221
 St. Paul's Cathedral, 1878.

XI.

KNOWLEDGE WITHOUT LOVE 239
 The "Pride" Sermon. Preached before the University of Oxford, November 23rd, 1879.

XII.

THE ETHICS OF FORGIVENESS 257
 Preached before the University of Oxford, 1880.

XIII.

THE HAPPY SERVANTS AND THE UNHAPPY SON . . 275
 Preached before the University of Oxford, 1881.

XIV.

MORALITY AND DOGMA 293
 Preached before the University of Oxford, 1881.

XV.

THE BIBLE HUMAN AND YET DIVINE 309
 Preached at the Jubilee of the Peterborough Auxiliary of the British and Foreign Bible Society, Peterborough Cathedral, April 18th, 1882.

THE SEEKER AFTER A SIGN AND THE SEEKER AFTER WISDOM.

B

THE SEEKER AFTER A SIGN AND THE SEEKER AFTER WISDOM.

An Ordination Sermon, preached at Whitehall Chapel, London, Dec. 23, 1860.

> "For the Jews require a sign, and the Greeks seek after wisdom: But we preach Christ crucified, unto the Jews a stumblingblock and unto the Greeks foolishness; But unto them which are called, both Jews and Greeks, Christ the power of God, and the wisdom of God."
>
> 1 Cor. i. 22—24.

TWO facts are here recorded by St. Paul as the result of his experience as a preacher of the Gospel. First, that this Gospel provoked hostility wherever it was preached; that it was rejected, not by men of one nation or of one creed alone, but by men of all nations and of all creeds. No two races, no two types of the human mind, could have been more widely different, more directly the opposite of each other, than the Jew and the Greek. The very fact that the Gospel was displeasing to the one might therefore have led us to expect that it would be sure to please the other. And yet Jews and Greeks, who agreed in nothing else, agreed in rejecting Christ. "He was to the Jews a stumblingblock, and to the Greeks foolishness." Nevertheless, St. Paul tells us, in the second place, this Gospel possessed just those very qualities, for the seeming want of which Jew and Greek refused to receive it. The Jew rejected it for its seeming want of power; he demanded "a sign," an evidence of its Divine origin, greater than any it had ever given. The Greek rejected it for its seeming want of wisdom; and yet Christ crucified was "to the called, both Jew and Greek," both wisdom and power; nay, the perfection of wisdom and power. "Christ the power of God and the wisdom of God."

Christ, then, was, according to the experience of Paul, just what the Prophets had foretold He should be; at once the "desire of all nations," and the "despised and rejected of men." "The messenger of the Covenant, in whom they should delight" and yet "He in whom they should see no beauty that they should desire Him. He was at once all that men most needed and all that they most disliked.

And it is in the union of these two facts that we have the strongest proof that Christ crucified is really God's gift to man—the Father's provision for the wants of His suffering children; for it shows us that Christ is all that man wants, and yet that the human mind could never have imagined a Christ. If the Gospel had really been deficient in any one element of human happiness, if it left the need of any part of man's nature unsatisfied, then it could not have been, what it claims to be, God's good news—God's revelation of blessing to all men. But, on the other hand, if this Gospel, which is so wonderfully adapted to our nature, which does so completely satisfy all our wants, had been universally and at once received by all men, then it might have been said, This Christ the Saviour is but a thought of the human mind; He is only the dream of a suffering humanity picturing to itself a deliverer from all its woes—the mirage of the human soul in its fever-thirst for happiness. Now, against this notion stands the fact, that, so far from the idea of a Christ being the natural product of the human mind, it was just what the mind of man naturally disliked and rejected. Christ crucified was no Jewish legend; He was "to the Jews a stumbling-block." Christ crucified was no Greek myth; "He was to the Greeks foolishness." Most precious, then, amongst the evidences of our faith, is this record of the twofold experience of its greatest missionary, proving, as it does, at once the fitness of the Gospel for man's need and yet the odiousness of the Gospel to man's prejudices, and going, therefore, far towards proving that the Christ of the Gospel is, indeed, nothing less than the " wisdom and the power of God."

But for those who inherit Paul's mission, for all preachers of the Gospel, these words are more than an evidence; they are a prophecy. His experience is that of all who preach Christ crucified. They find, in every age, that the Gospel contains all that the age requires and yet that this is just what that age complains the Gospel does not supply. They find that the desire of the generation in which they live, that thing, be it what it may, for which men are crying out most earnestly, is just that very thing which the Gospel, and the Gospel alone, can give. So much so that, in fact, the complaint of each age against the Gospel will always indicate, unerringly, that very aspect of it which most needs to be brought out in the preaching of it. Nay, more; not only is the experience of St. Paul thus broadly and generally fulfilled in that of all preachers of Christianity, but it is repeated in all its circumstances and details. All true preachers of it encounter the very same opposition that he did, arising from the same causes. For the opposition which the Gospel met with in St. Paul's day was not of that day alone. The Jew and the Greek, the seeker after the sign and the seeker after wisdom, exist always. Still, wherever the Gospel is preached, must the preacher expect to hear from each of these the same demand that Paul heard; still must he find, with Paul, Christ crucified a stumblingblock to the one and foolishness to the other. For these two—the seeker after the sign and the seeker after wisdom—the man who would rest all religion, all philosophy, all social polity, upon authority alone, and the man who would rest them all upon reason alone—this Jew, with his reverence for power, his love of custom and tradition—which are the power of the past—his tendency to rest always in outward law and form—the power of the present—his distaste for all philosophical speculation, his impatience of novelty, his dread of change—leaning always to the side of despotism in society and of superstition in religion,—and, on the other hand, this Greek, with his subtle and restless intellect, his taste for speculation, his want of reverence for the past, his desire of change, his love of novelty, his leaning towards licence in society and scepticism in religion; what are they—these two—but the representatives of those two opposite types of mind which divide and always have divided, all mankind? Do we not find them wherever man is found, appearing at every great crisis, whether in religion, or philosophy, or politics, in broadly-marked contrast, and shaping, by their antagonistic influences, the history of every sect, and school, and state? Must we not expect, therefore, to trace the effects of these opposing influences, these two great currents of the human mind, upon Christianity, as upon all else? Must we not expect to find them, as Paul found them, displaying themselves, now in the denial, now in the corruption and the perversion of the faith; knowing as we do, that whatever tendencies induce a man, in the first instance, to reject any truth, will, after he has received it, tempt him to pervert it?

If we would therefore be truly the successors of the great Apostle; if we would prove ourselves, like him, able ministers of the New Testament—able at once to preach and to preserve the faith once delivered to the saints; able at once to feed and to guard the flock over which the Holy Ghost has made us overseers; if we would deal as wisely, as lovingly, as tenderly, as successfully, with those whose souls we desire to win for Christ, as he did, we must understand why it was that the Jew and the Greek alike refused to believe him, and how it was that he dealt with each of them. We must study carefully this account which he gives of the Gospel in its encounter with the wants and the requirements, the desires and the prejudices of his age.

Let us consider, then, first, *What it was that Jew and Greek demanded of Christ;* secondly, *How the Gospel, though refusing to give it in the form in which they asked for it, really gave the very thing they each desired?*

I. And, first; What was the demand of the Jew? He "required a sign." We know from the Gospels what this "sign" was; it was one particular miracle selected by the Jews as the test of our Lord's claims; "the sign from heaven," or "the sign of the Son of Man in the heavens," which they so repeatedly asked for. The miracles of Christ did not sufficiently prove His mission for the Jew, who knew that there might be false miracles as well as true,—nay, that false teachers might work real miracles.* However great, therefore, or however numerous the miracles Christ wrought, they still left the question undecided whether He was or was not the Messiah. The Jews demanded, therefore, such a miracle as would leave no room for doubt; some sign from heaven, some glory or wonder in the sky, wrought manifestly and undoubtedly by God Himself, which should compel all who saw it to believe. This was that "sign" which they were always demanding of Christ, and it

* Deut. xiii. 1—3.

was that sign which our Lord would never give.* Never would he grant them such a display of Divine power as should leave no need for attending to all the other proofs of His mission; all the moral evidence of His spotless life and of His words of wisdom; all the scriptural evidence from the Law and the Prophets which testified of Him. And because He would not do this—because He would never force them to believe in spite of themselves, because He would never give them such a demonstration of His mission as would relieve them from the difficulty and responsibility of judging for themselves and the necessity of bringing themselves into a fit condition for judging impartially—they refused to believe in Him. If He would only have complied with their requirements, if—divesting Himself of all those conditions of humiliation and weakness which offended their prejudices and provoked their unbelief—He had appeared in all the overwhelming glory of His divinity, silencing at once all doubt by the manifestation of power and of power alone, they would have received Him; but because He would not do this they rejected Him. A Christ appearing in glory in the heavens, Him they would receive; a Jesus walking in lowly goodness on the earth, dying on a cross from which He will not descend at their bidding even to win their belief, Him they will have none of. "Christ crucified is a stumblingblock to the Jew."

Exactly opposite to the demand of the Jew was that of the Greek. He asked for no sign, he cared nothing for the supernatural, he had ceased to believe in it. He believed only in nature; he sought only for wisdom to understand himself and the world in which he lived; he asked from Christ only light on those problems in

* Matt. xii. 38. Mark viii. 11, 12.

external nature, or in himself, on which his subtle mind was ever working. He wanted a perfect philosophy, or, at least, a perfect morality, which could justify itself to his intellect by solving all those difficulties which beset all other philosophies and all other systems of morals. Could Christianity do this? Could it tell him what was mind, and how it differed from matter? Could it tell him whether he was governed by fate or by free-will? Could it tell him whence came evil? If it could, he was willing to listen to it and to believe all that it could prove. But then for such teaching there was no need of miracles any more than there was for the teaching of geometry. All that was true in it he would receive on its own evidence, and he would receive nothing that did not so prove itself to be true.

This Gospel, then, displeased the Greek just because it would not give him what he wanted, and because it offered him exactly what he did not want. It left unsolved those mysteries which he was always trying to solve, while it required him to accept miraculous legends which he despised. To the eager, ambitious questionings of that daring intellect that would fain scale Heaven itself in its search after knowledge and demand from Him who sits upon its throne reason for all His deeds and proof for all His words, the Gospel gave no answer. It revealed still the same horizon of impenetrable cloud that bounds the view of all the dwellers upon earth, though it declared that beyond that veil of cloud there shines the light to which no man can approach. Or, if it shed at all a clearer light upon any of those things he had desired to know, it did so but as the telescope resolves for the astronomer some dim nebulous mystery of the heavens only by bringing at the same time some remoter and hitherto unseen mystery into view. It told him, if not of the origin, at least of the end of evil; but it did so by revealing to him the mystery of the Atonement by which he was redeemed from evil. It told him that man was not the slave of Fate; but it did so by revealing to him the mystery of the Incarnate Christ, his living Lord and Master. In one word, it showed him POWER—the power of Christ the Saviour, supernatural, miraculous, mysterous, divine; and to this power it demanded his submission; and, because it did this, he would have none of it. A Jesus, a wise and pure teacher of a pure system of morals, he might receive; but a Christ incarnate, redeeming, atoning, rising from the dead, a supernatural being with supernatural claims to his obedience, this was no better than the old fables of his own mythology which he had long outgrown! This was "foolishness" to him.

Thus we see that the Jew rejected the Gospel of Christ because it had not enough of the supernatural; the Greek, because it had too much: the Jew, because it did not give the miraculous evidence he demanded; the Greek, because it had any miracles at all: the Jew, because it did not compel him to believe; the Greek, because it required him to do so: or, in the words of our text, the Jew, because it was not all power; the Greek, because it was not all wisdom.

But so long as the Apostles were faithful to their mission they never could have preached the Gospel so as to satisfy the demand of either Jew or Greek. For they were sent into the world not to propound dogmas nor to teach a philosophy, but to relate a history. They were sent to testify to what they had "seen and heard and their hands had handled, of the word of life;" sent to be witnesses to the facts of the birth, life, work, words, death, resurrection and ascension of Jesus Christ. These they were to tell to men; and so long as they told these facts fully and faithfully, they must necessarily have offended both the seeker after the sign and the seeker after wisdom. For their story describes a Christ neither altogether supernatural, as the Jew required Him to be, nor yet altogether natural, as the Greek required Him to be; but a Christ who is both. Perfect man in all the reality of His human nature; perfect God in all the mystery of His Divine essence. The story reveals for the Jew a sign and a wonder *from* heaven, but not *in* it; not flashing out from the sky in awful majesty, but dwelling on the earth in lowly and loving goodness. It is a Galilean carpenter, who stills the sea and wakes the dead. It is round the cross of a condemned criminal that the heavens grow dark, and the earth quakes; and from this cross Christ will not descend to win men's belief. The Gospel is the story of a Christ *crucified*. On the other hand, it reveals for the Greek a human teacher speaking words of wisdom such as never man spoke before; but it bids him believe this Man to be the great power of God. It shows him Jesus on earth; but shows him, too, heaven opened and angels ascending and descending on the Son of Man. It shows him a cross and a grave; but it bids him say at the foot of that cross, with the Gentile witness who stood there, "Truly this man is the Son of God:" it bids him look into that grave spoiled of its tenant, and worship Him who rose from it.

This Gospel then, this simple narrative of the life and death of Christ, is that which makes it impossible for the preacher of it, so long as he is faithful to his mission, to accommodate Christianity to the demands of his age. It is the *history* of Christ crucified which opposes ever an insuperable resistance to every attempt to explain the *doctrine* of Christ crucified into a philosophy, or to darken it into a superstition; and it is this history therefore which made, and will ever make, the Gospel "a stumblingblock" to the superstitious seeker after a sign, and "foolishness" to the philosophical seeker after wisdom.

And if the Apostles had attempted to satisfy the Jew or the Greek—if they had accommodated the Gospel to the demand of the one by adding to it the amount of miracle he asked for, or to that of the other by divesting it of all its supernatural character—then their Gospel would not have been worth the preaching; it would have ceased to be the Gospel; God's good news for man. For what is the good news of the Gospel? It is salvation from sin; it is the deliverance of man from the evil that is in him and has become a part of him. And what is this evil? It is enmity to God. The curse of the fallen man is that he does not love God; does not believe that God loves him, that He is the Father who in all His commands only wills his happiness. Man does not believe this. He distrusts God. Now, until this distrust and dislike of God is removed, man is not and cannot be saved; any change wrought on him, short of this, is not a saving change. It would not suffice, for instance, to place him in circumstances in which his disobedience, which is only the expression of his distrust, should be restrained by terror; nor again, to give him such clear knowledge that his unbelief, which is only another expression of distrust, should have no provocation; for in such a case the nature of the man would remain still unchanged, the unbelief and the disobedience would be repressed, not eradicated. Remove the terror that enforces his submission; give any new revelation which passes beyond the bounds of his knowledge, and the distrust breaks out again at once in disobedience or unbelief. The revelation of God, then, to man, which is to save him, must not be one which makes it impossible for him to doubt or disobey; it must rather be one which makes it possible for him to believe and to obey; one which, leaving room for doubt and disobedience, yet enables him to overcome doubt and to subdue disobedience; one which enables him to wrestle with, to conquer, to slay the evil in him, not one which merely lulls that evil to sleep. It must be, in short, a revelation which brings him face to face with his first temptation, and bids him hear again the question, "Hath God said?" yet which does not force him, but only helps him, enables him, if he *will* do so, to say, "Yea, God hath said, and I will trust Him and obey."

Let us suppose, for instance, that the Jew had obtained his wish, and that the sign of the Son of Man had appeared in the heavens, in all the awful splendour of His Divine Majesty. There would certainly have been no room for doubt in the mind of those who saw that sign; sore afraid, they would have owned the dreadful power of a present God: but neither would there have been room for faith or love. There could have been no possibility of that free play of all the spiritual faculties, that contest of opposing forces, that strife of faith and hope and holiness, with doubt and fear and sin, by which the spirit-life in man grows and strengthens. No change would have passed on the spirit of the Jew; he would not have loved or trusted God one whit the more for all the glory or the terror of the sign that displayed His power. We know this, because we know that there will come a day when the dream of the Jew will be realised, when "the sign of the Son of Man shall be seen in the heavens in power and great glory;" and yet those who see it shall not be moved to love or trust: they will "cry to the rocks to fall on them, and the mountains to hide them from the wrath of the Lamb." No! power may compel assent, but never can create trust. "The devils believe and tremble."

Again, suppose that the Greek had had his wish, that all miracle and mystery had vanished from the Gospel, and that it had become a mere moral philosophy; there would have been no room for doubt here certainly, but as surely no room for faith, no discipline of the heart, no training of the spirit, no moral progress. The Gospel would have been a philosophy, like any other; showing him what he ought to be, but giving him no power to become that thing it described. He would have had no more difficulty, it is true, in receiving it than in receiving the truths of mathematics, and it would have done him just as much good as mathematics; it might have added to his knowledge, might have sharpened his intellect, or elevated his fancy, or refined his taste, but it never could have changed his heart. It would have given him wisdom, the "wisdom of this world which comes to nought," just because it is of this world, beginning and ending with this life to which it belongs; but giving him no knowledge of, bringing him no help from, the higher and the diviner life without which he perishes. "Plentifully declaring" to him, in all its wise saws and moral axioms, "the thing that is;" telling him that "virtue alone is happiness," and that "vice is unworthy of man;" bidding him "cease to do evil, and learn to do well:" but only omitting to tell him *how* he is to cease to do evil, and *where* he is to get the power to do well; such wisdom as this it would have given him. But it could never have given him that "wisdom of God" which, because it is from God, *does* reveal to man the mystery of a higher life—the power of the world to come—which *does* tell him how he may obtain those things beyond this life "which eye hath not seen, nor ear heard, neither hath it entered into the heart of man to conceive;" but which—because it must be received, not by the intellect, but by the spirit of man, revealed to it by the Spirit of God in words which that Spirit teacheth—is foolishness to that "natural man which receiveth not the things of God."

Thus we see, that, widely different as the demands of the Jew and the Greek seemed at first, they were really asking one and the same thing; they were asking for an *unspiritual religion;* a revelation that should not deal with the heart at all in the way of trial or discipline, which would spare them the great trial of being called on to trust and to love, in spite of doubt and difficulty. What they sought for, in one word, was knowledge without belief. The Jew demanded a demonstration of God to his senses; the Greek demanded a demonstration of God to his intellect. The Jew required a revelation that should compel assent; the Greek required one that should give no occasion for doubt. Both demanded a religion without faith, both asked to see, both refused to believe in, an invisible God, and, therefore, both rejected a crucified Christ.

II. We have seen, then, what the Jew and the Greek demanded of the Gospel, and why the Gospel refused it. We have to see, in the next place, that the Gospel really gives in another form just what they demanded. Their demand was certainty; the certainty of knowledge. Let us see if the Gospel gives this.

The Gospel reveals Christ crucified; that is to say, it reveals to us, invites us to trust in, a person. Now, there is this difference between assent to a fact or a proposition and trust in a person; that in the one case perfect knowledge is absolutely necessary, in the other it is not. I must know the whole of an alleged fact before I can believe it; I must understand the whole of a proposition before

I can assent to it. But in the case of a person knowledge may be imperfect, and yet it may be enough to warrant the most implicit trust. I may know the being in whom I trust so far that I may feel assured he is utterly incapable of deceiving me; I may find in his teaching such wisdom and beauty, such knowledge of me and my wants, I may find in all his conduct such tender love and care for me, that I would sooner die than doubt him. And yet there may be much concerning him of which I may be ignorant; much of his previous history may be unknown to me; many things he says I may not understand; all his purposes I cannot fathom; and yet I trust him with my whole heart. Thus, you see, there may be perfect trust, and yet imperfect knowledge; such, for instance, as that of the child who trusts his parent implicitly but understands him imperfectly, who trusts, not because he knows, but in order that he may know; whose belief is, in fact, the necessary condition of all his knowledge.

But then, be it observed, this trust of mine will depend entirely upon my moral condition; will depend, that is to say, upon whether I am like or unlike the being I am asked to trust in. If I am unjust, untrue, unloving, I cannot believe in his truth and love; I cannot so much as imagine them, or understand them when I see them; I shall be jealous, suspicious, distrustful, hostile: and, on the other hand, it will be only in proportion as I am like him, only so far as I have in me some truth and righteousness and love, that I shall trust him. And thus my acquaintance with such a man will be at once a moral test and a moral discipline. It will always depend upon my own will and my own life how far I shall understand him and trust in him.

And is not this just the test and the discipline to which the Gospel submits us? It reveals an object for our trust—Christ, the righteous man, holy, harmless, undefiled, tender and compassionate, loving and faithful even unto death; Christ the all-powerful Son of God, mighty to save. And we are bid to trust in Him, to believe that He can save us; to believe Him when He says that He has come from God His Father, to seek and to save us, the lost and the perishing; to trust Him when He tells us that He is as powerful as He is good, as able as He is willing to save us; to hearken to Him when He calls us to rise up and leave all for His sake; to obey Him, as, calling to us from the cross on which He hangs a sacrifice for us, He bids us take up our cross and follow Him, and promises us that in the might of that cross we shall overcome the world, even as He has overcome it. And the trial is, will we trust in Him? The discipline is, to learn to trust in Him. He will not dispense with that trial and that discipline by forcing us to believe or to obey in spite of ourselves. He will, indeed, make it reasonable that we should believe. As He comes to be the restorer of the life of our spirits, so will He, in token of this, be the restorer and the giver of life in all the lower domains of life. As He comes to give us a diviner and a truer wisdom, so will He speak words of heavenly wisdom. But neither His wisdom nor His miracles are such as to divert our attention from Himself, His goodness, His holiness, His truth. "Believe me," He still says, rather than My works. And therefore it is that He veils His glory in weakness and hides His wisdom in parables and mingles with His gracious words hard sayings that offend; so that those who trust Him not may reject the sign and those who love Him not may deny the wisdom: while those, and those alone, who love and trust Him, will reply to every doubt, to every temptation to desert Him,—"To whom shall we go?" "He, and He alone, has the words of eternal life." And thus He is ever a test and a trial to all who behold Him. Those who *will* see Him, as He is, may; those who will not, who wish not to see him, shall not. But for those who do there is a daily growth in trust and love, an ever-increasing assurance that He is the wisdom and power of God; "For to as many as believe on Him to them giveth He POWER to become sons of God."

And thus the Gospel does at last give us that very certainty of knowledge which it seems at first to refuse. Christ crucified, received into the heart, works there the very sign; gives the very wisdom that the Jew demanded and the Greek sought for in vain. He works in the heart of man a greater, a more convincing miracle than any recorded in the Gospel. He wakes the dead soul to life, feeds it with heavenly food, casts out the unclean spirits that have made it their abode, and enters in and dwells there, stilling the war of its wild elements, rebuking the winds and waves of its stormy passions into peace; and he who feels himself the subject of this miracle, sees in his soul the true sign of the Son of Man, knows, with the same absolute certainty that he knows any object presented to his senses, that Christ in him is "the power of God." Again; in the soul of the believer, He sheds abroad that light of heavenly wisdom by which it sees God and itself, lighting up all the mysteries of the word, shining down into the depths of man's spiritual being, showing there "the wondrous works of the Lord," making him wise with that unction from the Holy One, by which he knows all things; and he who has this light in his soul sees, as plainly as he can see any fact in nature, any demonstration of science, that Christ in him is "the wisdom of God." And yet in this inward assurance, this experimental evidence of the Gospel, there is no fanaticism, no mysticism, no exclusive appeal to an inward light, dispensing with all other sources of knowledge. The Gospel is still the Gospel of Christ crucified, still links itself with real and objective fact. It is the Christ of history, the Christ whose deeds and words we know, the Christ who instituted the church and the sacraments, who is, in the soul, wisdom and power. For the Gospel of Christ, because it is to save the whole man, addresses itself to all the man; not to the senses alone, though it has power as its evidence for the senses; not to the intellect alone, though it has wisdom as its evidence for the intellect; not to the emotions alone, though it speaks to the heart: but to all three, and all three together. Christianity is not a merely intellectual, nor yet a merely sensuous, nor yet a merely intuitional religion; but it is all these, and all of them together. And thus we see how the Gospel does give what men ask, only not *as* they ask. They desire certainty, the certainty of *knowledge;* it gives the certainty of *trust*. They ask for knowledge without faith, and the result is, they obtain neither knowledge nor faith; the Gospel requires faith in order to knowledge, and those who receive it gain knowledge as the reward of faith. "They *know* in whom they have believed, and are persuaded that He is able to keep that which they have intrusted to Him;" because He has been, because He is becoming for them, more and more in their own soul's experience, "Christ the wisdom of God, and the power of God,"—Christ in them "the hope of glory."

III. And now that we have seen what was the demand of the Jew and the Greek in Paul's day, is it not clear that the Jew and the Greek exist still, have always existed; that the Gospel, then and now and always, has to encounter the demand of those who ask for the sign or who seek after wisdom? On the one hand, do we not see the craving for the sign—for the display, that is, of supernatural power, crushing and silencing all doubt—resulting in all superstitious corruptions of Christianity? For what is superstition, but an appeal from wisdom to power, an effort to silence the reason by the terrors of the senses? Once the seeker after the sign believes that he beholds it, is it not obvious that, by the very conditions he has imposed upon himself, he has lost all right to ask for further proof, or to question the utterances of the oracle he has himself chosen? If the Jews were prepared to believe in Christ, in spite of all that seemed to them unscriptural in His teaching, provided only He gave them the sign they demanded, then it is clear, that if ever any one should come who would give, or seem to give them this sign, or any other which they might hold to be sufficient to demonstrate his mission, they would implicitly believe him, whatever the character of his teaching might be. The very idea of doubting or denying any word of such a teacher would be blasphemy; and the greater the difficulty, the greater would be the merit in believing. Thus, the demand for the sign and the sign alone, as the sole reason for belief, leaves the seeker after it liable to be deceived by every false teacher who can only persuade him that he possesses it; makes him the slave of him, whoever he may be, who seems to hold the talisman that he has bound himself to obey. It was so with the Jew. The nation that rejected and crucified the true Christ, believed in and shed its blood for more than one false Christ. Thus has it ever been with all the seekers after the sign. The demand for a religion which shall dispense with the exercise of reason and the discipline of thought, is ever punished by belief in a religion which outrages all reason and, at last, silences all thought. Superstition is still the Nemesis, not of faith, but of unbelief. And every such superstition necessarily grows always grosser and darker as it grows older. For the desire of the teacher for power, combining with the desire of the taught for certainty, must tend always to efforts at making the SIGN, which is to secure both, still more awful and convincing, by still greater and more awful attestations. A fresh miracle must still be provided to silence each fresh heresy, a new prodigy to confirm each new dogma. And thus stranger and still stranger legend, falser and still falser doctrine, must multiply more and more to meet the increasing demands of the system upon the credulity of its followers, until, at last, it resembles some great tropical forest, all choked up with the rank luxuriance of its own undergrowth, the old pathways obliterated, the shrines where men once prayed, the homes where they dwelt, concealed and mouldering in the dark embrace of its tangled parasites. What else but this has been the whole history of Romanism, with all its superstitions and all its false signs and wonders to attest them? What is it all but the result, the necessary result, of an attempt to give men the infallible certainty they crave, in the shape of a living and speaking infallible judge, silencing all doubt, terminating all controversy by its decisions and enforcing its authority by repeated miracles? What is all the long and ever-lengthening chain of her legends, from its first pious fraud to its last and newest prodigy? What are they all, but one constant and increasing effort to make more and more clearly visible the ever-waning sign, to recover the ever-wavering allegiance of men by fresh appeals from the obstinate questionings of the intellect to the terrors of the senses? And what is that strange charm and witchery of this system, by which it has held in subjection in times past, by which it bows to subjection in our own day, so many a noble intellect, in spite of all the grossness of its errors and incredibleness of its superstitions? Is it not this, that, proclaiming the revelation of the SIGN, it professes to give that *certainty*, that absolute freedom from all doubt in matters of faith, which men so earnestly desire? Is it not that, to minds worn out with the strife of controversy and the agony of doubt, it offers repose from all the painful effort at deciding for themselves questions for which the human intellect can never find a satisfactory solution? To souls exhausted with the feverish anxieties of freedom, it offers the rest of despotism. To the weary and heavy laden, borne down with the burden of their own doubts and difficulties, Rome speaks ever, in cruel and misleading parody, those comfortable words of Christ, "Come unto me, and find rest for your souls." Still does she stand, the false representative of Christ, by the well-side where come those who thirst for truth, and telling them ever that they "have nothing to draw with, and the well is deep," bids them ask of her, and she will give them water, which if they drink of "they shall never thirst again." Who is there among us who has thought earnestly and deeply on those vexed questions that are trying men's souls in this day of doubt and controversy, when all creeds are challenged, all opinions disputed, when we are driven to search ever deeper and deeper for the foundation of all our faith and the ground of all our hope, who has not felt the terrible fascination of this temptation to repose? Who has not listened with a longing, an almost yielding heart, to the voice that whispers to us—Cease to doubt, cease to dispute, cease to think. See this sign,—obey and rest?

But, on the other hand, there has always existed in the Church the opposite school of thought—that which demands a demonstration, not to the senses, but to the intellect — which is, therefore, impatient of mystery, incredulous of the supernatural, rebellious against authority—which seeks ever to divest Christianity of all that is mysterious or supernatural and to reduce it, as much as possible, to a purely natural religion, to something that can be weighed and measured by the understanding, or that approves itself to the feelings; to something, in short, that is self-evident to the natural man. To this source may be traced all those heresies which may be described as *negative*, which consist in the denial of some of the supernatural facts, or the rejection of some of the mysteries of the Gospel. From the earliest days of Christianity to our own, the Catholic Church has had to contend with those who denied the great miracles of the Incarnation and the Resurrection of Christ and the Inspiration of Holy Writ, or sought to explain away the Great mysteries of Redemption and Atonement and Regeneration. All these denials of the supernatural, all these attempts at getting rid of the mysteries of the Christian faith, are but the efforts of the human mind to attain to absolute certainty, but which seeks to gain it in a demonstration, not of power for the senses, but of wisdom to the intellect.

At this moment we are suffering from a reaction in this direction. The age in which we live is intellectual, self-reliant, sceptical. The human intellect—resenting the long tyranny of tradition and authority in science and in philosophy—is insisting loudly upon its right to be the supreme and only judge of all questions. Religion is experiencing the effect of this revolt against authority. Men are demanding everywhere that religion, like philosophy or science, shall be received only so far as it can make good its claims at the bar of the intellect. As the evidence of miracle was once held sufficient to prove any error, so the claim to such evidence is now held sufficient to discredit any truth. The mind of man is revenging itself for its long slavery to usurping superstition, by an attempt to overthrow the lawful authority of revelation. As men once demanded power without wisdom, so now they insist upon wisdom without power. They ask for a religion which shall be purely and entirely human, set forth in a revelation, not *to* man, but *of* and by man; a Bible which is not inspired; a Christ who is not incarnate; a Church which has no Divine and indwelling Spirit; a Gospel which tells us no truth which we could not have discovered for ourselves and reveals no wisdom which it did not first derive from us. This is that Gospel for the age, freed from all the errors of the past, the remains of Hebrew superstition, from which Jesus of Nazareth did so much to free religion in His day, but of which He left so much for us to free it from in our day. This is that Gospel of wisdom without power which the age demands, and with which so many are endeavouring to supply it.

To effect this all the resources of learning, all the ingenuity of criticism, are put forth. No hypothesis is too wild, no interpretation is too extravagant, no assertion is too bold, if only it disposes of a miracle, or dispenses with a mystery. Especially are these attacks directed against the story of the Gospel, that obstinate history of miracles, that record of a life which is all one miracle, which records in its every line the manifestation of a great power of God dwelling among men. For if this were once disposed of, it were easy to deal with all the rest of Scripture. Indeed, if this story of the life and death of Christ be not a true one, if Christ were not all that Christianity proclaims Him to be, the miracles and prophecies of the Old Testament, which were only the announcements and foreshadowings of Him and of His kingdom, become utterly useless and unmeaning. And, on the other hand, if we accept the one great miracle of the Incarnation, there is no reason why we should reject the lesser miracles that precede or attend it. If we believe that Christ did, indeed, come down from heaven to reveal God to man, there is no difficulty in believing that God spake before from heaven to tell men that He was to come, or that signs and wonders should herald or accompany his appearance upon earth.

The Gospel history then, the life and character of Christ Himself, must be, is becoming more and more clearly, the ground on which the battle of Christianity with the scepticism of the age is to be fought out. The controversy is rapidly narrowing itself to this one issue,—"What think ye of Christ, whose son is He?" It is against this rock, the rock on which He built His Church, even the record of the life of a Christ who claims to be the Son of the Living God, that the wild waves of unbelief are rising ever higher and higher, dashing themselves ever more and more fiercely. Could they but once sweep over it, the light of the Word, the light that now shines out, the only beacon over the wild waves of human passion and human sin, were quenched for ever. For with that story vanishes all certain evidence of a power of God, working among men and in man, of a love of God, redeeming, seeking, saving man. With the Gospel vanishes the whole book of God, and with the book the God of the book, the living, personal God, the ruling, loving, Father of men. Nature would take the place of the God of Nature, and the idolatry of law be substituted for the worship of the lawgiver; until at last the seeker after wisdom end his search in the fool's discovery that there is no greater, no diviner wisdom or power than his own, and stand at last in the despair of hopeless atheism, in a world from which he had succeeded in banishing the sign that reveals and that alone fully reveals, the wisdom and the power of the God who made it.

My brethren, my reverend brethren, into the midst of this strife of contending principles, you are advancing to take your part. It has come to your turn to bring the Gospel to bear upon the wants and sorrows, the doubts and difficulties, of the age. And if I have spoken to you this day of those doubts and difficulties, rather than of the practical and every-day duties of a minister's life, it is because I am convinced that to encounter these difficulties, to meet these doubts, will be your practical, your most practical, duty wherever your lot be cast. Not only in the active intellectual life of the university or the theological college, not only in the retirement of our studies, but by the wayside and in the market-place, from the lips of the cultivated man of the world and of the ignorant peasant, in the simple questions of the little child, do these doubts haunt and waylay us. Everywhere, anywhere that we meet with man, we must expect to be called upon to hear and to answer the questions of the superstitious or the sceptical; for the questions they ask, the demands they make, are not of this, nor of any age, but of all ages. They are but the utterance of the desires, the expression of the needs, of our common human nature.

Woe to us if we cannot answer them! Woe to us if we can only listen in silent terror to the cry of those who feeling themselves drifting away from the old moorings out into a sea of doubt, ask us for help and counsel, and we have no help or counsel to give them.

What, then, should we do,—we who are called to preach Christ crucified, in an age of contending doubt and superstition? In the first place, we should not be surprised nor dismayed at what we see. It is no new thing that we are contemplating. As it was in St. Paul's day so is it now, Christianity must still encounter the seeker for the sign and the seeker for wisdom. The Gospel of Christ crucified must always stand in irreconcilable antagonism alike to those who would harden it into a superstition, and to those who would dissolve it into a philosophy. The temple of which we are the guardians has always been endangered alike by those who would darken the light of the Word within it, as well as by those who would raze it even to the ground. And yet it stands still, as it has ever stood, resting upon that rock against which the gates of hell shall never prevail—"Christ Jesus, the same yesterday, to-day, and for ever." High on its summit, above the clouds and mists of human ignorance and unbelief, stands still revealed the sign of man's salvation, the cross of Christ; and still is the prophecy of Him who hung upon that cross fulfilled, that if He be lifted up all men should come unto Him. Nation after nation, age after age, have heard in their turn the joyful sound of those messengers of glad tidings who bid them look upon that cross and live. In every nation and in every age there have been those who saw in it but a stumbling-block or foolishness. But there have been, also, and shall ever be, those who, feeling that they need a Saviour and that it displays to them the only Saviour for their need, come humbly, come lovingly to its foot, and, kneeling down beneath its shadow, feel, as it falls upon them in all its healing and sanctifying influence, that Christ crucified is, indeed, "to them that are called, the wisdom and the power of God."

In the next place; as we have no reason to fear for the Gospel, so must we take heed that we are sternly faithful to that Gospel; that we never attempt to accommodate it to the age, by softening down any of its peculiarities, or by reserving any of its doctrines. The inducement to do so will always be a very strong one. Our own temperament or education will necessarily incline us, more or less, to one or other of those two great parties that I have endeavoured to describe. And we shall naturally be tempted to call in the aid of the one to help us against the other. The authority of a visible Church, if we could only rest in it, would so completely silence all doubt. A philosophical and natural religion, if we could only receive it, would so completely free us from all doubt. And even if we needed not such aids for our own faith, how strong the temptation to provide them for others—to win the superstitious by presenting to them the Gospel in its aspect of power rather than of wisdom, or to win the sceptical by presenting to them the Gospel in its aspect of wisdom rather than of power—to strain the Gospel message, in order to conciliate the prejudices of one side or the other. Yet all such attempts are useless, as they are sinful. "The children in the market-place" will not be satisfied with us unless we dance altogether as they pipe and lament altogether as they mourn. We cannot stop short with the first concession; each one draws on another, until there be nothing left to concede, and we find ourselves landed either in the superstitions of Romanism or the cold negations of Infidelity. We must never, then, be afraid to say, to all who ask us for *certainty*—for a demonstration of the Gospel that we preach—We have it not to give. There is no demonstration of the Gospel possible for the natural man. We can demonstrate it for you neither by the authority of an infallible Church, nor by the reasonings of an infallible philosophy; Wisdom is justified of her children, and of them alone. Believe it, and you shall know its truth. Try the remedies we offer you, and you shall experience their efficacy. But in no other way is it possible for you to know with absolute certainty of this "doctrine, whether it be of God or no."

Thirdly; we must as strongly maintain that there is a demonstration to the regenerate, a "demonstration of the Spirit" in His divine power, "bearing witness with our spirit that we are the sons of God."

That evidence we must seek to strengthen in our own souls, that we may be able to speak of it to our people with the assured and assuring certainty which springs from personal experience. Let the Christ we preach be a Christ in us, crucifying our affections and lusts, subduing us to Himself, revealing Himself ever by the cross within us, and we shall speak with no stammering nor uncertain lips as we preach that cross to others. Nor need I remind you how our lives as well as our lips may testify to the power of the cross. As men recognize in us those graces which we tell them are the gifts of Christ — as they see the presence of the indwelling Spirit of our Lord manifesting itself in all we do and all we say, proving that there is, indeed, a wisdom that is not of this world and a power that overcomes this world—we shall be evidences of Christianity to thousands who cannot read our books nor understand our arguments, but who read and understand *us* thoroughly. And our people, so convinced, so won, shall be in turn most certain evidences to us of the truth of Christianity. The miracle of conversion, the perpetual miracle of spiritual resurrection, shall prove to us that Christ is with us still. As we see the tears of godly sorrow, as we mark the fruits of repentance, as we trace the growth of the divine life in men once dead in trespasses and sins, as we stand by the bedsides of saints departing in faith and hope, giving glory to God, braving death and triumphing over the grave in the name of Him who hath made them more than conquerors, we shall see surer and still surer evidence that the Gospel of Christ is, indeed, "the power of God unto salvation to every one that believeth."

This should be our aim, and this, if it be our aim, will full surely be our exceeding great reward. From the lips of those we have taught, from the lives of those we have trained for God, shall come to us an ever-ready and a powerful help against the doubts and the difficulties, the trials and the temptations of our ministry. Heavy, at times full heavy, is the burden of the cross we bear aloft as an ensign to the nations. Ever the higher that we lift it do our weak hands tremble the more beneath its weight. But we bear it in the name and we may bear it in the strength, of Him who will give, to all who believe, wisdom and power. So may it be, my reverend brethren, for you, wherever your lot be cast. So, brethren and friends, let your prayers now ascend to God that it may be for all His ministers, and especially that He may give these His servants grace ever to "witness a good confession," wisdom to know and defend, power to preach, grace to exemplify, the doctrine of "Christ crucified, the wisdom of God, and the power of God."

THE FINAL OVERTHROW OF EVIL.

THE FINAL OVERTHOW OF EVIL.

OXFORD LENT SERMONS, 1866.

"O thou enemy, destructions are come to a perpetual end."
PSALM ix. 6.

IN the vision of the Church in heaven, granted for the encouragement of the Church on earth, the victors in the strife in which we are engaged are described as singing "the song of Moses the servant of God, and of the Lamb." That is, they are described as keeping perpetual remembrance of the conflict they have endured. Their song is not of the future, but of the past. The host of the redeemed are pictured as looking back, like the host of Israel on the morning of their deliverance, over the troubled waters through which their long night march has led them, and mingling with their triumph over the utter destruction of their enemy the memories of that night of weakness and weariness and fear. They sing the song of "the servant of God," the song of all good and faithful servants, no small portion of whose joy it will be to remember that good fight in which they were more than conquerors through Him that loved them. They sing "the song of the Lamb." By the power of sympathy they enter into the joy of their Lord—that deep joy He knew, when He, the true Moses, passed before His people through the depths of the grave and hell, and came forth leading captivity captive, destroying by His death him that had the power of death. The whole history of the Church's pilgrimage here on earth, all the greatness and the mystery, all the weariness and the agony, all the patience and the faith of her long warfare, as well as all the glory of her last crowning victory, find their utterance in the song of Moses and the Lamb.

In that song it is our privilege even now to join. As it will be the joy of the Church triumphant to remember the trials of the Church militant, so it should be the joy of the Church militant to anticipate the rest and the peace of the Church triumphant. By faith the Church, while yet on earth, can ascend and dwell in heavenly places with her risen Lord; can see her warfare accomplished, her enemy vanquished; can take up her song of victory over him, and say now, even in the hour of her sorest and weariest strife, what she shall yet say in the hour of her final triumph, "O thou enemy, destructions are come to a perpetual end."

It is this sure and certain hope of the future that gives so peculiar a character both to the prophecy and the history of Scripture. It turns the prophecy of Scripture into history. The prophet, as in this Psalm, sees the future so certainly accomplished, that he speaks of it as already passed; he does not say, thus and thus it shall be, but thus it is, thus it has been. On the other hand, this certainty turns sacred history into prophecy. The narrator of some partial victory—some local triumph of God's people or judgment on God's enemies—exults over it in strains of praise that take, ere he is aware, a louder and a deeper tone than fits the occasion: as they swell into the notes of the last great song of the Church triumphant, he sings, though all unconsciously, "the song of Moses and of the Lamb."

It is in this spirit that we should ever seek to

interpret all history; not merely all Scripture history, where the conflict between good and evil is distinctly traced, but all history whatsoever. The history of our own hearts where flesh and spirit wage such deadly war; the history of the Church of Christ, from the first proclamation of enmity between the seed of the woman and the serpent, down to the last good word spoken or brave deed done for Christ, that proves the Captain of our salvation to be with us still; the history of the kingdoms of this world, with all its strangely intermingled good and evil, its terrible preponderance and triumph of evil over good; in all these, through all these, one thought should still be present with us, one clear, assured conviction sustain and guide us still,—" the end of all this is fixed, certain, appointed from everlasting; evil shall be cast out of our world, good shall triumph in it everywhere and for ever; the destructions of the enemy shall come to a perpetual end."

It is of this assured certainty, it is of this ever-present vision of the final overthrow of all evil, which God has given to His Church, I have to speak.

I. And first, I would remind you *that this certainty is God's gift to His Church, and to His Church alone.* The final overthrow of all evil is a truth of pure revelation. From the written Word of God, and from it alone, do we learn the fact that the conflict between good and evil which we see and feel, is not eternal; that a time was when it was not, and that a time is coming when it shall no longer be. We are too apt to forget this. Like other ideas which the Bible reveals to us, this idea of a final triumph of good over evil has happily so leavened and possessed the minds of men, it seems so natural now to all of us to expect it, that we forget how entirely it rests upon the authority of revelation, how utterly impossible it is that it ever could have made a part of merely natural religion. So completely is this the case, that those who are most loudly calling on us to cast off our old superstitious belief in miraculous prophecy, are loudest in their prophecies of the final triumph of good and the utter destruction of all evil. They are for ever assuring us of "the good time that is coming," when mankind shall have improved themselves by the aid of physical science and political economy and natural morality into universal virtue, wisdom, and peace.

But when turning away from this book which they bid us reject, we look upon those other revelations of God which still remain to us,— the visible world; human society; our own experience; all that we may call natural, as distinguished from supernatural,—what ground do we see for this hope? What voice in all these tells us that destructions are to have a perpetual end?

Not the voice of nature; for that, ever interpreted more and more clearly by science, speaks of one great, awful, all-embracing law of vicarious suffering, by which the happiness, the progress of the race is purchased by the suffering, the destruction of the individual;—the law by which the weak and the imperfect perish, that the strong may grow stronger and more perfect; the law by which the death or the agony of one sentient being makes the life or the pleasure of another;—the law by which an ever-wasting destruction is called in to check an ever-needlessly multiplying life;—laws which with one voice proclaim, that physical evil and pain must be as lasting as physical good, that suffering must still be the shadow of joy, and death still the condition of life, and therefore that destructions shall never, can never, come to an end.

Is it the voice of human society and the course of human history which give us this assurance? More and more clearly are these revealing the working of that terrible law by which the happiness of the few is made dependent upon the suffering of the many. What is it that conditions that high civilization of which we boast ourselves? The law which governs all human society, and which is the necessary condition of all civilization and progress, is the law of unequal distribution. All cannot have an equal share of wealth and leisure and learning; all cannot be equally cultivated. It is the law, then, of society, that many must be poor to allow of some being rich, many ignorant to allow of some being learned, many overworked to allow of some having leisure. Civilization, then, and progress, mean just this—the refined, the graceful, peaceful lives of the few, purchased by the toil, the temptation, the weariness, the shortened, saddened lives of the many. Civilization has still, like all things human, its darker as well as its brighter side; its law of degradation, as well as its law of progress; and the one is still seen to be the necessary condition of the other. You may endeavour to lighten the pressure of this law, by the enactments of statesmanship, or by the counteracting influences of Christian benevolence; you may lessen these inequalities, war against these evils, but you never can eradicate them.

And what is history, for the most part, but the record of the efforts men have been making to shift from one class or other of society the burden of this law? What are the wisest or the wildest political movements, but attempts to adjust its pressure? None have ever perfectly succeeded: no social polity has ever yet been seen, so perfect as not to inflict some suffering or wrong on some one class; none so lasting as not to need perpetual readjustment. There is a decay of institutions, as of men. New births there are, too, for these, but they are still preceded by the sickness and death of the old. Not gently and peaceably, but with convulsions and agonies does the old perish and the new come to life. Here, too, the law of suffering seems eternal; these destructions seem to know no end.

Are we then to look into our own hearts? Who ever there saw evil finally overthrown, good finally triumphant? Who ever could say, At last the warfare within me is over, and my will, in perfect accord with all the laws of right, rules absolutely and without effort all my nature? Who does not know that it is still the wisest and holiest of men who mourn most over the perpetual warfare they must wage against evil within them; how its destructions never cease, but threaten ever the wreck of their virtue and the ruin of their peace; how it compels for its conquest, the severest self-denial, the most ruthless sacrifice of many a joy and many an innocent delight. And after this life-long struggle there awaits us, if in this life only we have hope, the undistinguishing grave, that involves in one common annihilation all alike; —the grave, beyond which the soul untaught of God can but send a guess or a wish, but never gains the vision of a sure and certain hope; the dark curtain, with its terrible inscription of "perhaps," that drops at last upon the stage of our conflict. Here is no assurance of the final overthrow of evil, not here do we learn that destructions come to a perpetual end.

Nor do we gain this assurance by resorting to a general belief in the goodness and benevolence of God, a persuasion that, because He is good and loving, He must at last end all evil. For although creation does, on the whole, testify to the goodness of God, yet, it is clear that the idea of His goodness which creation gives us, can never rise beyond the amount of goodness revealed in creation. If that be, as it clearly is, a goodness which allows of evil,—nay, which seems to have interwoven it in the whole plan of the universe,—how can we argue from the exhibition of such goodness, that evil is ever to be destroyed? If its existence is consistent with God's perfect law now, why not for ever? An instant of unnecessary evil or pain under the rule of an Almighty and All-loving Being, is logically as inconceivable as an eternity of it; an instant of necesary evil seems to insure an eternity of it. If, therefore, we are to judge of the purposes of God only by what He has done and is doing in creation; if we are to judge of the future of the world only by the past, or the present, we must believe in the eternity of evil. The stream can rise no higher than its source. A natural religion can never rise above the teachings of nature, and if these declare one fact more clearly and more uniformly than another, it is that evil, whether moral or physical, is natural, —is an inherent, inseparable element in all forms of creature life; and that to talk of final deliverance from it is not to believe, but to contradict, the Bible of nature.

No! the word which tells us of the deliverance of nature from what seems an essential part of it must be supernatural. Nature can tell us nothing of her future, for she can tell us nothing of her beginning. It must be another voice than hers that gives us a Genesis and a Revelation. If we would know this, we must listen to the voice from heaven, which calls to us—as we seek hopelessly and wearily amidst the desolate places of earth for a sign that desolation shall have an end, or a promise that joy shall endure—" Come up hither, and I will shew thee things to come." "Ascend up above the region of nature, that thou mayest learn the true aim and destiny of nature;" and the voice that so calls to us, is the voice which in the beginning said, " Let us make heaven and earth."

That voice it is, and that alone, which tells us that in the beginning evil was not; that there was a time when all was very good. That voice alone can tell us that evil is not God's work, formed no part of the original constitution of things; that it was no imperfection in the material which He found to His hand and which imposed itself upon Him as an indispensable necessity in all His work, but that it was a foreign element introduced into this world of ours from without; introduced by the evil will and power of a being, not of this world, and which may, therefore, be removed by a higher will and by a mightier power. It is God who tells us, and it is He alone who can tell us, " an enemy hath done this."

But He tells us more than this. The knowledge that an enemy has introduced evil into this world gives us no certainty that it shall ever be cast out; for, as we have seen, if God Almighty could for a moment permit the existence of evil here, we have no right to say that He will not permit it always. The reason for His tolerance of it, for aught we can tell, might be eternal, and so too would therefore be the evil. We need, for the certainty of its end, another revelation; we need, not only that God should say "an enemy hath done this," but that He should say, "the destructions of that enemy shall come to an end." And this is the revelation He has given us. He has given it, not only in the express words of those prophecies which from the first foretell this end and which fix, though in mystic dates and figures, the date of it. He has given us a still more certain assurance. To the word of His prophets He has added a sign. He has shewn us evil already overthrown, our great enemy completely vanquished. This Book reveals just that one fact of which all nature supplies no single instance, one case, not of partial and temporary, but of complete and final victory over evil.

Our Gospel, our good news for man, is this, that humanity, represented in its great Head and Chief, has encountered the Evil One, has foiled his temptation, endured the worst his hatred can inflict, passed through his prison-house of death; has risen, has ascended to the heaven from which he fell, and dwells there for ever. The voice which speaks from heaven of the end yet to come, is His voice—the voice of Him "who was dead, and is alive for evermore;" of Him, whose promise to us is that, because He lives, we shall live also; the voice of Him who, in the crisis of His great strife, saw the travail of His soul already accomplished; saw the world for which He died, given Him as His eternal inheritance, purchased with His Blood; saw the glorious future of that reign which must continue till all things are put under His feet; and seeing it, exclaimed, "It is finished!" That word of His it is our right to repeat. In the life, death, resurrection and ascension of Christ, we see the pledge of the resurrection, of the ascension of humanity beyond the reach of the Evil One; we see the works of the Devil destroyed by the manifestation of the Son of Man, and we too say, "It is finished." "O thou enemy, destructions are come to a perpetual end."

Viewed in the light of this revelation, nature, that before could tell us nothing of the end, now gives us a mighty assurance of it. For every proof she gives of the enmity of the destroyer, becomes a pledge of his destruction. The more pitiless the havoc the wider the desolation he has wrought, the deeper grows our conviction that our Almighty and all-loving Father will not, cannot leave the enemy to work this cruel havoc an instant beyond that time which He has set wherein to work by evil a greater good. The "remainder of wrath" must be restrained, and restrained for ever. And thus, as we look upon each scene of ruin which tells that the destroyer has been there, it tells us that the restorer is yet to come. The once pleasant places, the gardens of our delight that he makes desolate, foretell by their very barrenness the hour when they shall blossom as the rose. The fenced cities of our joy, that he lays into ruinous heaps, proclaim the hour when they shall be replaced by the city of God, the heavenly Jerusalem, through whose gates no evil thing shall ever enter. The thirst of our souls, fevered by the poisonous wounds he has inflicted, foretells the cool and refreshing streams of the water of life, beside whose banks grows the Tree whose leaves are for the healing of the nations. The very pains of creation thus become prophecies of rest: it groans, but it groans in travail; it travaileth with the birth of the new creation, where destructions shall be unknown. And so the old word of triumph of the victor becomes ours, "Out of the eater comes forth meat, out of the strong sweetness." We raise against our enemy our song of triumph, though we sing it often with quivering lips; and by the anguish with which they quiver, and the sorrow that chokes our speech, we know that the morning of joy shall succeed the night of weeping, and we exclaim, 'O thou enemy! By the deadliness of thine enmity, by the cruel ingenuity of thy torture, by the fierceness and pitilessness of thy wrath, we know that "destructions shall come"—aye, we can say in the assured certainty of faith, are come—"to an end" for ever!'

THE FINAL OVERTHROW OF EVIL. 43

II. In the next place we observe that, *while the date of this overthrow is concealed, the manner of it is largely revealed.*

The date of it is concealed. "Of that day or hour knoweth no man," because such knowledge would be hurtful to the Church. Nothing can be more injurious to the real, earnest, patient Christian life than a spirit of eager, impatient curiosity, which is for ever peeping and prying behind the veil that God has interposed between us and the future; writing perpetual supplements to the Apocalypse; announcing, with all the solemnity and precision of a herald, the very day when the great procession of judgment is to appear and assigning to each personage his exact place in it: announcements which the course of events is sure to contradict, and which their author must forthwith replace by new ones, given with as much confidence as if the old had not just proved a failure. We say nothing of the mischief that such Christian soothsaying does to those without by the ridicule which it casts upon the awful themes which it profanes; but we would earnestly impress on you the mischief it does within the Church; the spiritual dissipation, the love of excitement, the distaste for sober, practical study of God's Word, that it is sure to generate. We only remind both those who indulge in it and those who, because of it, scoff at prophetical studies, that for such sensational treatment of prophecy Scripture gives no warrant, and that against it, it gives more than one express and solemn warning.

But just as it is not good for us to know or to guess at the precise date of the end, so it is good for us to know and meditate on the manner of it; and therefore He who will not tell us the time of His coming, does tell us that concerning the manner of it which is calculated to help, and not to hinder, our Christian life meanwhile.

Two things He more especially tells us. First that it will not be brought about by the gradual wasting away of evil and the gradual growth and spread of good ; that we are not to look to see our present Christendom gradually conquering all heathendom and growing the while more and more perfect and Christ-like. On this point our Lord's words seem decisive when He makes His coming in judgment to Jerusalem the type of His last final coming to judge the world. He tells us how it is to be preceded, not only by manifestations of the power of evil in the world of nature—by wars and famines and earthquakes—but by manifestations of its power within the Church, of which those outward ills are but the shadow ; by apostacy and false prophets, by wide-spreading heresies, by waxing iniquity and waning love, by the dying out of living faith from the earth, until the carcases—the dead forms of dead religions and churches—lie waiting and inviting the gathering of the vultures of judgment to cleanse the earth of them for ever.

So St. Paul foretells the "falling away" first, "the revelation of the man of sin," to be destroyed only "with the brightness of the Lord's coming ; " so, in the vision of St. John, the shadows grow darker and the lights fainter as the vision draws to its close, while the forms that rise up out of the abyss grow more bestial and horrible. So the beast succeeds the dragon, and the mouth of the beast speaks still fiercer blasphemies, and Babylon the great grows still mightier, and she, whose name is Mystery, drinks deep, even to drunkenness, of the blood of the saints, and the witnesses lie slain and unburied in the streets of the great city, and the woman flies into the wilderness ; until at last heaven is opened, and He who

THE FINAL OVERTHROW OF EVIL. 45

is faithful and true comes forth to judge and to make war in righteousness and to win the great victory that proclaims Him King of kings and Lord of lords.

Of the exact meaning of all the details of these mystical pictures we know very little; but surely this much at least is clear, that they all foreshadow, not a great growth of good and decay of evil, but rather a great growth of evil and decay of good, to be ended at last by a sudden and final overthrow of evil at the coming of the Lord.

It is good for us to remember this. It preserves us from a false estimate of the Church's mission in this dispensation. The Church must be known by her work, but we must take care that we understand what that work is, or we shall be unreasonably expecting that from her which she was not sent to do. Her work is warfare against evil everywhere, complete conquest over evil nowhere. Not by the completeness of her conquest over evil, but by the completeness of her antagonism to all evil, are we to judge how far she is true to her mission. To look for more than this is sure to lead to disappointment, perhaps to unbelief; to look for less than this is sure to lead to carelessness and sloth. To look only for this; to understand that we are to contend against every possible form of evil and yet that we shall never succeed, in this dispensation, in completely casting out any one form of it; to work as if all were to be done by us, to wait as if nothing were to be done by us; to know that the warfare is still to be ours, and the victory at last, not ours, but our Lord's; this is "the patience and the faith of the saints."

Again we learn another truth concerning the manner of this overthrow, and that is, that it will be visibly and unmistakably miraculous, that it will be seen to be solely and exclusively God's work and not in any way man's work, nor yet the result merely of an increase of what we call the ordinary workings of His Spirit amongst us, but rather such a manifestation of the Divine power in the person of Christ as shall bring out distinctly before men and angels the true character of this great conflict as a strife, not of forces, nor of laws, but of wills, of persons; a war, not of *good* against *evil*, as we might imagine it to be now, but of the *Evil One* against God and His Christ.

As to the nature of the tokens that are described as ushering in that last great convulsion there may be doubt and debate. How far those physical signs and wonders in the heaven and the earth which we are told are to accompany it,—the darkening sun, the waning moon, the falling stars, the heavens shrinking as a scroll,—how far these are to be regarded as strictly literal, how far symbolical, the end alone will tell; but of the general purport of them, so far at least there can be no doubt, that such signs and tokens shall accompany it as shall prove it to be the work, not of nature or of natural forces, but of nature's God. Whatever other sign shall be revealed, one shall be seen above all—the sign of the Son of Man in heaven. The power that destroys all evil and restores all good, shall be seen to be His, and His alone.

And it is well for the Church that she does possess this prophecy of the manner of the end. It helps to keep alive her faith in God; her faith, that is, in God in the only sense in which the word of God has any religious meaning; her faith in a will—not a pervading force, nor an eternal something outside us which makes for righteousness, but a supreme, all-ruling, all-ordaining personal will, in which we can trust, to which we can pray—a will, the thought of which delivers us from the sullen tyranny of soulless, unintelligent, mechanical law. And it is this faith, the very ground of all religion, which so greatly needs in these latter days to be strengthened against the ever-growing idolatry of law, which threatens to supersede the worship of the law-giver; that worship of the creature rather than of the Creator which in one form or other has been the world's great temptation to the Church; a temptation which is seducing Christian men not only to misinterpret the phenomena of the natural, but even those of the spiritual world: a temptation to narrow as far as possible the limits of the supernatural and to enlarge as much as possible the limits of the natural; an eager and fussy anxiety to make it easier than the Scripture narrative makes it for Almighty God to work miracles in the world He has created, and which has been trodden by the feet of His Incarnate Son; a desire to shew in how very low and merely natural a sense we may speak of the Bible as God's word to man, prayer as man's speech to God, or the sacraments as God's gift of supernatural grace; a striving to shew how all these things may be made ingeniously to fit in with a system of laws and forces which may be seen and measured and weighed and calculated; an attempt, in short, to explain away God out of the Bible and the Sacraments and the Church, because it is the fashion just now to explain Him away out of the world.

Now against this idolatry of nature—against this dread and dislike of the supernatural even in the kingdom of God—this temptation to subordinate the Church, whose laws are supernatural, to the world, whose laws are natural, and to make the constitution of the physical and material the rule by which to interpret the constitution of the spiritual,—against this, God has armed His Church by revealing to her the great antagonistic truth that it is not the world whose natural history conditions and limits that of the Church, but the Church whose supernatural history shapes and rules that of the world; that the destiny of man is not to be learned by investigating the laws of nature, but that the destiny of the world is to be learned by a knowledge of the true history of man. He reveals this to us in that great supernatural fact—the central fact of the world's and of the Church's history—the Incarnation; He reveals to us in that fact the transcendent importance of that human history, in the course of which God became man; He shews us that the whole world—nay, if needs were, the whole universe—were fitly regarded but as the temporary platform on which this great fact was to be wrought out; how all its physical history, through all that infinity of ages science tells us of, were sufficiently accounted for, if it existed for this only; how its utter annihilation were but a small matter compared to the loss of one soul for which Christ died.

He shews us, too, how the whole of that history of man, which thus dominates the history of the world, is truly supernatural. That it is in some degree unnatural we have already seen. It is unnatural that the evil will of an enemy should introduce disorder into God's order, lawlessness into His law. It is unnatural that man's will should continue in rebellion against the will of his Creator. But it is a supernatural thing that the Divine will should suspend the operation of that great natural law by which death should instantly have followed sin; that Omnipotence should hold apart for a time acts and their true consequences, crime and punishment, desert and reward. Not judgment inflicted but judgment delayed, not goodness triumphant but goodness suffering, not right and might miraculously united for ever, but right and might miraculously separated even for one moment,—this is the real wonder, the great mystery of mysteries.

This is the word of history; and the word of prophecy is like unto it. As history reveals to us disorder unnaturally introduced and supernaturally restrained, so prophecy reveals to us order supernaturally restored; shews us that Divine will, which now overrules evil, appearing at last to overthrow it; shews us the true order of the world replaced; the law of righteous government working the true unity between right and might, purity and happiness, on the one hand, and between wrong and weakness, wickedness and misery on the other; shews the whole history of our race on earth to be one long supernatural pause and parenthesis in a far vaster history, whose deeper laws and mightier forces embrace and girdle in from the first our lawlessness and our unrest.

And these two great lessons mutually strengthen each other. Believe in the will that supernaturally overrules, and you have less difficulty in believing in the will that shall supernaturally overthrow all evil. Believe in the will that is supernaturally to overthrow evil, and you will have less difficulty in believing in a will that is controlling and overruling it now.

III. And now of the result of that great overthrow, of the new heavens and new earth which are to come forth at God's command from the ruins of the old, what have we to say? But little, for God has told us but little. "It doth not yet appear what we shall be." It could not yet appear. The mortal cannot comprehend immortality, nor the corruptible conceive of incorruption. The language which foretells these changes becomes accordingly mystic and symbolical. The vision of a city whose gates are precious stones and whose streets are gold, that needs not the light of the sun nor the moon, through whose streets flows a mystic river, by whose banks grows a mystic tree of life,—what does it tell us, save that the language which men speak on earth has no words in which it were possible to reveal the joys of heaven? Nay, even those words which seem most intelligible, those which tell us rather what we shall *not* be, than what we shall be,—that there shall be no sin, nought that defileth, no curse—that sorrow and sighing shall flee away, and God Himself wipe away all tears from all eyes,—even these, when we ponder on them, seem full of mystery; for with the vanishing away of all that is evil, it seems to us as if there must also vanish much that is good. There are many of the noblest elements of goodness that seem impossible, save as existing in antagonism to evil. To say there shall be no evil in the world, seems to be equivalent to saying there shall be no pity, no mercy, no benevolence, no fortitude, no courage, no self-sacrifice; that is, it seems to say that, though this life be our preparation for another, yet that some of the very chiefest of the lessons we shall have learned here, shall be useless there. All this may serve to shew us that a condition of pure and unmixed good, of which we talk so familiarly, is really quite as inconceivable as, perhaps more so than, one of unmixed evil, and that heaven is quite as great a mystery as hell.

One thought, however, respecting our future life we can with some distinctness grasp; it is the one suggested in our text; namely that it must be a state of infinite progress; a life, not as we too often think of it, of progress arrested, a life in which humanity, once and once for all perfected, has before it only an eternity of virtuous repose; but rather one of intense and incessant activity. The promise of eternal life necessarily implies this, for life is something more than mere existence. Life, in its truest meaning, is the highest and happiest manner of being; it is existence, with every power of our nature in its fullest, freest exercise. Whatever falls short of this, whatever checks or restrains any one faculty of our nature, whatever of weariness or weakness there be in us, comes from the imperfection of our life, comes from its invasion in some measure by its great antagonist death. And so we call it "this mortal life." This life, whose every breath, whose every movement, is one half death, —for such a life rest is essential, because the waste of it is incessant. But the very idea of a perfect life, that knows no strife with death, that needs to defend itself against no destruction, to repair no waste, implies, not eternal repose but eternal activity. It means the existence of a spiritual, intelligent, immortal creature, whose whole being, whose every power and faculty lives, intensely lives, in the glorious activity in which perpetual service and perpetual rest are one. "They rest, saith the Spirit, from their labours." And yet "they cease not day or night," proclaiming by all the unwearied actings of their glorified natures, saying, with the eternal hymn of an eternally happy life, "Glory, and honour, and power, be unto the Lamb for ever!"

For such a race there must be eternal progress, for there must be eternal acquisition without the slightest loss. How much of our present life is lost in our perpetual warfare against death! How much in the labour for the meat that perisheth! How much in those low, wearing, petty cares and anxieties that weigh down to earth the noblest souls! How much of each life, how much of the sum of all lives, seems wasted in the mere effort to live! And, then, for the whole race in any one age, what hindrances, what interruptions to its progress in these destructions of the enemy! How much of the experience of each life perishes with it! What glorious treasures of knowledge are buried in each generation over and over again! What long, long ebbings of the tide of progress, what irregularities and uncertainties in its flow! What precious things does it carry and sweep away! How small a portion does each generation inherit of the intellectual or moral wealth of its predecessor and how little does it leave to that which succeeds it!

This is the "great destruction" wrought by our "enemy." A mortal race can never be a perfect race. But think of the infinite progress, in glory and honour, of a race that possesses immortality; a race, each individual of which is for ever contributing, to the common inheritance of knowledge and happiness, the imperishable gifts of a spirit made perfect! Think of the eternity of a race to whose advance there is actually no limit, save that which forbids the finite to become infinite, which leaves therefore to the creature, who still adores and contemplates and approaches to his Creator, still an eternity of progress!

And this is the hope set before us in the Gospel: the "inheritance incorruptible, undefiled, that fadeth not away," of which nature gives no promise, science no prophecy, history no hope; the inheritance which the miracle of redemption has purchased and the miracle of revelation made known, and which the miracle of regeneration conveys. These are "the good things" which God hath "hidden from the wise and prudent,"—too wise to believe in the invisible, too prudent to trust in the undemonstrated,—but which He "hath revealed to babes," to loving, trusting hearts whose highest wisdom is to know their Father's voice, and whose deepest prudence is to trust their Father's word. To these, and these alone, it is given here to sing this song of triumph and of joy; they, and they alone, can say "O thou enemy, destructions are come to a perpetual end!"

The song that shall fully utter all that such hope implies, cannot be sung on earth; it is that "new song" which those whose pilgrimage is still unaccomplished, whose warfare is still unended, have yet to learn. Nay, even that song of victory whose notes we have been trying to catch to-night, we cannot often sing. It is our war-song here; we chaunt it at times as we enter into the battle; but in the strife it is replaced by the sigh of weariness and the groan of pain and the cry of dismay. Into that strife each one of us, who lives for God, enters as he leaves this place. The long narrow path through the troublesome waters stretches out before us again; and instead of the safe shore and the bright day dawn and the overthrown enemy, we see only the next step before us, and that but dimly as the clouds of doubt and perplexity gather above us, while behind us rings the shout of the pursuer and our hearts grow faint and our feet weary, as we pass on slowly, uncertainly, fearfully often, no song of praise upon our lips, happy if we are always able to speak the needful prayer for help. Aye, and sadder than this, we too often find it hard to remember that we are pilgrims at all. The vision of glory grows dim, the song of victory faint,—not only in the night of spiritual trial and the weariness of spiritual warfare,—but in the broad glare of the working-day world and the noise of the great battle of life.

Let us bear away with us, then, as helps, to be availed of at some future moment of temptation, these two truths that we have been contemplating. Against the overmastering tyranny of the visible which ever wars against the power of the invisible let us set the thought of the awful, the truly supernatural character of this present life, the terrible strife of wills, in a world in which Satan contends with Christ for the souls of men. Against the weariness and faintheartedness that feels the reality and the importance of this life, but feels too its weariness and its risk, let us set the thought of the assured and promised victory revealed in the Church's song of triumph, "O thou enemy, destructions are come to a perpetual end."

THE MISSIONARY TRIALS OF THE CHURCH.

THE MISSIONARY TRIALS OF THE CHURCH.

Anniversary of the Church Missionary Society, St. Bride's Church, Fleet Street, London, April 30, 1866.

"Then was Jesus led up of the Spirit into the Wilderness to be tempted of the Devil."—Matthew iv. 1.

IT is the awful privilege of the Church of Christ that she is called to a share in the work of her Lord. The ministry of reconciliation which He has committed to us is still His ministry on earth. The mission of ambassador for God to man, on which He entered in the days of His flesh, He is accomplishing still through His Church by the Spirit. As the Father dwelt, in all the fulness of the Godhead, in Him whom He sent into the world, so does Christ, in all the fulness of His Divine Sonship, still dwell in His mystical body, the Church. The Word is still flesh, still tabernacles among men, still manifests through human form the glory of God and speaks, with human voice, the message of God's love.

"Go ye into all the world;" "Preach the Gospel to every creature;" here is the Word that clothes the Church of Christ with His prophetical office. "Behold, I am with you always;" "He that heareth you heareth me;" here is the Word that tells her that her voice of prophecy is still His voice. So when, as ambassadors for Christ, we beseech men, it is as though God did beseech them by us; when we pray them in Christ's stead to be reconciled to

God, we are working together with Christ. It is in us, with us, by us, that Christ, for whom we work, is working for and with God.

This is an awful privilege! A privilege, because with the work of our Lord we inherit His reward. To him that overcometh will He give to sit with Him upon His throne, even as He overcame and hath sat down with His Father on His throne. But it is an awful privilege; for to share the work of Christ is to share His trial and His temptation. His work is a warfare. It is the invasion of the kingdom of Satan by the kingdom of God, and it provokes still all the deadly enmity of Satan that it provoked at the first. The servant is as his Master, the disciple as his Lord. We must drink of His cup and be baptized with His baptism. The measure of His sufferings must be filled up in His body, which is His Church. And just so far as our work is identical with His will the nature of our trial be identical too. Whatever weapon was chosen as most likely to wound the Captain of our salvation at any particular moment of His life or work, is just the weapon that will be used against His Church at any similar moment in her life or work; and ever the nobler the work, the sorer the temptation. The closer the disciple draws to His Lord, the nearer does the tempter draw to him. The more the presence of the Lord fills His Church, the more does that presence attract the fiercer assaults of the enemy.

And if this be so, then it follows that the missionary work of the Church must have its special dangers and temptations. It is so entirely work for Christ, it is so truly work in the doing of which the Church grows truly Christlike and in which His presence is so specially promised, that in it she must expect especial assaults of the tempter and must need against these a double portion of the Spirit of her Lord.

It is of some of these dangers and temptations and of the safeguards against them I am about to speak.

Of the duty of missionary work you have often heard from this place; of the encouragements and successes God has graciously given to it you will hear to-morrow, as we trust and believe you will hear year after year. For God is very good to us; He gives, as He is wont, "far more than either we desire or deserve," and blesses our too-scanty sowing with many a glorious reaping. But I will ask you to bear with me if I venture to speak, here and now, rather of temptations to be encountered, dangers to be avoided and safeguards to be availed of in the mission work of the Church. If God shall give me grace to speak wisely of these, I shall have helped the great cause we have at heart; for our warfare will prosper or will fail just in proportion as we who are engaged in it are contending lawfully. Work for Christ is successful just in the degree in which it is done in the Spirit of Christ. If we should learn therefore to-night from our Lord one word only as to how He would have this great work done—one word of warning as to the dangers we are exposed to in the doing of it, one word of teaching as to the true safeguards against these dangers—not in vain shall we have gathered here in His name and in His presence; not in vain shall we have besought Him that He who sends us forth to do His work may give us wisdom to know His will, as well as "grace and power faithfully to fulfil the same."

It is from the story of Our Lord's own temptation that I propose we should endeavour to derive these lessons. I do so, not merely because that story records His great lesson to His Church in all times concerning all temptation; but because there is in that scene a special, perhaps a primary, reference to the temptations and difficulties of missionary work. It is as the founder of the kingdom of God on earth that our Lord seems in that temptation to have been specially assailed. It is just as He has concluded His long preparation for His ministerial work; just as He is entering on His great office, immediately after that consecration to His Heavenly Father in baptism which typifies the self-sacrifice of all His ministry; just after the voice of God's messenger on earth and the voice of God Himself from heaven, had owned and proclaimed Him the Messias, the sent of God, the only and well-beloved Son; it is then that—filled, as He must have been—with the sense of his great mission, He is led away to encounter temptations, every one of which is aimed at inducing Him to say or do something inconsistent with that mission, something opposed to the spirit of that kingdom He had come to set up. And when that temptation has passed away and, filled with the Spirit that had sustained Him throughout it, He returns from the wilderness to the scene of His labours, His first word is of His prophetic office—" The Spirit of the Lord is upon me, because He hath anointed me to preach the Gospel to the poor." It is as if Christ, who, in His temptation, says to all tried and tempted souls, "Learn of me," has here a special word for those whom He hath anointed to preach the gospel. It is as if He said, "Before you enter on your great office, come apart with me into the wilderness; see how the tempter sought to mislead me as I was entering on mine. As he tempted me, so will he tempt you. See how, in answering him, I have taught you the true nature of my kingdom, the true laws of your mission : study these, that you too may have wherewith to answer the tempter in your time of trial."

And surely there is a special suitableness in this scene to the season and the occasion of our assembling here. Now, when the servants of Christ are coming together from all the many and varied scenes of their labour, to gladden one another with fresh proofs that the Lord is indeed still with His Church, and that our mission is indeed divine; now, when we meet to renew the vows of our dedication, and hope to return, each one to his work of the ministry wherever God has cast it, with a fresh baptism of His Spirit, with a brighter, clearer vision of the open heaven and the glory of Him who stands there at God's right hand, with a deeper echo in our hearts of that voice which speaks to us in every new triumph of the cross—" This is my beloved Son, hear ye Him;" now should we especially remember that the tempter and accuser will assuredly be present too; now especially have we need to listen, not only to the voice which speaks from heaven words of approval and of encouragement, but to the voice which speaks from the wilderness words of loving warning and counsel. It is our Lord and Master who speaks these words for our learning; let us hear Him.

In choosing, however, the subject of Our Lord's temptation for our consideration on such an occasion as this, it is not of temptation in its coarser or lower forms that I am about to speak; not, for instance, of temptation to weariness of our work, to forsaking it after putting our hand to it, to doubting if it be our proper work or a work for God at all. There may be times when such temptations assail the Church; but such a time is not now: not at this moment, not by those who are here assembled, are these likely to be experienced. But there are other temptations which beset earnest, zealous, loving workers; there are those trials, not of the darkness and of the night, but of the day; trials that come as our Lord's must have come, addressed to all that is best and brightest in our nature and our aims; temptations which beset us, not in the measure of our unlikeness, but of our likeness to our Lord.

And in the first place; all who are earnestly striving for the spread of Christ's kingdom on earth—all who say from their hearts and by their lives, "Thy kingdom come,"—are exposed from the very earnestness of their seeking and striving to one great temptation, the one which really underlies all the three temptations of our Lord, and to which He was exposed all His life long—the temptation to promote His kingdom by means which are not in agreement with that one fundamental law according to which alone it can truly develop itself.

What is that law? It is the law of conquest by self-sacrifice. The kingdom of God, which Christ has set up, is, in the end, to prevail over and cast out the kingdom of the devil. But His victory is not to be that of mere force. It has pleased God, of His mysterious wisdom and His love, that the establishment of His kingdom on earth shall not be effected by the sudden flashing forth of that awful brightness of His coming that shall consume all things evil; but by the veiling of that brightness in the form of human weakness, by the Eternal Son emptying Himself of His glory, "becoming of no reputation, taking upon Him the form of a servant," becoming subject to the lowest conditions of humanity, sin only excepted. By weakness, by suffering, by death, even the death of the cross, is Christ the Son of Man, as man, to win the inheritance which shall yet be ruled by Christ the Son of God. "He hath appeared to put away sin *by the sacrifice of Himself.*"

But if this law of conquest by self-sacrifice be the law of His kingdom to which He was Himself from the first to be subject, it was one which must have made His life one long temptation. It was a law which every circumstance in His position and His ministry must have been a provocation to break; for it forbad Him ever to use the power of His divinity in order to escape from those conditions of weakness and suffering in which His humiliation consisted. Never once might His power as Son of God be used by Him to do that, without effort or without suffering, which it was appointed He should do as Son of Man by effort and with suffering. Never, for instance, might the word of the Son of God save the Man of Sorrows one moment of grief or of weariness; never might the shield of His divinity interpose between His soul and the darts of the enemy; never might the sign of the Son of Man in the heavens be revealed to silence the opposition of His enemies or win the adherence of His people; never might the hour of Christ the King be anticipated in order to accomplish more speedily or more easily the work of Christ the Priest or of Christ the Prophet. To have done this in any one instance, to have poured out but one drop of the cup that was given Him to drink, would have been to have undone so far the work of the Incarnation; it would have been to have separated Himself so far from His brethren, to whom He came to be made in all things like; it would have been, so far, to have returned to that better country He had left, to have resumed the glory He had resigned, to have sought again the Father's presence without having first entirely accomplished the Father's work. And yet this is what every hour, every moment of His life must have presented temptations to do. Not only in that hour of supreme trial, when the flesh shrank from the bitterness of its coming agony and the spirit, even in the willingness of its self-sacrifice, utters its cry of deprecation—" If it be possible, let this cup pass from me;" not only when, as He hung upon the cross, the voice of the tempter spoke once more in the taunting cry, "If thou be the Son of God, come down from the cross, and we will believe;" not only then was this temptation present, but all through His life it must have haunted and waylaid Him. The power over His life was always His. He had "power to lay it down or take it again," to save it or to lose it, as he pleased. Legions of angels were always at His call; heaven always at His disposal for His work on earth. For His own needs, for His own sorrows, for the convincing of His disciples, for the silencing of His enemies, for the salvation of His country, over whose coming woes He wept, at every moment was the occasion and the temptation present to make Himself a King, to establish on earth the kingdom of God without the cross. And it was in this daily trial and in this daily resistance to and victory over it, that He, the Captain of our salvation, the Chief among many brethren, Son of Man as well as Son of God, was made "perfect through suffering."

This temptation is the deadliest and most insidious that can assail those who do the work of Christ, for it is addressed at once to the weakness of the flesh and the willingness of the spirit; to the flesh, in that natural and lawful instinct of our nature by which it shrinks from pain and desires a happy existence; to the spirit—the loving, zealous, devoted spirit, inflamed with love to God and man, longing only for the coming of the kingdom of righteousness and joy—in the desire to gain a speedy triumph for that kingdom; to hasten in eager impatience the work of God that we may see it. In one word, His temptation—as it is ours when we are most like Him and specially when we are most engaged in His work—is that sorest of trials to all earnest and ardent minds, the temptation to accomplish noble ends by unfitting means. It is the temptation to gain a great right by a very little wrong; to do God's work, to do it zealously, lovingly, earnestly, but without sufficient care that we do it exactly in God's way; to give Him, as we believe, the sacrifice of ourselves and yet, unconsciously perhaps, in our haste to sacrifice, to neglect to search and see that no leaven of self-will have mingled with our offering; to serve Him, and yet to choose in some degree the manner of the service. In all such temptation self comes stealthily creeping in; there is an avoidance of the cross, an easing, a saving of self in some form or other. But it is so subtly introduced; it comes so veiled and disguised in the form of zeal, devotedness, earnestness, love for God and man; it comes with such visions of the greatness and the glory of the end, such artful concealments of the unlawfulness of the means, that it is no wonder if in the trial which it needed all His perfect faith and wisdom to resist, our imperfect knowledge and feebler faith give way and the tempter whom He discovered and denounced is welcomed by us as an angel of light.

And now let us proceed to trace the manifestation of this great law through these three temptations of our Lord. Let us place ourselves in succession in each of the scenes of His trial, and in each of them contemplate Him as our example.

First, there is the trial of the wilderness. To the Son of Man, in His hunger and peril of loss of life for lack of food, the tempter says, "If thou be the Son of God, command these stones that they be made bread." Here the temptation is manifest: it is a proposal to preserve the human life of Jesus by means of His divine power; that is, to preserve it by a violation of that law of His kingdom which, as we have seen, forbade Him thus to save Himself. If He had done this, He would have been securing His humanity from suffering by the power of His divinity; He would have been emancipating Himself from those conditions to which He had voluntarily submitted Himself. Had He done this, He had refused the cross. And yet how very subtle was the temptation to do this! The act proposed was in itself a lawful one. He was more than once in His after life to work miracles of like kind for others, why not for Himself? It was no sensual indulgence either that He was asked to furnish Himself with, only a supply of the merest necessaries of life. Nay, more; the end was not only lawful, but in this case all-important; the life imperilled in the wilderness was the life of the world; on it depended the accomplishment of God's greatest work; it was consecrated to the noblest of tasks. How if it perished then could that task be completed? Like the life of Isaac, the seed to whom the promise was given, this life of the true Isaac seems essential to the fulfilment of the promise of blessing to all the nations of the earth. Not for the sake of avoiding trial, but to preserve Himself for greater and sorer trial, even the endurance of the agony and the sacrifice of the cross, let the Son of God provide for His human life the sustenance it needs. "Command these stones to be made bread."

And now, mark how our Lord replies to this temptation. He does so not, as He might have done, by simply pleading duty, by the answer, "God hath said;" nor yet by any explanation why it would have been unlawful in this case to have done what He was asked to do. For our sakes He goes deeper; He goes, in His answer, to the root of the temptation itself, that He may arm us against all trials of like nature. He has been tempted by the desire to preserve life. His answer is, that His so doing would not preserve life, but destroy it. "Man"—observe how He graciously identifies Himself with His people. "Man"—for I the Son of God am and will here be only man—"doth not live by bread alone, but by every word that proceedeth out of the mouth of God." Man's life—so far even as it is mere animal life—is not supported by food alone: the life-sustaining word of the Creator must accompany the food, or it will not nourish. Life in the meanest thing that lives is a Divine mystery: it lives and moves, and has its being in God: there is in it something more than eating and digestion and assimilation and growth; there is in it the creating and sustaining word of God. But the life of man, the spiritual, the immortal creature, in whose nostrils the breath of life was breathed by God, consists in the redeeming, regenerating, sanctifying word of His Heavenly Father. To know God as by His word He reveals Himself, to love Him, to serve Him, to dwell in and with Him, this is man's life eternal. To do His will, is meat and drink. To lose that word of revelation, to disobey that word of command, to want that word of blessing, is for man to die: to know it, to love it, to obey it, is to live. Therefore it is that for man it is possible to lose his life and yet to save it; to save it and yet to lose it. Therefore it is, that for us it never can be necessary, in order to preserve life, to disobey the very least word of God; for it is by that word we truly live. Not by food alone, whether food corporeal or food spiritual; not by the abundance of all that we possess for body or for soul; not by the wealth that supplies the bodily sustenance; not even by the wealth of grace that supplies the spiritual sustenance; but by the life-giving word of God, does man live.

In that one word of faith which lifts us above the means of life—above life itself—to the Author and Giver of life, our Lord provides His Church with a perpetual defence against all the temptations and the terrors of sense. From the love of life and the fear of death; from the love of all that makes life sweet and death terrible; from all fear, all love, save the fear and love of God, Christ sets us free. In the spirit of this word, we fear to lose, we love to keep, nothing save the love of God! It is not a necessary thing, it is not even a desirable thing, that we should enjoy this present life, or that we should preserve it, if life, or the joys of it, come into competition with the word of God.

This is the martyr spirit of the Church; the spirit that comes from the knowledge of what it is in which our true life consists. It was in this spirit that the Church, in her earlier days, went forth, "led of the Spirit into the wilderness" of heathendom, to be tempted of the devil. In this spirit it was that the first Christians went forth to their great missionary work in days when every Christian was a missionary, and every missionary was in peril of becoming a martyr. In this spirit it was that they endured their great fight of affliction, taking joyfully the spoiling of their goods and the shedding of their blood, thankful if only they were thought worthy to suffer for His name who sent them. In this spirit it was that the first martyrs and confessors faced the sword of the executioner, the rage of the wild beasts, and the hideous ingenuities of the torture. Through famine, through nakedness, through death in all its most terrible forms, from the noble army of martyrs and confessors came still the same unhesitating, unwavering answer—" Not life, but the word!" "Man doth not live by bread alone, but by every word that proceedeth out of the mouth of God." It was in this martyr spirit the early Church conquered the world. It was beneath this banner of the cross her warriors went forth to victory. And it was not until her wilderness trial had ended—not until the enemy had changed the nature of his temptation and tried her, not with danger and suffering, but with safety and ease—that her missionary zeal abated, her first love grew cold, and she left the heathen half won, and the uttermost parts of the earth unclaimed for her Lord!

Such martyr spirit should be in all our work for Christ now. It is in it largely still. It is to be seen wherever the missionary goes forth, severing the ties of home and country, leaving the pleasures, the advantages, the noble and lawful ambitions even, of civilized and Christian life, to encounter the fatigues, the perils of his sojourn in the lands of the heathen; or—harder still perhaps to bear—the utter isolation, the sick weariness of heart that falls on him, who, day by day and year by year, dwells with inferior natures to whom he must for ever minister, from whom he can receive nothing, whose soul's life grows faint and sad as he finds himself thus alone in the wilderness! It is to be seen, though in far lower degree, whenever the Christian at home gives to the cause of Christ—not the nicely-calculated superfluity that remains when every want is provided for, and every taste indulged; not the regulation subscription which remains the same, though the means of life become trebled or quadrupled; but the gift which requires for the making of it that something be subtracted from the enjoyments of life —the gift that is a sacrifice. In this, too, there is the acknowledgment, "Man doth not live by bread alone." And this, therefore, is the Church's special message to the world. In a soft and luxurious age—in an age in which the art of making the most of life, of living comfortably and pleasantly, seems elevated almost into a virtue—this is still her message, "Man's life consisteth not in the abundance of the things that he possesseth." To ourselves when tempted to covet inglorious ease and slothful comfort; to the youth who, with his life choice yet to make, is hesitating between a course of lawful advancement and gain here, and of nobler self-sacrifice in his Master's service; to the man of wealth, and to the man of pleasure—our message still is, "Man doth not live by bread alone, but by every word that proceedeth out of the mouth of God."

But there is a deeper lesson given us here, and against a still subtler temptation. There is a life of churches, of institutions, of societies, as there is of individuals, and there is the temptation to preserve this life too by unlawful means. Religious institutions have their secular life. They live as it were by bread, by means, by money, by all that machinery for obtaining money with which all who work our great societies are so familiar. Such means are useful and lawful, just as the means of maintaining bodily life are lawful. But the use of them is attended with the danger of forgetting that the society or the institution does not live by these alone; that it has a nobler life than that which these sustain, even a spiritual life, which consists in the sustaining word of God.

There is a temptation, we may call it of the wilderness, when some zealous worker for our society, who finds himself in a strait for help, is tempted to say, "The life of the society must not be weakened, the interest must be kept up. I must appeal to some lower motive, conciliate some local prejudice or influence, do or say, or avoid doing or saying, something, because of gain or loss to the society." This is to make an idol of the society, to prefer the life of a cause, of an institution, of a party, to the Word. Let us take care that we are not guilty of such idolatry. Honoured as we believe this society has been of God, and loved and honoured as it should be by us for His sake, yet, let us not forget that God can do without the Church Missionary Society if He choose, but that not for one instant can the Church Missionary Society do without God. The life of our Society does not consist in crowded meetings, interesting and eloquent speeches, powerful patrons, zealous collectors, numerous subscriptions, an overflowing treasury. It lives by all these, but not by these alone: its life consists in the presence of Christ in the hearts of Christian men. Not the great meeting nor the great speech, but the Spirit of the Lord that fills the meeting and the speaker; not the great patron, but the love of Christ in his heart that makes him willing to cast his honours at the feet of Christ; not the large gift, but the loving self-denial that accompanies it: these are the things in which its true life consists. Let us never forget this. Let us, who necessarily resort so much to the use of all these means, beware of the idolatry of means; let us beware of supposing that these are indispensable to our success, or that they are to be preferred, in the very least degree, to the word of the Lord. Let us remember that here, too, we need the martyr spirit; that here, too, we must be ready to sacrifice life for duty; here, too, we must remember we do "not live by bread alone, but by every word that proceedeth out of the mouth of God."

II. And now let us follow our Lord to a very different scene of trial; from the wilderness to the temple, from lowliness to prominence, from weakness to power, from fear to security. In the wilderness the Son of Man stands confronted by physical dangers and terrors, by peril to life from circumstances beyond His control as man. On the summit of the temple He stands safe from all physical danger, master of circumstances, secured by the promise of supernatural protection In the former case the temptation was to save life; here it is to risk it. There it was, "Command these stones to be made bread," or thou canst not live. Here it is, "Cast thyself down," thou canst not die. And as in the wilderness—the region of the natural—the temptation was mainly to the flesh; here in the region of the spiritual, in the centre and summit of the religious and ecclesiastical polity of His day, the temptation is altogether to the spirit. "Cast thyself down," for angels shall bear thee up. Surely this was not a temptation to the merely childish glory of a supernatural flight through the air just to try if God's promise of safety would be kept. This, which would scarcely be a temptation to any wise and sober man amongst us, could not have been the temptation chosen for Him. But if He had done this, and if angel-ministers had borne Him safely to the ground in the sight of the multitudes of Jerusalem, what would this have been but the very sign of the Son of Man in the heavens which their unbelief was always demanding? Had this sign been seen, the nation of the Jews must have owned Him as their Messias, His kingdom must have been established at once in all Judea, a kingdom which the same supernatural power that preserved Him in his descent might have been expected to preserve against the Romans. Here was a temptation to the prophet and to the patriot, a temptation to Jesus the son of David, who, even then, might have wept over the foreseen agonies of Jerusalem that would not accept Him in His humility, but would have accepted Him in His power and glory. Here is the old temptation reappearing—the kingdom without the cross—the king's part to be done without the pain of the priest or the weariness of the prophet.

Had He done this, it is conceivable that He would have converted His nation—but to what? To a kingdom and a king of their own making, not of God's appointment; to a false ecclesiastical polity, a spiritual despotism, based on false traditions and mistaken interpretations; to a worldly Messias reigning over an impenitent and unregenerated people. Christ will not do this. To this temptation to set up a false kingdom of God instead of the true one—a kingdom of corrupt ecclesiastical power instead of a kingdom of purity and truth—He answers by shewing wherein consists the true power of His kingdom. "Thou shalt not tempt the Lord thy God." The promise of the Divine presence and support is not absolute : it is conditional. Not in all ways, not whithersoever He goes, will God be with the Son of Man, but in *His* ways, in all ways appointed for Him ; not in the way of self-will, but of obedience ; not for the presumption that chooses its own way, but for the humility that walks only in God's ways, will this promise fulfil itself. And this is the condition of God's presence with His Church throughout all time : He will be with her in all her ways, but only in these so far as they are her appointed ways. Let her err from these; let her follow, not the ways of His appointment, but of erring desire or presumptuous choice ; let her cast herself down in her madness from the place where He has put her, and she shall not be preserved from shameful and grievous fall. Let the Ark of the Lord be borne unlawfully into the fight, it shall become a prey to the Philistines.

The history of this second temptation is written at large

in the history of the visible Church. When she had emerged from her three centuries of wilderness trial, she found herself on the pinnacle of a nobler temple than that of Jerusalem. The centre of the world's spiritual life, the summit of ecclesiastical power and dominion in the great Roman empire, was hers. The very agony of her previous struggle for life and the greatness of her victory, had helped to exalt her to this high place. God had delivered her, had made her to triumph over all the might of heathendom; the idols had fallen before the Ark of the Lord even in its captivity; and now, in the hour of her triumph, what might she not expect? How great her power; how glorious her dignity; how her robes, washed in the blood of martyrs, shone with dazzling brightness; what a crown of pure gold had her faithfulness won her; what supernatural powers were hers! God will be always with her, and the gates of hell prevail against her never! As she said this they were prevailing. She was already presuming on the promise, forgetful of its conditions; already listening to the tempter's whisper, "Cast thyself down," thou canst not go wrong. Infallible, imperishable, go thou on thy way; give the multitude the sign they ask, overawe all doubt, compel universal submission by the display of supernatural power. "Cast thyself down!" Alas that she did so! Alas that from the height of her victory over the hostile world, she stooped to ally herself with its sins, sunk lower and lower down as she corrupted her sacred deposit of truth with the errors of Judaism and the superstitions of Paganism; grew more and more a corrupt and carnal ecclesiastical kingdom, whose ever-increasing pretences were maintained by ever-increasing claims to supernatural might. The false miracle, the pious fraud, the wilder and still wilder legend bore her up like evil angels, a power and a wonder; but still they carried her away from the pinnacle of the temple, and bore her, slowly but surely, downwards to her fall.

And we, too—reformed, purified as we believe our Church to be—we need to remember this lesson of our Lord's trial and these warnings of history. The pinnacles of success, the high places of spiritual triumph, are giddy and slippery places. The head grows dizzy at such heights with the pride that precedes a fall. The tempter is there ever ready to whisper the temptation to presumption and to rashness. The individual is tempted to carnality and carelessness of life, presuming on the Divine promise. The Church is tempted to the carnality of priestly dominion, or to careless toleration of errors or heresies; to such carelessness and sloth, for instance, as fell upon the Church in the last century, when men were ever ready to defend her claims and rights, rarely to speak of her duties; when, on the summit of her prosperity, the Church could only see the worshippers around her, and had no vision, no thought of the heathen, her true inheritance. This was a danger: it may prove a danger still.

In our institution, in our missionary work, we are not free from this temptation and this danger. The wilderness hour of this great Society, her time of weakness and peril, is passed. The time when five men meeting together in a room in London looked out on the desolate wilderness of the world, and asked, "What shall we do for the heathen?"—the time when the power of a Christian state was arrayed, not for, but against missions and for heathendom; the time when to advocate missions was to incur, as its least punishment, the open contempt of the wise and prudent and even of the good;—has long since passed. Our Society has won her way to high and honoured place in Christendom; she stands on the very pinnacle of the edifice of Christian effort. Let us beware! The hour of prosperity is the hour of trial. Remember, the promise is still that God will be with us only in our appointed ways. Ever the wider our field, and the greater our success therein, the greater is the need of humility and caution; need, in our missionary churches abroad, of wisdom and power and a sound mind in dealing with all the difficult questions that arise in new and growing churches; wisdom in avoiding all offence, save the offence of the cross; faithfulness, strict, rigid faithfulness in dealing with the errors of heathendom; wisdom and gentleness in dealing with the prejudices, the infirmities, the traditions and customs of those weaker brethren whom we win from heathendom. Ever as our churches grow, will grow their difficulties from these sources. False doctrines, heresies, schisms, have yet to be encountered. The struggle of the earlier Church is for existence: as she grows, her trial is to order her life aright.

More than this: we need to remember that neither Society nor Church can live merely on the strength of what it has been. Not by repeating the traditions of the past, but by doing as men of the past did; that is, by doing with our present as they did with theirs, bringing still new as well as old out of their store-house; not by persuading ourselves that we have—that any institution, school, party, sect, or church has—a monopoly of Divine grace, or an exclusive promise of Divine presence, save so far as it walks in the Divine ways, can we maintain the life of our Society. Remember that if He is present to bless, He is present amongst the golden candlesticks to trim or to remove the waning light! Let us not be high-minded, then, but fear. Let us pray to be delivered by the love of Christ and of His truth from the sin of tempting the Lord our God by spiritual pride and presumption, by self-seeking and a spirit of party.

III. And now let us follow Christ to His third and last temptation. The place of trial changes once more. From the pinnacle of the temple—the summit of ecclesiastical power and supremacy—our Lord is borne away to a great and high mountain, the Scripture symbol of world power and dominion; from the sight of the city of God and the house of prayer and the worshipping crowd, which represent the supernatural office and functions of the Church, to the vision that reveals the might and the glory of the world. The great kingdoms of the world rise up before Him, glorious and terrible, in all the vastness of their extent and the pride of their civilization and learning and wealth. All that great heathendom that girded, like some great mountain range, the Holy Land, and high over-topped and over-shadowed the highest pinnacle of the house of the Lord;—all these in vision lie before Him; all these may be His for the asking. "All these will I give thee." All these and all their power and glory; not merely to possess and enjoy—that were a poor temptation to the Heir of heaven and earth—but to rule for God. The power, the noblest that the earthly ruler possesses, of swaying men to their own good; the glory, of moral conquest and of righteous rule; this would have been His. The tempter's offer was nothing less than the surrender to Christ of all the power he had possessed and all the glory he had usurped—the power to rule men, the glory of empire over the beings whom God had made in His own image. It was this empire—not merely material, but moral—over the kingdoms of men, that the tempter offered the Son of Man.

And all this is offered Him on one condition—"Fall down and worship me!" One act, not of adoration, but simply of homage; one single act of acknowledgment that the world is Satan's and that he may give it to whom he will; one act of vassalage to him, as the prince of the world's empire; an act which seemed to imply no after servitude, no further rendering of homage or duty, and all should henceforth be His. The world to rule, to teach, to bless with all the blessings of His Kingship, if He will only do homage to the Evil One for it! In that one word the Evil One stands revealed as the usurper of this world, the rebel against God. The act he tempts to is one of open disloyalty to God. To take and hold from the Evil One God's world, or any part of it, is to own him as our God and Lord; it is to choose him as the author and giver of our good things instead of the Lord our Maker; it is to prefer possession on the Devil's terms to inheritance on God's terms. "Ask of me," is the promise of God to His Son, "and I will give Thee the heathen for Thine inheritance." "Ask of me," is the tempter's offer, "and I will give Thee the heathen for Thy present possession."

And, ever from that hour, the tempter tries, by the same temptation, the souls of Christ's disciples. One by one, he takes us up to some mount of vision, from which we see some larger portion of the world's power or glory, some gain, some advancement for ourselves, and offers it at his price, promises to give it, does, alas! too often give it, for one act of homage to himself. Truly it is possible for any one of us to have some larger portion of this world, if we will only pay the Devil's price for it. But we are dealing now with temptation to the Church in her ministerial and missionary work; and viewed in this light it would seem as if this temptation to compromise with the Devil for the possession of God's world is the great temptation of Christian churches and Christian nations in these latter days.

Ever since the era of the Reformation, when the

Church was in a measure delivered from her second great temptation to spiritual despotism, the scene and manner of her trial seem to have taken the shape of our Lord's third trial.

The learning, the knowledge, the civilization of the world, have become, since then, more and more distinctly and exclusively the possession of Christendom, and, with these, of course, the dominion of the world. All the great empires of the world are, and have long been, Christian. The weak, the effete, the decaying, are Pagan. Christendom has been, is now more and more becoming, the exceeding great and high mountain of worldly supremacy from which the Church of Christ surveys, far beneath her, the kingdoms of the heathen. The power over these, the glory of them, are in a large measure ours. Must we say at what price? Alas! no need to inform you, but great need to remember with shame and sorrow, how, through all the history of the discoveries and the conquests of three centuries, Christendom has been purchasing the realms of heathendom at the price of homage to the Evil One; how as, one by one, each new land was discovered, or each older kingdom of the heathen invited conquest, still the tempter made his offer—Worship me for this, forget justice, stifle pity, silence mercy in your dealings with the heathen, and I will give you their lands for a possession and their wealth for a prey. Some you shall spoil by fraud; others you shall cast out by violence, or waste by your vices; others you shall buy and sell like brutes that perish, turning their tears and their sweat into gold, buying your wealth with their lives, forbidding them the knowledge that might make them free, building the edifice of your power and your wealth on their degradation, as some of the savages you despise rest the foundation of their houses upon bodies of men, cruelly done to death that they may dwell in safety. Has it not been so? Does history know a sadder page than the story of how the nations of Christendom have won from the savage and the heathen the power and the glory of the world?

But for the Church, for the Christian ministry—in these days happily free from the guilt of even tacit acquiescence in this sin—there is another and a far subtler form of this temptation. The kingdoms of the world are the objects of the lawful ambition of the Church of Christ. To conquer them for her Lord is her aim and her success in that conquest is her true glory. But it must be *for* her Lord she conquers them; the cities she wins must be called by His name and not by hers; it is His kingdom, and His alone, she is to establish. That kingdom is the kingdom of the cross, the cross of Christ. The cross not of Jesus, the great moral teacher, with its lesson of merely sublime self-devotion of man for men, but the cross of Christ, the Saviour, with its revelation of the infinite love of God for man. Not the cross, as some would have it, whereon hung only a patient, loving, self-sacrificing man, whose death distresses us by its cruel injustice and whose life perplexes us by its inconsistencies and its errors, but the cross on which was offered up the spotless victim provided from everlasting for the sins of men. Not the cross, as men would have it, with its inscription, "Behold the first and best of men, the model man, but nothing more." Not the cross which we may stand around to pity and admire, while we gently criticise Him who hangs there; but the cross, as the Bible reveals it, with its divine inscription, "Behold the Son of God, the King of kings, and Lord of lords;" the cross with all its accompanying mysteries of human guilt and Divine forgiveness; its mysteries of atoning, and cleansing, and sanctifying blood; its double mystery of the death that was suffered that we might have life, the risen life that is our death to sin. This cross, and this alone, may His Church lift up; in this sign alone is she to conquer.

And what at this moment is the temptation of the Church? Surely it is to withdraw this cross from the eyes of men. The kingdoms of the world are vast and their power mighty; the progress of the army of the cross is slow. Compare all that we have done with all that yet remains for us to do; compare the millions of unconverted heathen with the thousands converted; the few missionaries with the myriads of false teachers; think of the long delay, the painful interruption, the sad retrogressions in our missionary work; and then hear the whisper of the tempter— Are you not somewhat too strict and tenacious in your preaching of theological mysteries? This cross, with all its abstruse, half-metaphysical dogmas, with its overbearing demand for absolute submission, offends, perplexes. Must you preach it? Is there not an easier way of winning the heathen? They, with all their errors, hold with you the great tenets of natural religion common to all faiths, all, perhaps, that is essential to any faith. Preach to them of these only; teach them to lay aside the superstitions and errors with which they have overlaid the great all-sufficing truth of one good God and Father of all; tell them that all that He requires of them is that they should love and serve Him; trouble them not with proofs that the book you bring them is a revelation from God; they need no book to reveal Him; they need but to look into their hearts and listen to their own spirits in order to find Him; say nothing of the mysteries of your faith, leave out all dogmas, resolve religion into a sentiment, doctrine into an emotion; meet the heathen thus half-way on the common ground of natural religion and they will meet you. The new Christianity shall conquer the world for the new Christ, and all men shall own the fatherhood of God and feel the brotherhood of man. Yes! "All these will I give thee, and the power over them," and the glory of winning them, if—if only thou wilt fall down and worship, if only thou wilt do homage to the father of all falsehood, by yielding the supremacy of truth. Only acknowledge that yours is not the true faith, but one of many, all partly true; only bow yourselves to me as you enter those temples where men sacrifice to me and these temples shall vanish away and in their place shall rise a great world-wide pantheon, where your Christ shall still have high place, though others take their place beside Him; only be disloyal to God and to His truth, and you shall have the world now.

We need not remind you that this temptation is, of all the three, the most fatal to our missionary work. Notwithstanding the success of the other two, there might still be room left for missionary effort. To preserve the life of the Church, even by unworthy means, would imply that we still thought it worth preserving. To maintain the power of the Church by unlawful means, would imply that men still believed in her mission. But once yield to the temptation to compromise truth with error, once own that the devil's lie may be God's truth, and what need is there of missionary effort? If all the world's beliefs are only one truth seen from various points of view—only different ways of worshipping one Great Father—why should we trouble ourselves to change any of those views? Why send men round the globe to tell the Hindu that his Vedas are as truly God's word as our Bible; or the Caffre that all our Bible has to tell him he knows already? Once believe this, and our missionary enterprise is the merest waste of time, the most solemn and laborious trifling men ever engaged in.

Against this temptation Christ our Lord has armed His Church in His answer to His tempter: "Thou shalt worship the Lord thy God, and Him only shalt thou serve." To the spirit of ambitious disloyalty He opposes the spirit of obedient loyalty. Let others seek, if they will, the false glory of large conquests won by treaties with the enemy which our Lord and King will never ratify. Let others seek, if they will, the easy triumph, the painless victory that avoids the cross of the Prophet —which is unbelief of His message—by concealing the doctrine of the cross that provokes it. For us there must be no truce in our warfare, no armed neutrality, no alliance, but war, stern, open, uncompromising war, for the truth, for all the truth of God against all the lies of the enemy; and most of all, against that greatest of all falsehoods, which proclaims his lie to be greater than God's truth, which bids us to do homage to the false in order to advance the true.

Against this temptation our missionary work is at once our protest and our protection. It is the Church's repeated proclamation of loyalty to her Lord. It is her perpetual refusal to set up a kingdom in His name without His Cross. It is our affirmation, year after year, that the ambition of the Church is not to win the world by surrendering the faith, but to win souls by proclaiming the faith. The glory of this warfare is ours. The glory of the final victory shall be His. It is for Him to wear the crown when he "takes to Himself His great power and reigns." It is for us meanwhile to bear aloft the cross, even though we faint beneath its weight. Every missionary meeting we hold, every missionary sermon we preach, every missionary who goes forth to proclaim

Christ crucified, is one more act of homage to the Lord our God, is one more refusal to do homage to the evil one.

Pray for the Church of Christ in this her last trial, that she may have grace to be faithful, grace to hold fast in all its integrity the treasure Christ has given her for the world, the faith committed to the saints. Pray that, undazzled by the glory of a conquest which is not to be hers but her Lord's, unawed by the power of the world's kingdoms that are His inheritance and must one day be His possession, unseduced by the voice of the tempter, she may make to his offers still her Lord's answer, "Thou shalt worship the Lord thy God and Him only shalt thou serve."

Pray, brethren, finally, for the Church of Christ, that against each of her three great temptations she may ever be armed by her Lord's example and filled with her Lord's spirit.

Christ in the wilderness tells us wherein consists the true life of the Church. Christ on the temple pinnacle tells us wherein lies the true power of the Church. Christ on the mount of vision reveals to us the true glory of the Church. Her life is the word of the Lord; pray that she may never prefer life to the word. Her power is in the promised presence of her Lord in all her ways; pray that she may never claim the promise while she errs from the appointed way. Her glory is in the loyal worship and service of the Lord her God; pray that she may never seek to win a present triumph by disloyal homage to His enemy and hers. Pray that she may be delivered from the spirit of cowardly and unbelieving selfishness, by the spirit of brave, self-sacrificing faith; from the spirit of presumption by the spirit of godly fear; from the spirit of false ambition, by the spirit of true loyalty. So, against the wiles of the tempter, may she "stand fast in the Lord, and, having done all, stand!" Stand in the name and for the sake and in the power and spirit of her Lord, strengthened with all His might, and, though tried with His temptation, still living His life of faith—the faith that waits as well as works—the faith that lives by the word of God, that walks in the ways of God, that labours for the glory of God! This is the faith that overcometh the world, for it is not only faith *in* Christ, it is the faith *of* Christ, the faith in which He lived, walked, triumphed, and in which He bids us live and walk, promising that we shall triumph with Him at the last, when, from the exceeding high mountain of His supreme dominion—the Mount of the Lord, lifted high above all the mountains of the earth—He shall see no kingdom, no power, no glory that is not His and ours with Him for ever and for ever!

REBUILDING THE WALL IN TROUBLOUS TIMES.

REBUILDING THE WALL IN TROUBLOUS TIMES.

Preached at the Restoration of St. Andrew's Church, Dublin, November 30th, 1866.

"And Judah said, The strength of the bearers of burdens is decayed, and there is much rubbish; so that we are not able to build the wall.

"And our adversaries said, They shall not know, neither see, till we come into the midst among them, and slay them, and cause the work to cease.

"And I said unto the nobles, and to the rulers, and to the rest of the people, The work is great and large, and we are separated upon the wall, one far from another.

"In what place, therefore, ye hear the sound of the trumpet, resort ye thither unto us: our God shall fight for us."—Nehemiah iv. 10, 11, 19, 20.

NO two scenes could well be more unlike than that to which our text refers and that which we witness here to-night. This band of returning exiles, rebuilding, at the hazard of their lives, the walls of their ruined city, contrasts strangely with this congregation, assembled in perfect security in a church rebuilt at no greater effort or sacrifice than that implied in a successful subscription list. And yet, unlike as these two restorations are, they have this, at least, in common, that they both illustrate a law which governs the whole history of the Church—a law which we must ever bear in mind, if we would understand any event in that history, whether great or small.

I mean the law by which the outward condition of the Church stands related to her inner life.

The life of the Church is a divine life. It consists in the presence of her Lord in her by His Holy Spirit. It can never, therefore, be dependent upon any outward event or circumstance whatever. Nothing that comes to her from without has power to hurt her. All things that so come to her may be made to help her. "All things are ours;" all things, whether in themselves good or evil; "Paul, Apollos, Cephas"—the ministry, that is, with all its powers—and "the world," too—"this present evil world," which that ministry seeks to overcome; "life," and also its antagonist "death;" "things present," with all their unalterable facts and circumstances; "things to come," with all their unknown possibilities—all are ours. All are subject to us and we subject to none of them, for "we are Christ's and Christ is God's." Our life comes from Him who has power to subdue all things to Himself, and who has bestowed on us the power, in His name and by His Spirit, to do so too.

But if the Church possess this power by virtue of her Lord's indwelling Spirit, then it is clearly hers only so far as she is indwelt by that Spirit. So far as that is at any time wanting to her, she sinks down to the level of a merely human institution, dependent largely upon outward events and circumstances. Her good and her evil come to her from without rather than from within. She loses her power of drawing good out of seeming evil. She is in danger of deriving evil out of seeming good.

There is, therefore, properly speaking, no such thing as a favourable or an unfavourable event in Church history. The same event will have the most opposite results, according as the life of the Church is strong or weak—according as she has or has not power to subdue it to herself. The persecution that at one time only purifies may at another time destroy a Church. The peace that at one time relaxes and enfeebles may at another time prove a season of refreshing, in which she shall "walk in the fear of the Lord and be edified." The result is in each case determined not by the outward circumstance, but by her manner of dealing with it.

Both the restorations we contemplate to-night serve to illustrate this law.

Seven years ago you sustained a great loss in the destruction of your parish church by fire. To-night we see this loss apparently converted into a great gain. Your former church has been replaced by one in every way superior to it. But what the real loss or gain of these events to you should be, has depended all along on the spirit in which you dealt with them. If the destruction of your parish church had found you insensible to the value of a house of prayer, or if the long want of it had made you so; if, in consequence, you had been quite indifferent how it were rebuilt or whether it were rebuilt or no, provided only that its rebuilding cost you nothing; then, whether this church were a meaner one than its predecessor for want of your help, or a richer one without your help, in either case you would have been no gainers by its restoration. You would have actually suffered in it a severe loss. You would have lost the opportunity of winning spiritual wealth by self-sacrifice, and the church, rich or mean, would have stood a perpetual monument of your spiritual poverty. If, on the other hand, the destruction of your church found you truly sensible of all the blessings of a house of prayer, and if the long want of it had made you still more so; if you rejoiced in the opportunity its rebuilding gave you of offering of your substance to God; then, even though it had been, from real honest want of means, as poor and homely as it is nobly beautiful, its restoration would have been to you a real gain. You would—may I not say you will—worship in it henceforth with a deeper love for all its services, a livelier interest in all the parish ministrations that will once more cluster round it; and thus it will be to you the evidence and the future source too of your spiritual wealth. But in either case the loss or the gain would have lain not in the event or the circumstance, but in the manner in which you dealt with them. According to that and to that alone, are you richer or poorer for this your new house of prayer.

And just the same lesson do we learn from the story of that other restoration with which I have contrasted yours.

When the Jews beheld their restored temple, we are told that those who remembered the former wept. They grieved for the lost glory of the holy and beautiful house where they had worshipped of old. They had sustained, they thought, an irreparable loss. And yet, could they have read that scene as we read it now, they would have rejoiced for all the gain that seeming loss had brought them.

The glory of their latter house was, even then, far greater than that of the former. Never had there gathered to the temple of Solomon in all its glory a multitude of worshippers as rich in all that makes the true glory of a house of prayer as were those who worshipped there that day. The lessons of adversity had been largely blessed to them. The courts of the house of the Lord had gained for them a new preciousness, as they sat and wept by the waters of Babylon when they remembered Zion. The Lord's songs had gained for them a deeper meaning, as in the bitterness of their hearts they refused to sing, in a strange land, the melodies that had been so long unheard in their own. They had learned the worth of all they once despised and the loathsomeness of all they once desired. As they stood there, few, despised, threatened, but chastened, repentant, believing, strong in the courage that faith and repentance bring, they were once more a great nation—a greater nation than they had ever been before. They proved themselves so. It was the Church of the Restoration, the Church of the Maccabees, that supplied that noble addition to the noble army of martyrs, of whom we read, that "they were tortured, not accepting deliverance, and had trials of cruel mockings and scourgings, of bonds and imprisonments, who were stoned, were sawn asunder, were tempted; were slain with the sword; who wandered about destitute, afflicted, tormented, in deserts and mountains, and dens and caves of the earth." And "these all"—saints, confessors, martyrs—were the ripened fruits of the good seed sown in tears upon the plains of Babylon. But had the Jews in any other spirit than this restored their city and their temple; had some earlier Herod, for instance, rebuilt these for them in all their old magnificence; had the whole impenitent and godless multitude that remained in Babylon been transported to their own country instead of the sifted and winnowed remnant who returned there of their own free will; then, indeed, those who read the history of their nation aright might have wept over all the splendour and rejoicing of such a restoration. On all the stately beauty of that new Jerusalem they might have read the old inscription, "Ichabod!" On all the strength of its new defences they might have seen the old words of judgment, "Take away her battlements, for they are not the Lord's." In all the magnificence of palace or of temple, they might have seen but what He saw who walked her streets four hundred years after—when her fine gold had once more become dross—the outside whiteness of the sepulchre that hid within it the uncleanness and the rottenness of death.

So here, too, we see how the gain or the loss of the Church comes to her still from within and not from without; how the outward circumstance is still to her just what she wills to make it.

I. And now that we have seen how this law governs all the history of the Church, let us try to read by its light that portion of it which most concerns us—the history of our own Church. Let us see if we can learn aught from the records of our past that may show us our duties and our dangers in the present, our reasons for hopes or fears for the future.

The outward condition of the Irish Church has been for centuries that of a territorial establishment secured by law. Whatever be the advantages of such an establishment for the spiritual life and work of ministers and people (and they are very great), she has enjoyed them. Whatever were the disadvantages of such an establishment in the peculiar circumstances of this country (and they, too, were many and serious), she has had to contend against them. Whether her help from the one were not more than counterbalanced by her hindrances from the other, this is not the place to inquire. But it is the place to confess that she has failed to accomplish the task set before her at the Reformation—the spiritual conquest of the Irish nation. It is the place to confess that whatever there was in her position to make that task a difficult one, there was nothing to make her effort for it impossible. It is the place to confess that such effort was not made. She might or might not have succeeded had she made it. She might have gained the glorious spoil of a nation won to the purer faith of the gospel, or she might have reaped all the spiritual gain of her failure, as century after century she toiled on, hoping against hope, borne up against disappointment by an ever-deepening faith and an ever-growing zeal and love. She might, by the power of her inner life, have so used all that was favourable, have so striven against all that was unfavourable, in her outward condition, that whether she succeeded or failed in her great task, she would still have grown richer as she toiled at it. We know how she failed to do this. We know how, instead of striving with all her might to be the Church of the Irish nation, she only too willingly acquiesced in the laws and the circumstances that made her the Church only of a section of it. We know how on her there fell—not more heavily, but, for her, more perilously than on other Churches—that lethargy of the last century, which fell upon all Christendom, but from which the activities of a missionary career might specially have preserved her. We know how, at last, the Church was all but lost in the Establishment. We know how, for the idea of a heavenly kingdom, with its heavenly powers and privileges, its heavenly aims and uses, men had substituted the idea of a merely earthly institution, with earthly powers and privileges and earthly aims and uses—how the meat became at last more than life, the raiment more than the body. Why should we hesitate to confess this? Why rather should not we, whose teeth are set on edge with the sour grapes that our fathers have eaten and whose burden is heavy with their neglects, loudly proclaim the fact, that in times past the inner life of the Irish Church was not strong enough to subdue, was subdued and all but quenched by, her outward circumstances.

And now we are told that the outward condition of our Church is about to undergo a great change. The endowments that have been hers for centuries are to be taken from her. The fence of a legal establishment that has so long protected her is to be swept away. Justice, it is alleged, demands, policy requires, this sacrifice of our possessions for the peace and well-being of our country. All round the walls of our Zion we hear the war-cries of our assailants—the exulting prophecies of their success and of all the wonderful results that are to follow from it. Whether their assault will be successful, or whether all the social and political blessings they anticipate would follow from their success, this is not the place to inquire. Let statesmen and politicians decide these questions. As citizens of this kingdom, you have your share in their decisions; see that you take it. It concerns you far more than it does us. The existence of an Establishment is a layman's question far more than it is a clergyman's.

But there is a question of far deeper concernment; one that touches you and us alike and one that well befits this place and scene. It is this. Suppose this change in our outward condition to take place, how are we prepared to meet it? Is the inner life of our Church so strong as to be able to bear the shock of so great a change? Would our Church survive, or would it perish with the Establishment—would the deprivation of her wealth be but the trimming, or would it be the quenching of her light by Him who walks among the golden candlesticks?

This is, indeed, a very serious question. It is one not of poverty or wealth, but of life or death. It is the question how far we have ceased to be a dead establishment; how far we have become a living Church filled with the spirit and the power of our Divine Master. Thank God, that on this point there is such large ground for confidence. Thank God, that this change, if it were to befall us now, would not find our Church as it would have found her fifty years ago. We know how largely she has shared in the revival which, since then, has been poured forth on the Churches. We know how largely life and zeal have replaced sloth and spiritual death. We know how many a token of this there is amongst us, that strangers do not and enemies will not see; and how many a token too, that none can deny. We know of Church extension and Church restoration, of services multiplied, of frequent communion, of fervent preaching, of diligent pastoral visitation, of earnest and self-denying efforts for education, of zealous missionary work at home, and large share in missionary work abroad. All this we see, and as we see it, we "thank God, and take courage." But still, the change we speak of would be a very great one. It would be like a sudden and extreme change of climate to a convalescent. Are we strong enough to bear it? Would it subdue us, or could we subdue it to ourselves?

It might help us to an answer to this question if we consider for a little what would be our special difficulties and dangers in that case, and what powers we should specially need to strengthen us against them.

II. Let us suppose, then, the destruction of our Establishment accomplished and our disendowed and disestablished Church left dependent upon the zeal and the love of her own members. Suppose the call to have come for Irish churchmen to arise and rebuild the walls of their Zion, who would answer to this call?

First—Those, and those only, who valued the ordinances of religion for their own sake; those for whom the loss of these would simply be the loss of the daily bread of their daily life, and who would, therefore, hold them cheaply purchased by the sacrifices which would then be needed to provide them. Certainly they could not be expected to make such sacrifices for whom it is now a matter of indifference whether they have a church to worship in or no, and who show their indifference by rarely or never entering a church. Those who can now be hardly persuaded to avail themselves of means of grace which cost them nothing, would hardly care to join in providing means of grace which would cost them much. Those who grudge the comparatively small payment with which their property is charged for the maintenance of a Christian ministry whose services they would willingly dispense with, could scarcely be expected voluntarily to charge themselves with the much larger payments which would then be required. The godless, the indifferent, the pleasure-loving, all who despise, or dislike, or simply tolerate religion now, would certainly make no effort to preserve it then.

Secondly—Of those who really valued the ordinances of religion, those, and those only, could be expected to help who really prized the ordinances of our Church. Those who were merely her nominal members, avowedly rejecting more than one of her doctrines and enduring rather than loving her services—those to whom it were a matter of indifference, not whether they worshipped at all, but where they worshipped, provided only they heard from the pulpit those doctrines which they approved of, could scarcely be expected to make any great effort to maintain one form of worship rather than another, especially if that form entailed a somewhat costlier maintenance.

To rebuild our Church would require therefore not only religious men, but religious churchmen—men who had for their Church not merely a languid preference, but a devoted and intelligent attachment—men whose churchmanship was not merely the accident of their birth or the habit of their lives, but the settled conviction of their understandings and the strong love of their hearts —men who would understand and act upon the principle, with which all other religious communities seem more deeply impressed than ours, that no institution can long continue to exist, whose own members do not heartily and thoroughly believe in it.

And then, when those who thus loved our Zion had gathered themselves to the task of rebuilding her ruined walls, what dangers, what difficulties would they encounter? They would have to resist, in the first place, dangers from without. Around that rising wall would gather formidable enemies; not the enemies of our Establishment—that would have ceased to exist—but enemies of our Church and of those doctrines and practices for which she testifies.

They would find themselves assailed, in the first place, by those who would fain uproot the very foundation on which they would build. "Other foundation can no man lay than that which is laid which is Jesus Christ." Not Jesus the half mythical hero of a religious romance; but Jesus the Christ—the Saviour, the Anointed One—the Christ of the Gospels and the Creeds, who "for us men and for our salvation came down from heaven;" who lived, suffered, died, rose again, ascended into heaven, where He sits on the right hand of God and whence He has sent down His holy Spirit to make us partakers of His divine nature. For the faith in this Christ "once delivered to the saints" they would need "earnestly to contend." For, without this faith, the Church has really no reason for her existence. If it be a superstition, she is an anachronism. She might perhaps continue to exist as an association for the promoting of moral and social science —a mutual improvement society—a benevolent club; but a Church, in the sense of a Divine kingdom of God amongst men, possessor of Divine gifts and powers, witness for Divine truths, she could no longer claim to be.

But our builders would have to contend against another enemy. All around them would lie a system whose errors consist, not in denials of the faith but in corruptions of it and additions to it; a Church which acknowledges the foundation, but which has built on it the wood, hay, and stubble of man's devices; a Church which owns the authority of the written word, but claims to add to it an unwritten word that is also divine; a Church which acknowledges the Saviour's sacrifice, but claims to repeat it—His priesthood, but claims to share it—His mediatorial throne, but erects another beside it; a Church in which the catholic truths of the creeds which she still holds loom dim and distorted in the mist of error with which she has encompassed them, and yet a mist so transfused with the colours of imagination, so warm with sentiment and passion, that men love to lose themselves in it. Against this system, with all its dangerous attractions, the builders of our Zion would need to maintain a resolute defence.

For to yield to it would destroy her existence as surely as would the yielding to the assaults of Rationalism. For if ever our difference with Rome should come to be regarded merely as a question of words, a difference only about forms of expressing the same truth and not about the truth itself, then our separate existence must come to be regarded as nothing but an unjustifiable and sinful schism. We should stand convicted of having needlessly and wantonly broken the unity of Christendom, and our first act should be, not to ask for explanations of formularies or relaxations of discipline, but for pardon for our revolt. The protest of the Reformation was either the assertion of a Divinely-given freedom, or it was rebellion against a Divinely-constituted authority. Between these two positions there is no middle ground. We can find none. Rome recognises none. She can hold no parley with rebels. No alteration of formularies, no toning down of articles, can satisfy her so long as our real guilt in her eyes is our having dared to draw up any articles at all. And as for imitations of her services or borrowings of her rites, these go just as far towards obtaining her forgiveness as the adoption of the drill or the uniform of the soldiers of the state would go to atone for the guilt of a band of armed and impenitent rebels.

Once more—The restorers of our Church would need to guard against another enemy. We pray to be delivered not only from false doctrine and heresy, but from schism. That is from needless division and separation, and from the dividing and separating spirit which is ever splitting off from the Church some new sect, with its new error, or its broken and distorted fragment of truth, sure to develop itself into some imperfect or distorted form of spiritual life. Against this schismatical spirit, even more than against the serious forms of error it has given rise to, our builders would need to guard. . These errors are each of them opposed to some one distinctive doctrine or practice of our Church and therefore are so far hurtful to her life. The error, for instance, which denies to little children their right to membership in the kingdom of Christ ; or that which provides, in addition to baptism, a new sacrament of instantaneous conversion, with its outward and coarsely visible signs as the further condition of admission to the visible Church ; or that which denies the need or the authority of an ordained ministry ; or the thousand and one crude notions that may be propounded from day to day by ignorant and fanatical teachers, who, unsent and unqualified, usurp the office of pastors in the Church of Christ, and who set up for themselves sect after sect in which to maintain their errors and themselves. Against each and all of these we should need to guard. But more than all these, against that error which is common to them all, and which exists within as well as without our Church; the denial of the great truth that Christ designed for His Church an outward and visible as well as an inward and spiritual unity; the notion that the possession of this inner unity of the Spirit by individuals makes the outward disunion of communities a matter of indifference, nay, rather an actual advantage; the notion that such separation is not schism, provided only that those so separated "agree in essentials," that is to say, that separation is justifiable precisely in the degree in which it is causeless, and that the less men really differ, the better right they have to break the peace of Christendom; the notion that, provided only we love Christ, it matters nothing what body of Christians we belong to, that is to say, that provided we love Christ, it matters not whether we obey or disobey His commandment. Against this doctrine, which is the very essence of schism, the Church, if she is to exist, must maintain the opposite truth, that Christ did design for His followers an outward unity, which should manifest to the world the inner union they have in Him. She must proclaim the truth that in the inspired descriptions of the unity of the Church, "one Baptism and one Body" have a place as well as "one Lord and one Spirit." She must not fear to say that to break this unity for any lesser cause than the preservation of that inner life of which it is the expression, is a sin, and that the smaller the cause of separation, the greater, not the less, is the fault of the schism.

This doctrine we should maintain, not only if we would maintain the right of our Church to her true position, but if we would hope ever to win back those who have departed from her. If we are ever to do this, it will not be by assuring them that because they are brethren we think lightly of their departure, but that we deplore it because with all our hearts we own their brotherhood. We shall win them, not by telling them that our differences are so slight that we are virtually one, but that if they be so slight there is the greater reason why we should be actually one; and the greater too our readiness to confess whatever there may have been of schismatical spirit on either side in unduly pressing things non-essential as conditions of union and to consider how we might remove or modify these, in order to reunion.

Such speech to our Nonconformist brethren, more truly liberal than that which so often usurps the name, would do far more for the reunion of Protestant Christendom than idle words about "sinking minor differences," which are sure to rise to the surface in the first earnest effort men make for their sect or Church, or about "holding out right hands of fellowship,"* which, alas, must be unclasped in order to partake of the Sacrament of union which Christ gave to make us one. Not by ignoring differences, but by seeking to remove them; not by reaching out hands merely for a passing salutation, but by joining them in Church membership, can we hope to heal "our unhappy divisions."

Against these three forms of error, then—Rationalism, Romanism, and Separatism—whether without or within

---

* Those who quote this expression as a Scriptural authority for indifference to all questions of Church membership, seem to forget that the occasion on which it was used is a remarkable proof of their importance. "The right hand of fellowship" was given by the apostles at Jerusalem—not to members of another communion, but of their own—to Paul and Barnabas; and it was given after formal and careful consideration of what the conditions of membership in the Church should be.—*See* Acts xv., Gal. ii. 9.

her communion, our Church would need to maintain a steady and consistent testimony.

Her danger from each of these sources would not, of course, be equally great. Most persons, indeed, would be disposed to smile at the idea of the Irish Church running any risk either from Rationalising or Romanising tendencies. They would say that whatever other peril she might incur she is safe enough from these.

And yet these are not altogether imaginary. Rationalism, we must remember, has proved, ever since the Reformation, the bane of Protestant Churches. Protestantism, valuable as it is in its original form as a protest for Catholic freedom against the usurped authority of Rome, is apt to degenerate into a revolt against all authority and an idolatry of the "right of private judgment," which is not so very remote from the spirit of so-called "free thought" that we should regard the spread of the latter amongst us as quite impossible because we are so thoroughly pervaded by the former.

And as regards Romeward tendencies, we must remember that Disestablishment, which deprives the ministers of the no longer privileged Church of the authority and influence that office in her gave them, tends to throw them back upon the assertion of whatever claims to authority can be found in the nature and powers of their order. And it is easy to exaggerate these until they grow into that "sacerdotalism" which, oddly enough, is supposed to be the special disease of Church Establishments, but which is really far stronger in the un-established Churches of our communion. An impoverished aristocracy are not generally the less, but the more tenacious of their rank, because they can no longer pride themselves upon their wealth. The more immediate peril of the disestablished Irish Church would doubtless not be from either of the two first-named causes: but he would be a rash prophet who should say that she will be always or even long secure from these.

There is, however, a danger arising from these which is really imminent, and against which we should need to be specially on our guard.

The indirect effect of error is often greater than its direct effect. It is often more mischievous because it is less looked for; coming, as it does for the most part, in the form of a recoil from error in one direction, which insensibly hurries men into some equally dangerous error in the opposite direction.

Rationalism, for instance, is a deadly evil. But the recoil from rationalism leads to very serious evils on the other side. It leads to a narrow and bitter dogmatism. It leads to clinging to every antiquated prejudice as if it were a revealed truth and to fighting for small sectarian shibboleths as if they were articles of the creed. It leads men to dread thought and to deprecate inquiry, and to refuse "to prove all things" lest they should thereby fail to "hold fast what is good." It leads to men holding their faith—not with the firm grasp with which a brave man holds some treasure whose priceless worth he knows, because he has proved it, and which he will not part from save with life itself—but with the frantic clutch of the drowning coward, catching alike at straw or bough; or rather with the blind tenacity, the mere instinct of adhesion, that binds the limpet to the rock, from which, if the waves once sweep it, it must toss at their mercy till chance shall cast it against some new resting-place.

Again; the evils of Romanism are serious, but the extreme recoil from them leads to evils on the other side. It leads to that most mistaken principle of measuring the right or wrong of our position simply by its distance from

Rome. It leads to an ignorant and bitter Puritanism; to the loss of catholic truth through dread of Romish error; the loss of apostolic order through dread of Romish despotism; the loss of reasonable and lawful symbolism through dread of Romish ritualism. Against this evil our Church would need to testify. She would need to teach that the remedy for Romanism is not Puritanism; that the remedy for superstition is not irreverence; that the remedy for ultra ritualism is not sacrilege. She would need to remember that if spiritual worship be hindered by a sensuous and gaudy ritual, it is not, therefore, promoted by poor and mean churches, nor bald and slovenly services. She would need to warn her members that errors of excess are not best cured by errors of defect; for this simple reason, that these are sure to lead by natural reaction to those very excesses against which they have been cherished as a defence.

In like manner the recoil from schism leads into serious evils on the opposite side. It leads to a truly schismatical denial of the inner unity of the spirit to those who lack the outer and visible unity of the body. It leads to the sin of refusing to recognize the likeness of Christ, the seal of His spirit, in all who love and serve Him, whether they walk with us or no. The remedy for dissent is not Romanism any more than the remedy for Romanism is dissent.

III. But with these dangers all around them, the builders would have to encounter difficulties also. They, too, might exclaim with the timid Judah: "The strength of the bearers of burdens is decayed and there is much rubbish." Weakened by the change that had dried up so many of their resources, they would have to contend with the "rubbish" —the debris of the wall of their old establishment, once a defence, then only a help to the ascending feet of their assailants. Old habits of thought and action suitable to a Church ruled by the State, but unsuitable to a Church self-supported, and therefore, in common justice, self-governed; old notions of political ascendancy or alliance; old slowness and difficulty of co-operation; old disuse of the proper machinery for Church government; old laxity of discipline; old want of flexibility in adapting Church life to the ever-varying conditions and wants of the times; all these remains of the old system would lie all around and hinder their building.

But far more would they be hindered by that difficulty which the prophet pointed out to the builders of his day as the most serious of all; the extent of the wall they would be called on to build and to defend, compared with the small numbers of the builders. The wall would, indeed, be "large and they separated far upon it!" Not merely the paucity of their numbers, but their wide and thin dispersion, would be their greatest weakness. The thicker populations of the towns might, at any time, shift for themselves, and hardly feel the change; but the outlying congregations, scattered in tens and twenties through the country, in perpetual danger of absorption in the surrounding mass of the Romish population, unable to provide their own ministrations, who would care for them? On you, the town congregations, would fall the burden, if your brethren were not to be left a prey to Romanism or dissent. Truly, the care would be an anxious one; you would, indeed, be "few upon the wall," and heavy, indeed, would be your task of building and defending it.

What, then, is the advice the prophet gave of old to those in like case? It is this: "DISPERSE TO BUILD; UNITE TO DEFEND." Let the builders scatter themselves all over the extent of their wall to labour at their task, few it may be and far apart; but at the sound of the trumpet that calls to battle, let them gather themselves together as one man. Let the missionary pastor go forth to his remote and isolated mission alone, but neither forgotten nor uncared for. At his first cry for help, let the sympathy, the encouragement, the aid of all his brethren be with him in his need. Let the separation, the isolation of diocese from diocese, parish from parish, pastor from pastor, that results from the dispersion of so small a number over so wide an area, be so counteracted by new powers of union and of rapid co-operation, that the whole strength and life of our Church should be free to concentrate itself upon any one point. Let the builders be really one; not by the mere mechanical cohesion of a heap of sand, held in by an external fence, from which almost any number of grains might be taken and leave it still one heap; but one with the unity of a living body, in which a wound to one member is felt by all and in which the life in each is shared by all. One, not by the identity of their opinions on all points, but in their agreement in the essential and distinctive principles of their Church. One, in the unity of a deep conviction of the preciousness of what they hold in common. One, in their zeal to build—one in their resolve to defend—one, above all, in the power of that living and inner unity of the Spirit which joined them each to other and all to Christ. Such a unity of the Church would surely then, at last, be recognised as the essential condition of her existence. Irish Churchmen, then at last, would feel that they were too few to afford needless divisions, too weak to survive internal strife. They would learn then not to look too suspiciously or jealously upon the brother who stood side by side with them, with his face to their common foes. They would learn to look upon him lovingly for his brotherhood, gratefully for his help, even though the posture in which he stood to build, or the manner in which he held his weapon, were not precisely identical with theirs. Then, when more than one cause of heart-burning and estrangement that now exists had been removed—then, when so much of the "rubbish" over which the feet of brethren now stumble as they reach their hands to each other, should have been cleared away; then would the watchmen of our Zion see eye to eye, and her soldiers man her walls a resolute, patient, loving, united band. Then would the city, thus at unity within itself, win the presence of Him whose dwelling can only be in abodes that are worthy of the Son of Peace. Then, indeed, might we hope our God would be seen to fight for us.

But if, even in that hour, Irish Churchmen failed to understand the need of this unity; if, for the strength of union, they had only the weakness of disunion; if bitter prejudice, or cold unbrotherly suspicion, or fierce party spirit sundered us then; if the trumpet-notes that were heard amongst us summoned us not to united resistance to a common foe, but to bitter strife of brother against brother; then would our building be turned to the confusion of another Babel, then would the taunting threats of our enemies find a sure and speedy fulfilment, and the meanest, the weakest assailant overleap or overthrow our half-built wall; the first hail-stones of any passing storm would suffice to beat down the stones we had daubed only with untempered mortar and their fall would be at once the proof of our folly and the punishment of our sin.

Brethren, members of our Irish Church, dwellers now within the outer walls of our beleagured Zion, if these would be our dangers and difficulties and these our helps and safeguards in the hour when that outer fence were swept away, surely they are our difficulties and our safeguards while it still stands, though besieged and assaulted. The religious indifference or half-hearted churchmanship that would desert us then is betraying us now. The enemies of our Church who would assail her then are the very same that are assailing us now. The "rubbish" that would help their assault or hinder our defence then, does it not need to be removed now? The missionary zeal that should send us forth to build, and the brotherly love that should unite us to defend then, are they not needed now? The defects that would then threaten our life now weaken it. The powers, the principles, that would then be needed to restore are needed now to strengthen and preserve.

It may be that the threatened change shall not come in our day. It may be much nearer than we think. But our duty is in either case the same, to build the inner wall of our Church. If this, our true defence, remain unbuilt, what avails it if the outer fence of an establishment be left? It would soon cease to hold aught worth the keeping. If, on the other hand, we build aright, then, though that outward wall were levelled with the ground, when the dust of its fall had cleared away there would rise to view another, stronger and higher far, resting on a far deeper foundation, built up all of living stones, guarded by far-seeing watchmen, manned by devoted soldiers of the cross. And as that band of brethren watched the retreating wave of each assault upon their fortress, clear and loud would rise their song of praise, all the clearer and the louder that its every note had been already uttered as a word of prayer: "God is our help and strength, a very present help in trouble; therefore, will not we fear, though the earth be removed, and though the mountains be carried into the midst of the sea, though the waters thereof roar and are troubled, though the mountains shake with the swelling thereof."

Listen, then, to the call to arise and build. The time, yea, "the set time" for that task has already come and we have each our appointed part in it. There is work for all. Some may be called to clear away the "rubbish;" others to bring the stones; others again to "hold the spears until the stars appear." But all may help to build. Each one of us may add to that building at least one living spiritual stone—himself; for in the City of God, each one is both stone and builder, even as He who shall one day place the corner stone is Himself the Foundation. On that Foundation we may learn to rest, with still calmer and deeper confidence, the basis of our faith. On it we may learn to raise with more and more skilful hands the superstructure of our spiritual life. Wider too, as well as stronger and higher, may grow the walls of our city, as to her master builders may be given the joy of adding to them many a living stone that once made part of walls raised in hostile siege against her.

Pray for this, work for it, live for it, and the answer to our prayers and our labours of love may be, that we shall see the wall rebuilt, though in troublous times; a newer, fairer Zion rising, though it were from the ruins of the past, the home of brethren who dwell together in unity, an habitation of God through the Spirit!

THE VICTOR, MANIFEST IN THE FLESH.

THE VICTOR, MANIFEST IN THE FLESH.

Oxford Lent Sermons, 1867.

"For the law of the Spirit of life in Christ Jesus hath made me free from the law of sin and death."—Romans viii. 2.

THERE is a remarkable likeness in these words of St. Paul, to those with which St. John concludes the preface to his gospel. When the Evangelist has told us of the Word becoming flesh and dwelling amongst men, he goes on to tell us how the fulness of that incarnate Word passed, "grace for grace," into the life of men. And he contrasts this "grace and truth," which came by Jesus Christ, with the "law which came by Moses," and which, though itself a divine gift, brought no such gift of life as that which God has bestowed upon us in His only-begotten Son.

This idea of a life which saves us, as contrasted with the idea of a law which has no power to save, is evidently the same with that which St. Paul sets forth in our text, and which appears so frequently in all his writings.

The "fulness" which St. John declares that he received from the Incarnate Word, is the same with that "spirit of life in Christ Jesus" which St. Paul declares has made him "free from the law of sin and death." The "law" which St. John contrasts with "grace and truth," is that same law which St. Paul pronounces too "weak through the flesh" to effect his deliverance. Those whom St.

Paul describes as walking "not after the flesh, but after the spirit," are those same "sons of God" whom St. John describes as "born not of flesh, nor of blood, nor of the will of man, but of God." One and the same idea, taught by one and the same revealing Spirit, is evidently present to the mind of each Apostle. It is the new idea of the deliverance of humanity, by the transforming power of a life, which Christianity has added to the older one of deliverance by the efficacy of an atoning death.

But though these two apostles teach us the same truth almost in the same words, they have arrived at it by very different ways.

St. John begins with the contemplation of the Divine nature which was made flesh. He tells us of "the Word which was in the beginning with God, and was God;" how "by Him were all things made," and how in Him was that life which is the only light of men; and so he comes down to the idea of that Word becoming flesh and dwelling amongst men and of their receiving from Him grace and truth. St. Paul, on the other hand, begins by contemplating that human nature which the Word came to redeem. He studies it in its infirmities, its sins, its struggles, its aspirations, and from these he rises to the conception of that new life which it is to gain from the Incarnate Word.

St. John describes for us our Saviour; St. Paul describes the salvation that we need. St. John, as it were, ascends to heaven to bring Christ down to us. St. Paul descends first into the very innermost parts of his own being, and learns what manner of a Saviour he must be who is to deliver him from the evil that he finds there. The one, with his calm, deep, solemn words, so full of mystery, and yet so full of love, seems like some angel messenger just lighted upon earth, strong and beautiful, the track of his path through the heavens still bright with light from the throne of God. But the other, with his words of passionate agony, his all but despairing cry for a deliverer, seems rather like some traveller through a dark, trackless forest, earth-stained, toil-worn, wounded by each entangling thicket through which he fights his way, but fighting it still resolutely, desperately, through every difficulty, on to the light and freedom that in his darkest hour he still believes he yet shall reach!

And we, who stand beneath the Cross where these two ways meet—we who hear the Divine harmony that these two widely-differing tones make as they blend in their utterance of the Church's hymn to Christ as God—we feel how ill we could afford the loss of either. We feel how inestimably precious to the Church is this twofold aspect of the great central truth of all her faith and all her life.

In the great theological definitions of St. John, we possess a fixed standard of dogmatic truth, by which we may test and correct our erroneous and imperfect conceptions of it. We see how the Spirit of God has lifted up in these for all time a sculptured likeness of our Lord, that stands clearly and sharply defined, high above the distorting mists and fogs of error and ignorance that are ever rising in the lower region of our fleshly nature. On the other hand, in the close, searching analysis of that very nature by St. Paul, in the clear light that he has thrown upon its essential elements, in the profound perceptions he gives us of its needs and desires, we have another safeguard against false and imperfect views of the Incarnation. For in thus deepening our idea of the deliverance that we need, he prepares us for deeper views of the deliverer who is to accomplish it. As we think of the one, so we may be sure will we always think of the other. We cannot have shallow views of our own nature, and deep and true views of the person and work of Christ. All creeds and dogmas notwithstanding, each one of us sees just that Christ, and no other, whom he believes himself to need. He who believes that humanity requires and can receive no higher influences than its own, will see in Christ no more than a man like himself. He who believes that all it requires is knowledge of virtue, will see in Christ a great moral Teacher and no more. He who believes that we need only a revelation of certain doctrines necessary to salvation, will see in Christ an inspired Prophet and no more. He who believes that we need only a great example, will see in Christ no more than an ideally perfect Man. But he who feels that the deliverance he needs is something far deeper than any one of these, or all of them together, is, so far at least, prepared to accept the idea of an Incarnate Saviour, that he can see that all those other Saviours men picture to themselves are no Saviours for him. Those reeds shaken with the wind; those prophets merely; nay, even those more than prophets, which men are ever going out into the wilderness of barren speculation to see, have no attraction for him; they fail, one and all, to satisfy the need of his soul. And on the other hand, he who does rightly believe the Incarnation of Christ, may gain fresh reasons for his faith as he sees how the deepest parts of his nature answer to this deepest mystery of his creed; as he sees how the Incarnation in which he believes can alone supply that salvation which he desires.

It is this aspect of the subject I ask you to consider with me now. I ask you to approach it—not as St. John does, by the way of revealed dogma—but as St. Paul does, by the way of human experience. Let us forget for a moment, as we are so often exhorted to do, the definitions and dogmas of our religious books and question only the soul within us, which we are told we theologians will not listen to, but which, if we would only suffer it to speak, would give us a religion deeper and truer than any of our creeds.

We take, then, the Bible to-night, not as a revelation of dogma, but as, what all admit it to be, a revelation, the deepest and truest we possess, of human nature. We turn to those who in this book have revealed for us the needs, the sorrows, the struggles, the aspirations of their souls. And of these we will question those and those only who had not heard of our dogma of the Incarnation, those who, believing only in "God the Father," had not yet learned to believe in "Jesus Christ His only Son our Lord."

I. The Bible records for us the experience of three men, who, above all others, seem to have been been tried with the question of the deliverance of humanity from evil. The first of these is Job. In him we see humanity contending with evil in its simplest and least terrible form, in that of outward circumstance only. The troubles of Job come to him altogether from without. They fall on him as so many blows dealt him by another's hand; he has not caused them, he can neither resist nor escape them. They sweep over him, wave after wave, and he drinks their salt bitterness and dreads the death they threaten; but he has no more to do with their coming or their going than the drowning man has to do with the rise or the fall of the tide. Like that other sufferer from a God's displeasure, who embodies for us the highest conception that uninspired man ever formed of the conflict of humanity with evil, conscious of his utter helplessness, conscious too of his integrity, he lies the victim of omnipotence, chained down to suffer all that resistless power can will to inflict.

But for the Hebrew Prometheus there is both an agony and a hope unknown to the Greek. Job cannot, like the sufferer in the Grecian drama, take refuge from his torment in defiance of his tormentor. He cannot conquer his conqueror by the calm, resolute power of the indomitable will that, mastering agony by endurance, lifts the righteous suffering man above the unrighteous cruel God. On the contrary, the very sharpest pang in all his trial, is the temptation to think and feel thus towards his God. For the God of Job is a good God, is the Father of his spirit, whom he has loved and served all his life, and he trembles at the thought that his sorrows and his sufferings should cause him to lose his faith in this God. At the thought of this a chasm seems to open beneath his feet, an abyss of evil into whose dark depths if he should once sink, he feels that he is lost for ever. For then the evil that before was all external to him, would have become a part of him; his very inmost self would have become enmity against God. Then would he have "cursed God and died"—died the eternal death of a spirit, that, separated from the true centre of its life and light, wanders hopelessly away into the blackness of darkness and despair for ever! Well might Job tremble and shudder as he saw this form of evil approaching him. It was the very shadow of his tempter!

But as this temptation comes from without, so deliverance from it would seem to come most naturally and easily by a change in those outward circumstances which cause it. Let God only "take away His rod from him;" let Him "cease to terrify him;" let him be no longer driven to and fro by the blast of His displeasure, like "a dried leaf

THE VICTOR, MANIFEST IN THE FLESH.

driven by the wind," and all will be well. This phantom of atheism that vexes and terrifies his soul has its home in that dark dungeon of outward circumstance in which he lies; it will vanish in the broad free light of open day. Give him back his old prosperity, his honoured, useful, happy life; make him the man he was in times past, when "the eye that saw him blessed him, and the ear that heard him witnessed to him," and the whole peace of his spirit will come back again; the world will be no longer in alliance with his flesh to assault and hurt his soul.

The deliverance, then, that Job desires is a deliverance from the evil that is in the world,—a victory *for* him, *for* his flesh, over the world. His "Redeemer" would be a restorer, a healer of outward nature, one who would stand for him and with him " on this earth," and enable him " *in his flesh* to see God," and to see Him as his Father. This salvation from outward evil is that which humanity, in its lower stages of spiritual development, alone can conceive of. This is the salvation of the heathen,—whose saviours were always heroes or gods who did heroic deeds, slaying the monsters that assailed men, destroying, that is, some one of the outward ills that flesh is heir to. And this is the salvation of too many Christians, whose only idea of a Saviour is of one who has saved them from some penalties attached to sin and who will some day make a great change for the better in their outward condition, by translating them to heaven.

And now we turn to question one who had, in large measure, attained to that very deliverance from evil that Job desired. Wise, learned, rich, powerful, he tells us that he applied all the treasures of his wisdom and power and wealth to fashioning for himself a paradise on earth.

No foreign war nor domestic revolt broke the peaceful prosperity, nor dimmed the glory of his reign. He tells us too what came of it all,—"vanity and vexation of spirit." He tells us how he "hated all his labour," how he hated his very life. Yes! Solomon in his glory was as ready, as Job was in his misery, to curse the day that he was born! And with better cause. The evil which Solomon endured was worse far than that which afflicted Job. The torture of satiety, the loathing of all things, that comes on him who has enjoyed all and wearied of all, is more intolerable far than that which the sharpest pain or sorrow brings, for it is hopeless. For the sufferer from this form of evil, no change of circumstance can bring relief, there is for him no good, and he is, therefore, in terrible danger of believing that there is no God. The atheism of pleasure is far darker, far deadlier, than that of pain.

Solomon's experience, then, of evil is more profound than that of Job. He sees, what Job did not see, that this evil is not in the world, not in circumstances, but in himself. It is because he has not "kept from all his eyes desired," because he "has not restrained his heart" from all the joys he cared for, because he gave himself too greedily to the enjoyment of the "good that God had given him under the sun," that he is thus weary and jaded and wretched. If he had enjoyed only in moderation, if he had observed the time and the mean that God had appointed for all things, he would have been happy. And accordingly, "the conclusion of the whole matter," the remedy for all the evil he has known, is self-restraint, obedience to those laws and ordinances of God which condition our enjoyment of this world. "Fear God, and keep his commandments, so shalt thou come forth from them all!"

Solomon's idea of deliverance from evil, then, is Law—a system of checks and restraints upon the appetites and passions of man, sanctioned indeed by the highest motives, by those of religion. His ideal deliverer would be a lawgiver, a prophet who should reveal to men new precepts and enforce them with powerful sanctions. His heaven would be a paradise, but one in which flaming swords turning every way should keep men from all forbidden fruit. This is victory, not *for* the flesh but *over* the flesh. This is the salvation of the heathen moralist and philosopher; it is the self-conquest they are always speaking of, the conquest of the lower part of our nature by its higher and better part, the triumph of the man over the beast in us. This is the salvation of the ascetic, whether heathen or Christian; the man who—believing that the seat of all evil lies in the material part of his nature, the flesh in its lowest and most literal sense—seeks his deliverance from it in the mortification, the torture, the very death of the rebellious flesh which opposes itself to his higher will. This is the salvation, too, of a far lower school, that coldly moral school of Christian teachers, who think of Christ as the Son of God come down from heaven chiefly to give us an "authoritative sanction" for natural religion, to prove His mission by miracles, and to reveal to us new motives why we should restrain from evil, new reasons, in His clearer revelation about heaven and hell, why we should "fear God and keep His commandments."

And now we pass to another; to one who has tried this remedy of Solomon's; to one who did indeed fear God with all the reverence of a devout soul and keep all His commandments, as he believed, with all the strictness of a resolute, self-denying will; to one who was "as touching the law blameless." And what is his experience as to the deliverance from evil that law, even Divine law, can effect? He tells us how utterly it failed to deliver him; how it became to him rather the deadliest and most terrible of evils; how when it "came" to him, when he really came to understand what law was, the sin he once thought dead in him revived in the presence of this restraining law, and "slew him," so that the commandment "ordained to life" he found to be "unto death."

For, this law, this external restraint, with all its awful power, wakes in him another and a mightier law,—"a law in his members," a law of lawlessness, an intolerance of all restraint, a force of resistance that no mechanical power of repression can restrain. And this lawlessness, this impossibility of subjection to law, is the very bent of his nature. It is his very self, and yet it is not himself. There is in him another and a better self that delights in law, longs to obey it, and yet cannot enable him, the whole man, to obey it. And so he finds within him a terrible strife, a conflict between good and evil, light and darkness, law and lawlessness, conscience and will, that rends him in twain, and forces from him, in the misery that it wakes in every fibre of his moral being, the exceeding great and bitter cry—"Oh! wretched man that I am, who will deliver me!"

And yet this is not all: within this deep there is a deeper still. The fear of Job falls on the soul of Paul with a tenfold dread. He sees that this evil bent of his nature, this lawless impatience of all law, is really "enmity against God" who is the Author of law; is the expression, therefore, not only of the lawlessness but of the ungodliness of human nature; is in its essence atheism, the refusal of the created will to own the will of the Creator, the miserable desire to be its own God and its own law. True, he has not consciously yielded himself to this evil instinct of his nature. True, in his inner man he still contends against this law in his members. But what if it should prevail at last? What if this carnal enmity against God were to rise up higher and still higher from his lower nature and invade, first his mind, then his conscience and his soul? What if the last utter victory of flesh over spirit were to change this miserable dualism in him into a yet more miserable unity, a unity of evil? What if the spirit within him, yielding itself to this double assault of passion and of understanding, should consciously, wilfully, deliberately, rebel against the God whose existence it can never cease to be conscious of? What if the "enmity," that in the lower nature shows itself only in the preference of the creature to the Creator, should in the higher nature develop itself into its completed and perfect form, the burning hatred of spirit against spirit—the fiend's choice—Evil, be thou my good! This were death, the worst kind of death, a life in death, a hideous consciousness of the dissolution that comes after death, the wild anarchy of all the elements of our nature when the vital force that held them all in check is gone! This was the death that Job saw afar off; but which Paul saw already begun within him, and that seeing he shuddered and groaned and cried out for a deliverer, a Saviour.

To such a cry what answer shall we make? Shall we tell this troubled soul that "humanity will be saved from evil when it once understands the great laws of its own being, and of nature?" or shall we tell him that there appeared in the world "a great Prophet who revealed a sublime system of Ethics," and enforced it by new and awful sanctions? or that this Prophet was "a sublime soul,

—an ideal man,—a glorious example of what humanity may attain to?" Nay, shall we even tell him that this man's death procured forgiveness of his sins and admission to heaven after death?

With what a sad, bitter smile, would this sufferer listen to such miserable comforters. You talk to me of law, he would say, of understanding, of obeying law. I understand what law is far too well already, It is my curse, my misery; it is that which is driving me to despair and to madness. I need no miracles to convince me of the authority of law, no prophet to tell me to fear God and keep His commands. I do fear Him, but I cannot keep His commandments, and my dread is, lest I cease to fear Him, lest the law within me drive me to outrage and defy Him. What is it to me that your perfect Man has realized the ideal of humanity, unless He can make me to do so too? What is that pure, noble, perfect life to me, but an object of hopeless envy? And even your sacrifice for sin, your forgiveness for the past, it is much, very much; but it is not all. It is forgiveness, but it is not deliverance. It may save me from the hell hereafter, but I need salvation from the hell in me now. I need deliverance from myself, from that human nature in which I feel that my misery lies. Not law, but the righteousness of the law; not restraint, but a nature that shall need no restraint; not a healing of this or that evil symptom in this or that part of my nature, but a cleansing of my whole nature from that original taint of lawlessness in its life-blood which fills its every vein with poison; not a victory *over* the flesh, but a victory *in* the flesh; a new law of life that shall free me from the law of sin and death; a new principle of unity in my nature by which, instead of the spirit growing carnal, the flesh shall grow spiritual; this, and this alone, can save me.

II. And now that we have learned, from these cries of the human soul in its conflict with evil, what is that deliverance which alone can satisfy its needs, let us turn to those despised dogmas, those abstract theological definitions which we are told have no relation to our real life, and see what they have to tell us. Let us hear again the answer of St. John to the question of St. Paul. "The Word was made flesh, and dwelt among us," "full of grace and truth." "And of His fulness have we all received, and grace for grace." What is it that these words tell us, as we read them in the light of that human experience we have been studying? They tell us of "flesh," of a human nature, really, truly human, dwelling amongst men, subject to all the conditions of their human life, bone of their bone, flesh of their flesh, but filled with "grace and truth." A humanity in which there was no untruth, none therefore of that unhappy falseness to its own ideal, that taint of evil ever making it untrue, which we feel in our nature and yet which we feel is foreign to our nature, is unnatural, is fatal to it. They tell us that in this sinless flesh we see, not a perfect Man merely, isolated from all other men by His very perfection, but human nature, the manhood taken into God and becoming, by its union with the eternal all-creating all-sustaining Word, a new source of life for all men, capable of imparting itself to all, so that of its fulness all men may receive, and "grace for grace." They tell us how this nature may become our nature, making us perfect with its perfection, pure with its purity, true with its truth. Is not this the deliverance and the Deliverer that we need? Not a Prophet merely, not an example merely, not an ideally perfect man; but a new humanity, a new life for men. Yes! the dry creed, the abstract dogma comes down, like Him whom it defines, and dwells amongst men, and we see that it too is "full of grace and truth," as it reveals to us the glory of the salvation and the Saviour that alone can satisfy the soul of man!

But is this idea of a triumphant humanity really fulfilled in the life of Christ? Was His life really so true, so perfectly sinless as we say? The sinlessness of Christ cannot be fully treated of in one, nor in many sermons; I can but suggest one line of proof, and yet one which seems to me very weighty. I ask, in the first place, what was the aim and desire of the whole life of Christ? It was undoubtedly righteousness,—perfect, unswerving obedience to the will of His heavenly Father. From the first word of His, that declared that He "must be about His Father's business," to the last word which proclaims that His Father's work is finished, one thought, and one only, seems to be the ruling passion of His life—" to fulfil all righteousness." Those even who will not admit that He succeeded in this, must admit that He ever aimed at this.

That law of righteousness, then, which St. Paul recognised as the ideal of his being, was never absent from the mind of Christ. How comes it, then, that in all His life there never once appears the slightest trace of St. Paul's consciousness of failure to realize that ideal? In no one of all His utterances concerning Himself, in none of the records of His temptations, His trials, His fears, His hopes, His most secret and inmost thoughts and prayers to God, do we ever find so much as a hint of His own imperfection. Never once do we hear from Him a prayer for forgiveness, a cry for deliverance from sin. How is this? Surely it is he who has the highest ideal, who is ever most distressed at his own failure to realize it. Surely we might have expected that the soul, which in all human history has the highest and loftiest ideas of holiness, would feel most keenly its own failure to be holy. How is it, then, that we find in Him only the most calm, serene, unbroken self-approval? How is it that the spiritual perceptions of Jesus seem at once so much higher and yet so much lower than those of all other men? How can He be at once so far beyond St. Paul in His ideal of perfection and so far below him in the consciousness of His own imperfection? Is His love for holiness an hypocrisy, or His belief in His own holiness a miserable delusion? Is this life of Christ, that for eighteen centuries has drawn to it the admiring gaze of friends and foes, nothing after all but the strangest and saddest of all moral monstrosities, the most inconceivable mystery of united contradictions? And if it be not this, what else can it be, but just the realization of that very ideal of humanity, the fulfilment of that dream of righteousness which has haunted every righteous soul that ever sighed, and sighed in vain, after perfection—a human nature freed from all taint of evil, all flaw of imperfection—a victory and a victor manifest in the flesh?

But if this human nature of Christ were truly sinless, was it exposed to trials such as ours? Did this sinless humanity really triumph over all those forms of evil to which we are exposed? Let us see. The temptations for our human nature from without, infinitely varied as they are in outward circumstances, are all of two kinds,—the temptation of Job and the temptation of Solomon. The trial from want, or from enjoyment,—the creature desired, or the creature possessed,—are the two forms under one or other of which man is ever tempted to prefer it to the Creator. Turn now to the life of Christ, and we shall see Him, in the first place, through the whole of it exposed to the temptation from the possession of the creature. The whole world of nature was His absolutely. All outward circumstances would change at His bidding. It needed but a word from Him to form round Him and His a charmed circle, within which, want and pain and sorrow should be unknown. He, "the preacher," might indeed have been "King in Jerusalem"—king of an earthly paradise, of which Solomon in all his glory never dreamed. And yet He never would do this. Never once in all His life does He use His miraculous power to save or serve Himself; never for any other purpose than the working out of His Father's will and His own mission. His was a life-long self-denial; a life-long restraint upon desires of the flesh, in themselves pure and noble. Here is that submission to law, that reverence for divine command, that subjection even of the sinless will of the creature to the higher will of the Creator, that breathes itself in His last prayer, but of which His whole life was but one long expression: "Father, not My will, but Thine be done." *This is victory over the flesh.*

But on the other hand, the temptation of Job was His likewise. The world was potentially His;—actually, He had not where to lay His head. The King and Lord of nature walked this world of His, a weak, weary, troubled man, in perils oft, in sorrow always; for the sorrows of all others were His own, by that intensity of sympathy which made Him truly one with us. Bowed ever with the burden of others' woes, the horror of others' sins; weeping with those that wept, burning with those that were offended, righteously indignant with all wrong, tenderly sympathizing with all who suffered, and yet isolated, too, like Job, by the intensity of His suffering, from those who, even though they loved Him, could not understand Him; He "the perfect and the upright man," whom Job alike in his righteousness and his sufferings foreshadowed, He appears the true type of Humanity tried by suffering, and conquering by endurance. For it is by endurance that He does conquer. He does not escape from suffering, He submits to it, and in submitting triumphs. His is the mastery, the only perfect mastery over outward circumstances; that which comes not from the power to change, nor even merely to endure, but from the power to subdue; the power to make that which is outwardly unfavourable minister to the inner life. He conquers want by wanting, weariness by wearying, pain by suffering, grief by grieving, death by dying. All these outward ills are His ministering servants; out of all these His life gathers its growth, its perfection. They minister to His glory, as earth and sun and shower bring forth the glory of the perfect flower from the life of the seed submitted to their influences. *This is victory for the flesh*; the only victory that fully and entirely overcomes the world. This is the victory that comes from the faith which places man above and beyond the world, which makes humanity the lord of nature and time and change and chance, because it makes all these subservient to that life, which has its source not in the creature, but in the Creator, not in the world, but in God.

Compared with this one great life-long victory for humanity, this conquest over all outward circumstances, those other occasional miraculous conquests of His,— those victories, not of endurance, but of change of circumstance, that strike us so much at first—seem infinitely smaller conquests. We might conceive of our being able to work all these works, and greater than these and yet gaining no real victory. What would it avail us, though we could turn stones into bread and water into wine, if our gluttony and intemperance made us slaves to the food and the wine we had miraculously produced? What would it avail us, if we could heal diseases with a touch, and recall the dead with a word, if the health we regained and the loved we called back, were to us more than God, were sources to us therefore not of life, but of death?

Is not this the mistake, the sad mistake, man is ever making, when he imagines that his discoveries of the powers of nature are giving him increasing power over nature. The truth is that they are all of them giving nature increased power over him. These new forces in nature which man discovers, as we apply them to the uses of human life, What do they do for us? They quicken the pace at which we must all live. We must live now faster, harder far than our fathers did. Steam and electricity are our masters, not we theirs. We are like hands in some great factory,—the faster the wheels revolve, the more unremitting and exhausting is our work to keep up with them. Circumstance is our master and conditions our life as much as ever. It is not in our surroundings—change or improve them as we may—but in ourselves that true power over nature is to be found. Which do you think is most truly lord and master of outward nature, he who could by one wonder-working word bind the old world and the new with such a link as binds them now, or he who could hear with patient trusting heart, with calm unshaken faith, the message those wires might send him, that all he loved and all he possessed in life were gone? The world might be the master of the one; the other would be the master of the world!

It is this mastery that our Lord has won for us; the complete triumph of humanity over circumstance, by its complete emancipation from the power of the creature. It is the reversal, point for point, of the victory won through the creature by the enemy of man over humanity. That was the subjugation of man to the dominion of the creature, which tempting him through the flesh, overthrew the lawful rule and supremacy of the spirit. This is the subjugation of the creature to the dominion of man, by the restoration of the lawful supremacy of the spirit over the flesh. That was the victory of the world, through the flesh over the spirit. This is the victory of the spirit, through the flesh, over the world!

And it is this double victory of spirit over flesh, and of spirit and flesh over the world, which constitutes the claim and proves the right, of his victorious humanity, to that universal kingdom which He won by it. He who would be king must first be priest. The consecration of self-sacrifice must precede the consecration to rule and dominion. The humanity that is to rule all things must first prove itself incapable of being ruled by any. It is because He did this, because in Him humanity has shown itself proof against its twofold trial from the creature,— the trial of want and of possession, of freedom and enjoyment; it is because He, the Second Adam, has passed victoriously through both the trials of the first Adam— that of the garden and that of the wilderness—the world under the curse, that brings forth still the thorns of care and sorrow, and that other world too, which might at His bidding have brought forth for Him nothing but delight, —it is for this that God has highly exalted Him, has given Him a Name above every name, has given Him the sceptre that He has proved may safely be intrusted to His hand; has raised Him to that throne which even He could not ascend, unless He first descended to its lowest steps on earth, and step by step, from suffering to suffering, from victory to victory, rose to its seat in heaven, to dwell there far above principalities and powers and dominions, crowned, because victorious Man!

And these victories are all to be ours as well as His. That nature in which He has conquered, that flesh which has thus in Him won its twofold triumph, He has come to bestow on us. Given *for* us first as our atoning Sacrifice, but given *to* us next as our sustaining life, this is that bread of life that came down from heaven, which he who eats of shall live thereby for ever!

He tells us how that flesh, that human nature, shall dwell in us, victorious in the law of the spirit of its life over that law of our fallen flesh which lusteth still against the spirit. He tells us how, by the power of that life, because He lives we shall live also, victorious *over* our flesh, crucifying it, mortifying its deeds, bringing its high thoughts into captivity and learning still obedience by the things that thus we suffer; growing still in our inner, our new nature, more and more like to Him, as that holy thing born in us of the will of God and of the power of the Holy Ghost, grows to the fulness of the stature of the man Christ Jesus, until at last we too become victorious *in* the flesh, until His last victory won for the flesh is accomplished in us. This new humanity of ours, proved like His in its double trial with the creature, conquering, unlike His, with many and many a sad defeat intermingled with its victories, but conquering still by enduring to the end, shall win of His infinite mercy the crown He won of right, the crown of life, perfect and eternal; shall pass with Him through its last struggle, know its last pain, sigh its last sigh, win its last victory by suffering, and then—freed for ever from its burden of the sin that He condemned in the likeness of sinful flesh—changed to the likeness of His glorious body, by the working of that power wherewith He subdues all things to Himself—shall reign with Him for ever!

Yes, victory *in* the flesh, victory *over* the flesh, victory *for* the flesh,—we need all three,—we need to see all three united in one and the same Saviour. There are times when our thoughts rise not beyond a victory for the flesh. There are hours when, in the sharpness of some sore trial, in the weary heart-sickness of some bitter sorrow, we only long to flee away and be at rest; when we see through our blinding tears but the far-off gleam of the walls of the golden city, and think how blessed to be within their safe defence, where nor pain nor grief can ever come! And, again, there are times when, with all our treasures round us, in the full enjoyment of all this life can give, we feel that this is not enough, that there is a higher, truer life than this, and that if we cannot attain to it, we have lived and loved in vain, and that without this, the joys of heaven itself would pall upon us at the last and we should loathe the monotony of its rest and the eternal quiet of its peace. Then we rejoice to think of that other, that higher victory won for us, the victory for the spirit over the flesh, the victory by which the soul of man can rise from the enjoyment and love of the creature to the enjoyment and the love of God and find its true life in Him. And yet, again—when we have won this victory, when in the might of this love we have accomplished some act of self-sacrifice for Him we love; when the spirit of the crucified one has triumphed over the flesh, has mortified, has crucified it even—we feel, by the pain of such crucifixion, that this victory is to be won only by a strife and an effort so exhausting, that heaven itself were dearly purchased, if it were to be held by such incessant warfare as this; we feel that its crowns of glory were but a mockery, if those who wore them still bent beneath so heavy a cross. Then we rejoice to see that other victory won, the victory not only over the flesh, but *in* the flesh; the victory not only of the Cross and Passion, but of the Resurrection and Ascension; the victory, final and complete, of the law of life in Christ Jesus, that even now as it works within us gives us the seal of our inheritance of the saints in light, but which then, fulfilling itself at last in all our nature—body, soul, and spirit—shall give us all the fulness of the gift of God, eternal life in His eternal love!

"Thanks be to God who giveth us *this* victory," through our Lord Jesus Christ!

SPEAKING PARABLES.

SPEAKING PARABLES.

PREACHED IN ST. PAUL'S CATHEDRAL, MARCH 24TH, 1867.

"Then said I, Ah Lord God! they say of me, Doth he not speak parables?"—EZEKIEL xx. 49.

THERE is a tone of remonstrance in these words. The prophet is evidently unwilling to speak to his countrymen all the message that God has given him for them. There is something in that message which he knows they will not like, something that he desires therefore to have altered before he utters it. God has given him a parable to speak to them. He has given him one of those revelations in figure and in symbol that the prophet so often received. He is commanded "to drop his word toward the south, to prophesy against the forest of the south field;" to foretel for some nation a judgment of God, that should be to them as the consuming fire among the trees of the wood. But what that nation is, and what the nature of that judgment is, he does not say. He does not seem to know himself. It is "a parable" he has to speak and there has been given him no interpretation of it. Now, it seems that the Jews in Ezekiel's day disliked these mysterious utterances. Where was the use, they thought, of warning them of judgment to come, if the warning was given thus mysteriously? How could they avoid it, if it was threatened for themselves; how could they profit by it, if it was coming upon others, unless they understood what it meant? And so they complained of these mysteries. They said, "Doth he not speak parables?" It was a natural feeling on their part, and it was natural for Ezekiel to wish to yield to it, not only for his own sake, not only for the sake of that popularity and influence that every honest, earnest teacher desires to have with his hearers, but for their sakes. These parables seemed to be a stumblingblock to his ministry, a hindrance to his usefulness. If he might only change just so much of his message; if only this part might be as plain as some other parts were, how much more useful his ministry would be; and so he expostulates with God:—"They say of me, Doth he not speak parables?" "If I might but leave out these parables, or if I might but explain them! Ah, Lord God, give me leave thus far to alter my message."

It was a very natural wish, but not the less was it a very sinful one: for the feeling that Ezekiel sought to meet was a sinful feeling. These mysterious words in his prophesy were not his own; they were God's words. If there was any one part of his message about which there could be no doubt that it was Divinely inspired, it was just this very part. These words that came to him, not from his own heart, but in mystic vision from without, could be nothing else than words spoken to him by the Lord God. When the Jews, therefore, who owned him for a messenger of God, asked him to change this part of his message, they were doing nothing else than dictating to the Almighty how He should speak to His people; they were refusing to hear their Maker, unless He spoke in such a manner as His creatures chose to prescribe to Him. This was infidelity. This was the very essence of infidelity. Infidelity is not disbelief of doctrine. A man may disbelieve many doctrines and be no infidel. A man may believe many doctrines and be an infidel. Infidelity is distrust of God. It is thinking of Him as if He were evil or ignorant, wishing our hurt, or not knowing how to do us good. It is regarding Him as if He were a Father who knew not how to give good gifts to His children so that, when they cry to Him for bread, He will give them, in cruelty or ignorance of their need, a stone. This demand of the Jews amounted really to the unbelieving denial of the great truth, that God is light, that in Him there is no darkness at all; that the gift which comes from Him, just as it comes from Him and in the way in which it comes from Him, is the very best gift and comes in the very best way for those to whom He gives it, and that if He bid his prophet speak parables to them, it was just because He, the loving Father, knew that so to speak that part of the message was best for those who heard it. When Ezekiel sought to yield to the wish of the Jews, he shared their sin. He too forgot who God was, he forgot who he was, when he dared to pray for leave to mend his Maker's message; he forgot, in his short-sighted presumption, that he might safely leave the result of his message to the wisdom of the Father who had shown His love in giving it; he forgot this, that be that result what it might, there was for him but one duty, to speak in the ears of those to whom he was sent *all* the words of the Lord, "whether they would hear, or whether they would forbear."

The sin of the Jew and the temptation of Ezekiel have not passed away; they exist still. They exist wherever the Church gathers together the world to hear the message of Christ. The Church inherits from Him the prophet's office, and with it the prophet's cross. Christ our Lord has bid her speak to men, partly in plain speech, but partly in parables; and she has to bear, as he bore, the rejection of that part of her message, which is spoken in parable. Christ our Lord has given to us very plain words to speak; and the world hears us when we speak them. When the Church utters her great message straight to the common heart of humanity; when she talks of its needs, of its sorrows, of its fears, of its hopes, of its joys, the world listens: it is all plain speaking. It is plain speaking when we say, "All we, like sheep, have gone astray. We have followed the devices and desires of our own heart;" it is plain speaking when we say, "In the midst of life we are in death. Of whom may we seek for succour, but of thee, O Lord, who for our sins are justly displeased;" it is plain speaking, and the heart of humanity echoes it, even while it will not obey it, when we say, "Let us arise and go to our Father:" this is plain speech; but this is not *all* our speech. We have to go on. We have to speak of the Son whom that Father sent into the world; of our sins being laid upon Him; of His mysterious nature, God and man; we have to speak hard words, parables, strange phrases concerning the Trinity and Incarnation and Atonement and Regeneration and Sacramental Grace; and when we utter these words, the world, that gave us audience until then, revolts, forbids us to speak these parables, and asks us, "What is the use of bidding us believe what we cannot understand? Why not give us the simple heart-religion of Jesus himself? Why give us all these dogmas? We will not have them. You shall not speak to us in parables." What answer, then, must we give to this demand? As we care for your souls, as we care for our own, we have but one answer to this request: we cannot do as you ask us; we must not, we dare not do so. These words are not our words. These mysteries are not of our making. We are stewards of the mysteries of God, and it is required of us that we be found faithful. We dare not do what you ask for our own sakes; we need not do it for yours, for the word that we speak is still a Father's word. God is no solemn tyrant proposing to humanity some cruel riddle which if it cannot solve, it dies; He is the Father of our spirits speaking to us from out of the cloud and from behind the veil, yet speaking to us with a Father's voice, bidding us draw near to Him and bow down before the cloud and kneel before the veil, and, even while we wait and pray for light, believe that the light we long for shall one day come from Him. This is our message, brethren, and we dare give you no other.

But though we may not give you religion without mystery, we may show you some reason why there should be mystery in religion; we may show you some reason why you should listen to us when we speak in parables; and, on the other hand, we may learn something from the objection that men make to our teaching; we may help the objector to a deeper faith and he may help us to a wiser teaching.

Listen to me, then, for a few moments, while I endeavour to deal with this complaint of the world as to the teaching of the Church, that she still speaks parables.

I. There are two objections that men of the world make to the preacher; they object to two kinds of religious speech: *the speech of religious doctrine and the speech of religious experience.* The Christian creed contains mysterious words and these are parables both to those who believe and to those who do not. Christian experience expresses itself also in mysterious words that are only understood by Christians. It speaks of Conversion, Faith, Assurance, Perseverance, Justification, Sanctification; and men who have not experienced these states of mind call these words unmeaning; they class them together under the head of *cant*; they speak of them as a kind of religious jargon and slang that religious men have among themselves, and which is unreal and conventional. I am quite certain that I speak the thought of more than one of my hearers when I say that what the age specially dislikes in the teaching of the Church are these two things: *dogma and cant, mystery and unreality.*

Now, let us do full justice to both these objections. There is truth, there is error, in each of them. Let us see what they exactly mean. And first, as regards the objection to mystery in religion. Perhaps the simplest way of considering this would be to ask whether it is possible to comply with it; whether it is possible to teach any kind of religion which shall be entirely free from mystery. Let us suppose, then, that in order to please the world, the Church were to give up her peculiar dogmas. Suppose we were to omit from our teaching all these parables that you so greatly dislike, should we then have got rid of mystery? Would the rest of our teaching be then as plain and intelligible as you would wish it to be? Certainly not, so long as we keep in that teaching two words, without which there can be no religion at all: one of them is *man*, and the other is *God*. What is religion? It is the drawing, the binding together of man and God. Who can conceive of all the mystery that lies hid in that one word *God?* Who can understand all the mystery that lies in that one word *man?* Have you ever pondered on your own being, your own life and history, and not felt what a strange, grotesque, unintelligible parable man is to himself? And, then, when you bring together these two great mysteries, God and man, the Creator and the creature—the Creator with his Almighty will, and the creature with his mysterious and awful power of rebelling against that will—the Almighty love that wills our happiness, and yet that seems ever to will it in vain, and the desperate recklessness of the creature that seems ever bent upon his own destruction—the living and the loving God "who heareth prayer," and the changeless, terrible law to which all prayer seems spoken in vain—we find ourselves all surrounded with mysteries; they rise up like mists out of the earth and gather round the meeting-place where men would draw nigh to God. Mysteries of Christianity! Ah, these are mysteries of all time and of all humanity. These are "parables" that vexed men's souls before the name of Christ was heard and that would continue to vex men's souls if the name of Christ were to be forgotten to-morrow; for these are mysteries arising not out of notions nor fancies that men may lay aside; they arise out of facts, of great, eternal facts, that will not come and go at men's bidding. Man is a fact; life is a fact; death is a fact; and that mysterious something, that power that seems to underlie all, to operate in all things, call it what you will—call it Nature, Force, Law, God—*that* is a great, an awful, and eternal fact. You cannot get rid of these; you must deal with them and you must think of them if you think at all, and you must, therefore, have your beliefs respecting them whether you will or not. Be your creed the shortest man ever believed and be your philosophy what it may, they will still have their mysteries in spite of you. Do not ask us, then, to give you no dogma, nor to explain all dogmas. Remember this: it is the smatterer, it is the pretender to science who tells you he can explain everything; it is the true man of science who tells you that he can fully explain nothing, for that mystery underlies all things. We cannot give up these "parables" of ours, but even were we to do so you would have to replace them by others of your own.

L

But those cant phrases that men so dislike, surely we can give them up. No, we cannot, and just for the same reason: they express, not notions, but facts. If a fact be a peculiar one, then the name for it must be peculiar too. Every science, every profession, every art has its own *cant* —has its peculiar technical expressions which are only understood by those who know the science or who practise the art. Religion is a science: it is the knowledge of God. Religion is an art: it is the art of holy living and of happy dying; it must, therefore, have its *cant* words. It must have these, because it is not an unreality but a reality, the deepest and the truest of all realities; because it is a life which must clothe itself in its own garb and have, like all living things, a language of its own. If you would understand our *cant*, you must be free of our Guild; you must learn our science, you must practise our art, and then you will understand our terms. Spiritual things are understood by spiritual men. Religion must have its *cant*, just as truly, just as fairly, just as legitimately as law and art and medicine and trade, have theirs. Nay, irreligion and infidelity have a cant too of their own. There is more of nauseous, offensive cant in one Frenchman's life of our most blessed Lord and Saviour than in half the canting books, as they are called, at which men of the world delight to sneer.

II. But though we may not give up our dogmas, though we must still speak those cant phrases that many men so greatly dislike, though we cannot obey the request that we shall cease to do this, there is a request that all men have a right to make of us and that we should do well to ponder when they make it. You hearers have a right to say to us teachers—"Take care what parables you give us. Take care how you add your words to God's and then call both of them His Word.

Take care how you claim for your doctrine or notion gathered by yourselves out of God's Word, the authority of that Word itself. Give us none of your merely human parables; none of your nicely squared and adjusted theological systems, your wire-drawn inferences, your half truths, that you are pleased to call *the* gospel and *the* truth. Give us God's message. Give us *all* God's message. Give us nothing but God's message. Give it in His own words and not in yours, as you stewards desire to be found faithful when you and we shall meet before His judgment seat." Undoubtedly you have a right to say this to us: and we, as I have said, do well to ponder it when you do say it; for the sin of adding man's word to God's, and giving both the same name, is one that we preachers are very prone to, is the besetting sin of all sects and schools and parties in the Church; and it is a great, though it is often an unconscious offence: it is the sin of making sad the heart of the righteous whom God hath not made sad; it is the sin of making the plain places rough and the straight places crooked; it is the sin of building up hills of difficulty and sinking valleys of despair between seeking souls and their loving and waiting Saviour. Woe to him who does this! Woe to him who, in his presumption, in his careless ignorance, in his reckless and unthoughtful zeal, or in the unsanctified bitterness of his sectarian spirit, incurs the punishment that falls on him "by whom the offence cometh!" We preachers should never forget this. We know of no more solemn, no more awful word for a preacher to hear from his congregation than this—"We do not understand you. You are mysterious. You speak to us parables." It may mean one of two things: it may be the unbelieving rejection of truth by an unbelieving soul, or it may be the anxious, heartbreaking cry of some struggling sinner whom we by our ignorance, by our error, by our rashness, are keeping back from God. Oh, let those who preach and teach in a day of thought and inquiry pray to be kept from this sin. Oh, you great multitude, gathered here from many congregations, listeners to many pastors, pray that God may keep your teachers from the sin of adding to His Word.

And there is another thing you have a right to say to us. You have the right to bid us take good heed that those peculiar religious expressions which we use shall be real and living on our lips; that they shall not be words merely, that slip from us carelessly, as if we only half meant them. There is such a thing as cant in this bad sense and a miserable and hateful thing it is. It is a miserable thing to listen to unreal speech, in the pulpit or out of it. Above all things miserable when this unreal speech is about religion—when you hear a man uttering with glib familiarity unrealities about the most awful of all realities. This, we admit, is a great danger; and yet it is one to which many beside the preacher are exposed; for it is a very common thing for men to use unreal speech, not because they are consciously insincere, but because the words they speak have lost for them their true meaning, because they have come to mean for them something less than they originally did. This is true of all language that expresses states of mind and feeling. Whenever we fall below the level of such speech it becomes untrue for us. There are words which as we speak them have a different meaning for different men. As I utter now the words—Truth, Honour, Justice, Love, Purity, they have a different meaning for my hearers, according as they are more or less truthful, honourable, just, or loving, or pure. When I speak the words—Repentance, Faith, Holiness, they have a different meaning for each one of you, according as you are yourselves penitent, or believing, or holy. So that you see it is still our life that makes our speech real. As it is, so will our words be for us.

Are there none of us here, brethren, who know how a single moment of a man's life may give new reality to his speech? Is there any one who has passed through some great life experience, who has not come out of it with a new meaning for some word or other that it never had before? Love! Joy! Fear! Hope! Remorse! Shame! Of this multitude who hear me, how many are there who can recall some dark, or some bright hour, when they said of such words as these:—"Ah, now I know what that means. I never knew it before." Why? Because in that hour into that word there passed your very heart and soul and it became a part of yourself; your dearest or your most bitter memories were mixed up with it for ever. Our words in this respect are like the figures and mottoes that we see in some great illumination. These, as you know, are very dimly visible or not at all until the light rushes within them, but when it does they gleam and shine out, and we see them as they shine. So our words lie cold and dim upon the surface of our minds; but let the light be kindled in the soul of a man, let the fire within him glow, and the cold, lifeless word gleams out all brightness: the pillar of cloud, that was but cloud in the daylight of his prosperity, gleams with a living fire in the night of his sorrow and trial.

We have, then, an awful power, every one of us, to make our words unreal or real. As our life is, so is our speech. A man may so live on that day by day, year by year, all higher, all nobler words shall become for him more and more mere parables; all things lovely, all things pleasant, all things of good repute shall become stranger and stranger to him; the old familiar words that he lisped when a boy beside his mother's knee, when the child's heart was wiser far than the man's brain—shall grow cold and strange and dim as the water-floods of his own iniquities drown him, and voices from heaven, nay, even voices from earth, reach him from afar, fainter and fainter still; for the heart of the man is passing away from him, and God in righteous judgment, is giving him instead the heart of a beast, so that he cannot speak with God, can scarcely speak as he ought with his fellow man. Nay, worse than this, along with this miserable ignorance there comes a still more miserable knowledge. Words, odious words, that once were parables to him in the days of his innocence acquire for him a new and horrible familiarity, as all things evil live and grow in him, until with the brute's heart there comes the brute's speech; and after that, if God in His mercy save him not from it, there comes the speech of devils. Oh, you on whose lips, familiar still as household words, are those that speak of love and truth and purity, pray God to help and save you whenever you find such words becoming to you unreal, for, as you thus speak them, your foot is on the first step of that descent which leadeth to destruction.

But, on the other hand, we have the glorious power of making our words real. A man may so live that, day by day and year by year, as he grows in knowledge and grace, all higher nobler words shall grow more and more familiar to him; better and still better understood. The son, as he grows more son-like, better knows the meaning of the word Father. The Christian, as he grows more Christ-like, better knows the meaning of the word Christ. The spiritual man, as he grows more spiritual, better knows the meaning of the word Holy Spirit. As we pray, as we repent, as we believe, as we grow in holiness, so do we still more fully understand the words Prayer, Penitence, Belief, Holiness. The soul, as it grows in wisdom, grows in power of spiritual speech. As the man becomes more and more conformed to the image of Christ, whole passages, whole books of Scripture, that for him were once parables, become for him familiar and dearly precious, as all the better memories of his life and all the brighter hopes of his future gather themselves into them and he draws out of them again into his inmost soul the peace and the joy of heaven and of God. Thus it is that, by God's grace, still clearer and clearer grows our knowledge as purer and purer grows our life. Thus do the light in the Book and the light in the life testify to each other; for "whatever doth make manifest is light." Thus as we draw nearer and nearer still to the Father of light—not (oh, thank Him for this!) as the infant crying in the night, not blindly groping our way up the world's great altar-stairs that lead through mist and darkness up to some unknown God—but with calm and patient, though it may be with tried and sorrowful hearts, may we ascend those stairs, the lowest step of which is by the foot of the cross of Christ on earth and the highest is by the footstool of the throne of the crowned Christ in heaven. On every step upon which we place our feet there beams a light thrown upwards from the cross and from the crown of thorns below, a light too sent down from the brightness of the throne of God above. Now, as we bend our weary faces, all but prostrate beneath the burden of our sorrows and our sins, we see but the light upon the step, now in some hour of reviving faith, we see heaven open and Christ standing at the right hand of God.

So may we learn to live, so may we gain, each one of us, a clearer and still clearer understanding of what is often for us the darkest of all parables—the true meaning of our own daily life. So shall there come to us still, in our darkest hours, the " light that ariseth for the upright," as still we hasten onwards to that Presence where all that now perplexes and distresses us shall be fully revealed, where we shall no longer " know in part and prophesy in part," but shall know " even as we are known."

THE CHRISTIAN THEORY OF THE ORIGIN OF THE CHRISTIAN LIFE.

THE CHRISTIAN THEORY OF THE ORIGIN OF THE CHRISTIAN LIFE.

Preached before the British Association, Norwich Cathedral, August 23rd, 1868.

"I am come that they may have life, and that they may have it more abundantly."—John x. 10.

THERE is a sense in which these words might and ought to be spoken by every true teacher. Taken in their lowest meaning, and yet in a very high and noble meaning, they express what should be the aim of every one who claims to have any truth to tell his fellow men. His motive for telling it ought to be this, and this only, that they "may have life, and may have it more abundantly."

This ought to be his aim because it is really his mission. The final cause of all science and all philosophy is the enrichment of human life; the quickening of its powers, the enlarging of its capacities, the increasing of its stores of intellectual wealth, the making it—in some respect or other—nobler, mightier, fairer than before. We know that there is no science, however abstract and remote from human life and its interests it may seem, which may not help towards this end. Nay, it is the firm belief of all true students of science that it must do so; if in no other way, at least in this, that the study or the discovery of it has enlarged, if it were only one human mind; has stirred with new and deeper emotions, if it were only one human spirit; has quickened into keener vitality one, if it were but one, of those particles of existence that go to make up humanity. So the life of the race has received a fresh impulse; has grown, by so much, more rich and vigorous; has its life so much "the more abundantly." And the true student and true teacher is he who most fully realizes this fact; who most deeply feels that his knowledge, his discovery, be it what it may, is not his,—is the property of all men,—is revealed to him only that through him all men may become possessors of it.

It is for this reason that he cannot rest until he has told it. It burns within him as he muses on it until he has spoken it out as his contribution to the wealth of human existence. And thus each student of nature comes from the scene of his toilful search for her hid treasures, with these words upon his lips; "I, come,"—I, with my newly discovered fact, I, with my new theory, I, with my philosophy, I, with my art,—"I come that ye may have life." Science has come at last to have, like earlier faith, her community of goods. Of all of her wealth that each man possesses "durst no one man say it is his own." Each pours his share into the common stock of knowledge, that every man may receive from it "severally as he has need." And so, as year after year the great Association now assembled here passes from city to city among us, it might proclaim as its motto these very words—more and more fully recognized as speaking its true aim and mission—we come "that ye may have life, and have it more abundantly!"

And in this sense, if our Lord had been no more than a great teacher—a teacher of the noblest of all sciences, the science of our moral and spiritual life—He might have used these words. Believing, as all true prophets and teachers must believe, in the vital importance of the truths they have to tell; conscious of the new and deeper tide of life that was to flow from the new fountains of truth He was about to unseal; He would have said, He could not but have said, " I come that they may have life, and have it more abundantly." He had been no true teacher nor prophet, if he had not said this. And we, His followers, have, in this sense, the right to repeat His claim. We have the right to say that on His lips it was no vain boast, but truest and deepest prophecy; that His words have been to myriads since the hour He spoke them, just what He said they would be, "spirit and life;" that they have strengthened, elevated, consoled mankind as no other words have ever done; that human life is made abundantly richer, nobler, happier for His teaching. As our association, His Church, passes on its mission from city to city, from home to home, throughout the world, we too have the right to say, " We come that ye may have life, and that ye may have it more abundantly."

And if this were all the claim we made for Christ and His Church none would dispute it. But this is not all we claim for Christ. It is not all that He claims for Himself in this respect. The sense in which He uses these words and others like them, is a far different and a far deeper sense. It is one in which no other teacher, before or since, has ever dared to use them. He claims to be, not merely the helper of the life of men, but the author and the giver of it; not merely to be the medium through which knowledge of this life reaches them, but that very life itself. " I am the life!" Not, I discover, or reveal, or illustrate, or strengthen this life; but I am it, it is from me it flows, it cannot be without me!

We know how constantly this, or some equivalent expression, is on the lips of Christ; we know how constantly it is repeated by His disciples. We know, for instance, how it fills and saturates the writings of one of the greatest and earliest of His followers, St. Paul: how he is for ever speaking of a new life, which he has from and in Christ; of a life which is not his, but which "he lives by faith in the Son of God;" of a "spirit of life in Christ Jesus that has made him free from the law of sin and death;" of "a life of Jesus made manifest in His body;" of "being quickened together with Christ;" "created in Christ;" "perfect in Christ;" "of Christ, being" in men "the hope of glory;" of "Christ who is our life," and with Whom "our life is hid in God."

No one can read these expressions honestly, and regard them merely as metaphors—merely as a figurative way of saying that Paul had found the words of Christ helpful to his spiritual life. Right or wrong, true or false, they mean something more and very different from this. Something, for instance, that St. Paul, filled, as he evidently is, with a sense of the worth of his own teaching, never dared to say of himself. Something that no followers of any other teacher ever dreamed of saying of their master. There have been other great teachers before and after Jesus of Nazareth; teachers whose words have stirred the souls and helped the lives of men. But of which of these did the most devoted and loving of his followers ever say what St. Paul and his fellow Apostles say of Christ? Who ever heard of men being "dead and their lives being hid" with Moses, or of Mahomet being "in them the hope of glory," or of Confucius "being fully formed in them, and dwelling in them"?

No! these words are unique; they express an entirely new and distinct idea, that of salvation by the life, the communicated life of Christ; and this is the distinctive idea of Christianity. It is that by which it essentially differs from every other religion the world has ever known. All the other dogmas of Christianity it shares in some degree with other religions. There is not one of them that has not at least its imperfect and distorted shadow in other faiths. But our religion stands alone and apart from all others in this idea of the life of its Founder being first given for and then communicated to His followers, so that they live in and by Him, and He in them.

Our claim, then, for Christ and for Christianity is this, that our Lord and Master founded on earth a kingdom within which is to be found that which is not to be found beyond its limits; a kingdom which is not "in words but in power,"—that is to say, is not produced by words or ideas alone, however true or however beautiful, but by a power, a vital force peculiar to itself; and that this force is the indwelling life of Jesus Christ—God and Man. In a word, we claim for Christianity that it is not a code of morals merely, nor a philosophy, nor a creed, nor a system of religious discipline; but that over and above all these it is a life, a new and real vital force in the world; a life with its own conditions of existence, its own laws of development, its own peculiar phenomena, as real and as distinct as those of any other form of existence which science investigates and classifies, and that this vital force is in the Christ we worship; for "this is our record, that God has given to us eternal life, and this life is in His Son."

Now this claim of Christianity is not admitted as is that other of which we spoke. It is largely rejected by those who admit that other. There are many who are ready to acknowledge that Christ, the Teacher, is helpful to the spiritual life of men, who will not acknowledge that He is necessary to it. They grant that we are taught by His morality and elevated by His example; but not that we are, or can be "saved by His life." He is for them a great moral teacher, but not a Divine Saviour. This is the world's controversy with the Church. It is one form of that long contest which, in one shape or other, has ever been waged between the Church and the world;— the contest between those who acknowledge only the visible and the natural, and those who believe in the invisible and the supernatural. The idea of a Teacher, whose words and example instruct men, is simple, natural, intelligible—it is accepted. The idea of a Saviour, whose life, communicated to those who believe in Him, shall give them a new life, is mysterious, inexplicable, supernatural, and therefore must be rejected. And the world on this point, as on every other where the supernatural comes in, challenges the Church for proof of its claim. "Prove, demonstrate to us," is the demand, "that Christ is this supernatural life-giver, and we will admit it; until then we refuse to accept Him as such, and it is unreasonable of you to ask us to do so."

Now to this demand the answer of the Christian should always be, we have no such proof as that you ask for. A demonstration of the supernatural is an impossibility: it is a contradiction in terms. No amount of evidence drawn from the world of nature can demonstrate the existence of a world above nature. The facts which we allege as evidences of the supernatural—such as miracles and prophecy—are themselves supernatural; and our adducing them *as such* in proof of the supernatural is a mere begging of the question in dispute. The supernatural is not to be demonstrated, it is to be felt; it does not prove itself to sense, it reveals itself to faith. Between the man who insists on seeing before he believes, and the man who believes in order that he may see, the dispute is endless. It is really as profitless as a dispute about tune between a man with a musical ear and one without one; or a dispute about the qualities of a picture, between one who looks at it from the proper distance and in the proper light to take in all its beauties, and one who insists upon examining it only through a powerful microscope. They have no common measure of the thing in question. They are not so much opposed to as utterly apart from each other. Each truly testifies to what he sees or hears; but one believes that he sees or hears more than the other. The answer and the only answer each can make to the other is this—Stand where I do, and you will see what I see and hear what I hear.

But though this must be the result whenever the question as to the existence of the supernatural is fairly reached, though we can never get beyond that point in our argument, yet it is a great matter that we should fairly reach it. It is a great matter that all needless difficulties be removed out of the way of the earnest searcher for truth. If there be a point at which he who walks by faith must part from him who walks by sight, let him at least endeavour that they shall not part before they have arrived at it. Are we quite sure that we have always done this? Have we always begun by inviting those whom we would win to follow us altogether—to go with us at least a part of the way? Have we fairly accompanied them and persuaded them to accompany us to the very verge of the natural and visible, before we asked them to own the supernatural and the invisible? Have we shown them all that they might see, before we asked them to believe in what they cannot see? It seems to me that we have not always been careful to do this. We have too often done the very opposite of this. What, for the most part, has been the answer of the Christian apologist to those who have demanded proof

M

that Christ was more than a great Teacher? Has it not been something in this fashion:—"Eighteen hundred years ago there lived a man in Nazareth who claimed to have come down from heaven and to be the Son of God, and who proved His claim by miracles. He re-edited the moral law, and enforced it by new sanctions. He declared that His death should obtain forgiveness of sins for those who should accept it on the conditions of repentance and amendment of life. He proved our immortality by His resurrection from the dead and His ascension into heaven. All this can be demonstrated by strictly historical evidences. Believe it, and you shall be rewarded by eternal salvation; believe it not, and you shall be punished by eternal damnation." Now, whatever effect this statement of our "evidences" may have upon the faith of Christians, it certainly has the effect of violently repelling those who are not Christians. The result of this hard, dry, logical attempt at demonstrating the supernatural to the intellect is, that the companion whom we would win starts from our side at once and refuses to walk with us another step. His fixed principle is that the supernatural cannot be.

But must this be so? Is this the only way of arguing this great question? Surely it seems a strangely unscientific way, to say the least of it. It is a method which we do not pursue in investigating any other subject. What is the claim that we are discussing? It is twofold. It is first the assertion of a fact; secondly the assertion of a particular theory to account for that fact. The alleged fact is the Christian life. The theory to account for it is that it is supernaturally given by a supernatural Christ. Christianity, living, existing Christianity, is a fact. Christian theology is the theory by which Christians profess to account for that fact. Now, surely the natural, the scientific method of investigating any theory whatever, is to begin by ascertaining the facts which it professes to deal with. Can anything be more absurd than to commence a fierce debate about a particular way of accounting for certain alleged facts, before we have decided the question, whether there are such facts at all or no. Ought not the first question in every such case to be, What are your facts? The next, What is your theory to account for them? We have reversed this process. We begin by insisting on our theory—that is to say our creed—and coming down from it to our facts, instead of beginning with our facts and ascending from them to our theory. We begin by reasoning down from God to Christ and from Christ to Christianity, instead of reasoning up from Christianity to Christ and from Christ to God. Let us try the other way. Let us approach this question from the side of the present and the visible facts within our own knowledge and experience. Let us begin by asking, what are the known and admitted facts respecting this Christian life?

Let us suppose then that we heard for the first time this claim of Christianity that it possesses a spiritual life peculiarly its own and that this is supernaturally derived from Christ. We look around us upon the sphere of this alleged life, upon Christendom as it is; and we ask, Where is this life? How does it manifest itself? What is it that we see? Much, very much at first to refute our theory. We see, in the first place, a kingdom divided against itself, not so much one Christendom as many Christendoms, a multitude of rival sects, contending sharply about nearly every one of the dogmas that make the creed of Christianity. In which of these contending sects that scarce allow to each other the name of Christian, are we to look for this Christian life?

Again, we compare the moral life of Christians generally with that of men of other religions, or of those who profess to be of no religion at all. Wherein are Christians in general better, or even different from these? The answer is, for the most part not apparently in any respect. We do not see that the average Christian is more chaste, more temperate, more truthful, more charitable and forgiving, more humble; a better husband, father, son; a better member of society than the average Jew, or Mahomedan, or Deist. There are many of these far better than many Christians. Probably there is the same average amount of morality and decency and respectability amongst them all. Whatever Christians may say they ought to be; in their actions, in the ordinary affairs of life, they are, for the most part, pretty much the same as other men. And as to those who fall below this average, as to the degraded, the vicious, the criminal, the great cities of Christendom have surely their full share of these. Is this then all we have to see? If so the claim of Christianity is an intolerable presumption. It is practically no better and no worse than other systems. It is a tolerably useful system of moral police, as many another religion might be, and it is no more.

But is this all? Is there nowhere to be seen within this merely formal Christianity, rising up above the level of this average respectability and morality, a nobler and a higher life; one that is more than merely moral and decent; that is devoted and heroic and saintly; a life that somehow impresses us with a sense of reality and power and beauty altogether its own; a life whose aim and motive is clearly seen to be, not self, but self-sacrifice and which reveals itself by its ceaseless war with all forms of evil; a vital force that is sending out every day those who are filled with it, to some task of loving effort or endurance; sending the missionary to the heathen, the pastor to the ignorant and the outcast, the Christian brother or sister to the bed of the sick and the dying; a life that is feeding the hungry, clothing the naked, visiting the afflicted, comforting the sorrowing, reforming the criminal, reclaiming the outcast; or again, a life whose quiet sustained energy accomplishes, unnoticed, unapplauded, the daily round of daily duty, bears with untiring love the burden of other's sins or sorrows, sheds along the daily paths of men a light which somehow we feel is light from Heaven? Are there no such lives to be seen here and there amongst us? Is there one here so unfortunate that he cannot recall at least one such? As that life then in its beauty and its power rises up, at this moment, before you, I ask, do you not recognise in it something of these two distinctive tokens, the cross and the crown—the cross of the helper, and therefore of the sufferer—the crown of the worker and of the conqueror? Do you not see a life which manifests itself in these two characteristics, that it "gives itself for many," and that where it comes men "have life and have it more abundantly?"

But this is not all that we know of this life. It is indeed all of it that is outwardly visible; for its truest and deepest manifestations are within. It is and always has been mainly a hidden life. But those who lead it have, from time to time, recorded their experience of it. They have breathed it in hymns and prayers and records of their inmost thoughts and feelings. Turn to these; take them at random from the religious literature of any one of the many contending sects we have been speaking of—nay, take them designedly from the most opposite and hostile of these. Take down from your shelves the memoirs, or the devotional writings of those Christians who in their day have stood most widely apart from each other, who seem to have had least in common with each other: lay aside with a smile or a sigh the half-forgotten theological controversies that seemed to them and to their followers so all-important; read the records of their inner life, hear them tell of the struggles, the sorrows, the temptations, the triumphs of their souls. You will see that they, one and all, speak of a life, a glorious and a real life, which is not their own and yet which dwells in them, a life by which they triumph over the deadliness of sin and the weakness of their own nature. They speak, all of them, of the joy of this life and of its power, of its sadness too and its trials; they tell how they grieved as it waned and exulted as it grew strong; how it helped them to pray in their hours of spiritual need and sorrow and to sing praises in their hours of spiritual rejoicing. We, too, pray their prayers, we sing their hymns; and as we see how they might have prayed each others prayers and sung each others hymns, we see that, spite of all outward diversity, they were one by the identity of this their inner life. Surely it is a remarkable fact that men who could certainly have learned nothing from each other, men whose lives were formed under such strangely diverse influences—Calvinist and Arminian, Huguenot and Catholic, Jesuit and Jansenist, high Churchman and low Churchman—show, each and all of them, this marvellous unity of life.

And then this Christian life has a history of its own quite as remarkable. It appears to develop itself with a strange capriciousness. No one can say beforehand where or when it shall be found. It is seen where we should least expect it; it is missing where we should most expect to find it. Now it starts up suddenly in its full strength and beauty in some dark den of vice and misery. Now it is feeble or sickly or wanting altogether in the carefully watched and cultivated garden of some Christian home. Now it startles us by the sudden conversion of some depraved and abandoned wretch, grown grey in wickedness or crime, and now we watch it gently and gradually revealing itself in the tender grace of some young innocent life, growing with its growth and strengthening with its strength. It is of all ranks, all conditions, all races, all ages. And yet under all this infinite variety of circumstances, still one thing never varies—the life itself; that is still everywhere one. The spiritual man is ever and everywhere the same. Always, out of all these strangely diverse materials, some unseen hand seems ever fashioning one and the same likeness; and as we see it, still the same, here and everywhere, now and for the last eighteen centuries, there grows upon us the conviction that we are tracing the history, not of a society or an association, but of a family, of a race, whose common features imply a common origin, and one too of such vital power that it has impressed itself upon the race indelibly and for ever.

Once more; it is a fact, that all those in whom this spiritual life is thus displayed are agreed as to its origin. They, one and all, agree in declaring that it is the supernatural work of a supernatural Christ. They, one and all, declare that they live this life by faith in Jesus Christ the Son of God. They say that it is only in the measure in which they trust in Him, pray to Him, draw near to Him in secret communion, that this life grows strong in them; that as they forget or fall away from Him it grows weak and cold. They say that His death has saved them from the guilt, is saving them from the power of sin; that He is in them by the might of His Spirit strengthening the life that He has given them, so that they in very truth live in Him and He in them. This again is simply a fact, as plainly ascertainable as any fact in the world of nature.

And now let us see whither our inquiry has conducted us. It has led us from ourselves back to Christ. From what we see and know and experience in our own lives and in the lives of living men—back through a long unbroken line of witnesses who all agree in testifying that they felt what we have felt, and saw what we have seen—back to the hour in which He was born whose life they one and all declare is their life and light, back to Him who foretold that they should have this life, who said that He had come that they might have it and have it more abundantly. Between that life of Christ and our own there is seen to stretch one long path of living light, thick set with clustering stars of grace and glory, or rather there reaches one long life, even that of Christ in the Church which is His body and in which His life repeats itself evermore.

And now we ask what are we to say of this life? Shall we deny its existence? Shall we say that this idea of a death of sin from which Christ saves men, and a life of righteousness which He gives them, has no corresponding reality, and that all these experiences of a new life with its joys and sorrows, hopes and fears, have been but one long hypochondria, a dream of disordered souls? Or if we admit its reality, how shall we account for it, on what theory shall we explain the facts which it reveals?

Our theory is a simple one. It is just this, that what all these witnesses say is true; that Christ has done for them, is in them, just what they say He has done and is. The opposite theory is that though this life really exists, yet that the idea of its supernatural origin is absurd and unnecessary; that it is not the supernatural power of Christ which has caused it; that it is sufficiently accounted for by the power of His ideas and the beauty of His life; that he was indeed a great teacher, who taught more powerfully and winningly than any other, the truths of the absolute religion which are common to all faiths, and that to these and not to Him—to the ideas of Christ and not to Christ Himself—all the power of the Christian life is to be attributed.

Here then are the two theories which profess to account for the facts of Christianity. The one the natural, the other the supernatural. According to the one, Christianity is a purely natural fact, it is only one of the many forms in which the natural religious idea common to all men expresses itself; the best perhaps it has yet attained to, but not the last; capable of improvement, nay, about to be improved by getting rid of all its peculiar dogmas about the person of Christ, all the old remains of superstition clinging still to His teaching, and retaining only His morality and His grand and simple idea of a common Father of all men. According to the other it is a new supernatural fact in the world, deriving its power from new and supernatural forces, born into the world with the birth of Christ, and living on in it by the power of His indwelling spirit.

Now, I am not about to dwell on the many objections to the theory of the merely natural origin of the Christian life. I do not propose now to show how thoroughly unphilosophical it is; how utterly it fails to account for some of the facts we have been describing; how utterly at variance it is with other facts in the history of Christianity. My object is not now and here to disprove this or any other theory as to the origin of Christianity, nor yet to prove our own. Let men compare them at their leisure, and they may find, perhaps, that ours is after all the easier of belief. All I seek now to show is, that our theory of the supernatural origin of this life, approached in the way in which we have just approached it, is not so violently improbable, so utterly impossible, that it must be at once rejected. For what is it that we have been contemplating? A life—a mysterious form of life—for which we assert a mysterious origin. Is it its mysteriousness which should make it improbable? Is not all life a mystery? Who has ever succeeded in analysing or in defining it? Who is there who, after tracing into the very inmost recesses of nature the ever vanishing spirit of life, can say I have discovered it; I know what and whence it is, and wherein it consists? Who can say I have ascertained what is that mysterious force, ever revealing itself in its actings, ever concealing itself in its essence, whose presence makes of the inanimate the animate, whose departure leaves the once living thing dead? Before the mystery of life, as before its twin mystery of death, science stands abashed and dumb.

It is to Science then herself that we make our appeal for aid to Faith. We call on her to yield her testimony to the existence of the invisible. We ask her to tell us whether she, too, has not her mysteries which cannot be defined, her dogmas which cannot be demonstrated. From the conceited half knowledge of the dabblers in science and smatterers in theology—with their parrot-like cant about the unreasonableness of mystery and the absurdity of dogma, their solemn platitudes about the irreconcilable differences between science, of which they know little, and theology, of which they know less—we appeal to the true high priests of science, to those who in the inmost shrine of her temple stand ever reverently with bowed heads before a veil of mystery, which they know they can neither lift nor rend, and yet through which they feel there ever streams a hidden and inscrutable, yet mighty power—a veil behind which they know there is a light whose source they cannot reach to and yet whose rays are still the light of all their life. We ask of these, whether mystery is a word so very absurd and intolerable to men of science that they cannot endure its presence in religion. We ask them whether it is not rather the very mysteriousness of religion that is its recommendation to the mind that has felt the mysteriousness of science; whether it is not probable beforehand that the science of the soul may have its mysteries as well as that of matter or of mind; whether the life of the spirit in man may not have—might not be expected to have—an origin as mysterious, at least, as that of his body, and whether therefore our theory that this life in its highest form is derived from another life—from a force outside our nature acting upon it—be so violently and preposterously absurd an hypothesis that it must not even be listened to by any one having any pretentions to scientific culture, who is not prepared at once to be scouted from the company of scientific men as a dreamer and a dogmatist. It is in the answer that such men will give and are giving to such questions, that there lies the germ of that reconciliation between faith and science (or rather between men of faith and men of science, for faith and science need no reconciliation), of which we hear so much just now. More and more deeply do we feel that it is in this direction that this reconciliation is to be sought. For surely if ever it is attained to, it will be, not at the point where the two kingdoms, the natural and the supernatural, stand in sharpest contrast, but at that point where they most nearly approach and melt, as it were, into each other. At that point, where the supernatural seems almost natural and where the natural almost rises up into the supernatural; there, where faith can produce within its domain facts which science will not dispute, and where science finds within her domain facts which she needs the help of faith to interpret; there, where religion, in the certainty and the regularity of its phenomena, becomes all but a science, and where science in the helplessness of its analysis becomes all but a religion; there, where the man of faith exclaims "I know!" and the man of science, "I believe!" there, where in the presence of life—that common miracle of science and religion—the disciple of each exclaims to the other, "Behold, I show you a mystery!" there it is that we men of faith feel our grasp to tighten on the hand of our too long estranged brother, the man of science; we draw him with us onward still and upward with a more constraining power, as we say to him, "Come with us but one step further, and you shall know what we know—the mystery of the life that is hid with Christ in God!"

And we can see, I think, some other advantages to be gained by thus conducting this great controversy. First, we may hope in this way to remove a great stumbling-block existing in many minds to the reception of Christian dogma, and that is the alleged relation between dogma and life. Nothing more shocks many minds in our day than the assertion that belief in any particular doctrine can have anything to say to man's eternal life; and put, as this assertion is too often put, on the ground of authority alone, the notion is a startling and a trying one. To say "This is a revealed opinion; if you receive it you shall be rewarded by eternal happiness, and if you do not you shall be punished by eternal damnation," is startling to many, and shocking even to some. The intellect revolts against being required to assent to any proposition under penalties. The heart revolts against the idea of punishment for opinions which men feel they cannot help entertaining. Put it, however, thus:—The Christian life, like all other forms of life, has its own laws of growth and development, its own conditions of being or of well-being. There is nothing, therefore, beforehand improbable, nothing shocking in the idea, that the effect of certain ideas or beliefs on the soul may be favourable or unfavourable to its healthy existence; any more than that certain conditions of the atmosphere should be essential to the health, or even to the existence, of human beings; or that certain forms of animal life should only be found within certain limits. Who shall say, beforehand, what conditions are or are not essential to the healthy state or even to the existence of this Christian life? Who shall say of this or that condition—it is impossible, it is shocking that this should be essential to it? Speak of life and death, or punishment and reward, as *arbitrarily* attached to certain beliefs, and you do shock and needlessly shock, the minds of men. Speak of them, or rather of the state of mind produced by them, as conditions naturally and necessarily more or less essential to the vigour and health of the spiritual life, and there is nothing shocking or improbable in the idea. It is mysterious certainly; but not more mysterious than the life it has to do with. Once more, then, we make our appeal to the man of science? Once more we ask of him whether he does not know of facts exactly analogous to these which we allege; whether, after all, the transition here from the mysteries he owns to the mysteries he rejects, is so very violent, so very difficult that it is impossible to make it.

In the next place, such a manner of approaching the question of Christian evidences is far more safe and healthy for ourselves. Who, that has ever gone through a regular course of the "Evidences," does not know the painful effect of such a study upon his own spirit. How—

as we begin, for instance, with the historical proof that miracles were wrought and prophecies fulfilled eighteen hundred years ago; and then proceed to the discussion as to what miracles, when themselves proved, can prove; and then plunge into all the historical, critical, physical and metaphysical questions that surround this question of the evidences, and so fight our way slowly, syllogism after syllogism, from proving God to proving Christ, and then to proving Christianity—somehow Christ himself seems to us very far off, seen through the far distance of eighteen hundred years, hidden by the smoke and dust of centuries of strife. His voice, reaching us faint and far off through the din of the battle, seems no longer the voice of our living Lord. The present Christ, "our very present help in time of trouble," the life of all our life, seems to have gone far away. We stand in the presence of the empty tomb from which we have syllogistically demonstrated that He has risen; but somehow we feel like one of old, who said, "they have taken away my Lord, and I know not where they have laid Him!" We long to meet once more the living Christ, to walk with us along the weary path of life; to reveal Himself to us by the burning of our hearts as He talks to us by the way, or breaks for us the daily bread of life; or, won by our entreaties, to abide with us when our day is far spent and our night is at hand. Well for those to whom their Lord, in pity to their need, thus visits again with His loving presence! Well for those who can hear the voice which asks, "why seek ye here the living among the dead?" "The living Christ lives not in the dead past, but in the present; seek Him and find Him there. Christ dwells in His church. If ye cannot find Him there, where He has said He will ever be, ye will never find Him here!"

It is thus that we are persuaded that our Lord designed we should begin the study of the evidences of our faith. Christianity is a present, an existing life, or it is nothing. It is as a living existence, therefore, that it should first be contemplated. The Christianity of evidences and dogmas alone no more realises it than the bones of the fossil creatures, which science collects and arranges, give us an idea of the living things themselves, as they once moved in the power and the beauty of their life. Study, if you will, nay, study because you ought— those of you who have leisure or ability for the study— these historical or logical evidences, this skeleton of Christianity. Trace the symmetry of its form, the minute and marvellous articulations of all the joints and bones, as it were, of its doctrinal system: but, remember, when you have thus reconstructed its frame, you have not discovered its life, any more than the knife of the anatomist can lay bare for him the life of the frame he examines. That is to be seen in its actings only. For that, you must leave the dissecting room of the apologist and even the museum of the divine, and come out into the world, where Christianity breathes, moves, and acts, a living thing. You must see it in the beauty, and the grace, and the might of its life. You must understand the conditions of its existence, the laws of its being, the manner of its sustenance, and then it may be that you may discover reasons for some of those peculiarities in its structure, which seemed to you in your study so utterly useless and superfluous.

One thing more we gain by such an aspect of our subject. By regarding Christianity, in the first instance, as a life to be contemplated, rather than as a series of propositions to be demonstrated, we gain a deeper sense of our individual responsibility for the exhibition of this life. Its phenomena are ours to display; they are ours also to conceal, to distort, to destroy. Whether this life of the Church shall be seen vigorous and beautiful, reflecting the glory of Christ, its author, as the material creation reflects the glory of the Father; or, whether it shall be seen only as a stunted, distorted, diseased, expiring life, rests with us. He has willed that it shall be so. "Let your light so shine before men that they may see your good works." "Ye are the salt of the earth!" Here is the word that proclaims all the power of that life He has come to give. We are to be the vital force that keeps the world from death! But if "the salt have lost its savour!" if the life that should be the light of the world dies out, "it is good for nothing." Here is the word which proclaims the awful responsibility of those who hold that life in trust for the world. No evidences, no arguments will restore its lost vitality, or make men believe that the thing that lies rotting at their feet has life in it. They hate it for its loathsomeness, they dread it for its poisonousness. They are right; for of all odious, of all poisonous things that rot and breed disease and death, the most odious, the most pestilential, is the corpse of a dead religion. Men gather together and bury it out of their sight lest it destroy them. So shall it be with our faith if ever it lose its vitality. If ever it degenerate into a mere creed and cease to be a life, it will die. And yet even in its death it would give proof of the truth of His prophecy who foretold that in such a case it would be sure to die. The expiring testimony of Christianity, if it ever should expire, would thus still be testimony to Christ. Thus, and thus only, can it ever die. Its enemies have more than once proclaimed its death. Again and again has the seal been affixed and the watch set over its supposed grave; yet, again and again, has it come forth in the power of its resurrection life. No merely natural force can hurt its supernatural vitality. No heresy, however cancerous, can entirely eat away its creed. No assaults of infidelity, however violent, can ever overthrow its evidences. Its death, if it ever should die, will be the departure from out of it of its soul—of the in-dwelling Spirit of Christ—grieved to departure by the sins and the faithlessness of Christian men! "He is come that we may have life;" but He will remain only on the condition that we will to have it. If we cease to will this, if our Christianity become to us only a creed, a sentiment, a bundle of opinions—if it cease to be for us Christians a vital power in all our lives, if Christ should be no longer to us a living and a present Christ and should become only a Christ who lived and died some eighteen hundred years ago—then, just because its life is supernatural, just because it is not one of those merely natural religions which spring from the earth and are of the earth only, just because God once breathed into it the breath of a Divine life, it must die. Its spirit, its life will return to God who gave it, and its body of theology and dogma resolve itself into its merely natural and earthly elements again.

Here, then, lies our duty. It is, first and above all, to realize this life, and then to display it. It is our task not merely so to argue, that the world shall listen to us when we ask, "Why do you not believe as we do?" but so to act, that the world of its own accord shall ask, "Why cannot we live as you do?" Leave—most of you must leave—you may safely leave to others the defence of the dogmas of Christianity, the strengthening of its evidences, the adjustment of its differences with the science or philosophy of the age. Wait—you may safely wait—to see more than one of these differences vanish, as others have already vanished, before a truer science, or a deeper philosophy, or before a deeper and truer theology. Watch—you may safely watch—the wholesome action of science and philosophy on religion, correcting, by their own advance, more than one erroneous form of expression that religion may have borrowed from the science or philosophy of the past; helping it to truer modes of expression; calling out, by their objections, old forgotten truths, or new aspects of old truths; moderating, by the calm judicial temper and critical spirit of scientific investigation, the heat and intolerance of our sects. Of all this you may be spectators—patient and willing spectators—sure that, from all this, true religion can only be a gainer. But one thing alone you should watch for with jealousy, one thing alone you should see with real terror—the decay of vital religion among Christian men. If this should ever come to pass; if the time should ever come, when, as this, or some like association of men of science, shall visit our cities—with its new facts, its newly discovered laws, its fresh gains in the exhaustless world of nature—its members should ask and ask in vain, for the facts of Christianity; if we could no longer invite them to contemplate the workings of our life, if we should have no tokens of progress to show them, no living saints, no great works of devotion to the good of men, no triumphs of our religion over the sin and misery around us—then faith would indeed have expired; the invisible and the supernatural would have faded for ever out of the life of men. Pray that this may not be. Resolve that this shall not be. Work still, with unceasing zeal, the works of Christ. Live still the life of Christ. And as you work, still pray that of His mercy He may grant you to realize His promised gift, still to " have life and to have it more abundantly."

THE BREAKING NET.

THE BREAKING NET.

Preached before the Dublin Church Congress, St. Patrick's Cathedral, September 29, 1868.

"And they beckoned unto their partners, which were in the other ship, that they should come and help them."—Luke v. 7.

THE Church of Christ, in this prophetic picture of her future, is seen passing through the two great trials of her life on earth—the trial of failure and the trial of success. As the first scene of this miracle opens on us, we see the disciples wearied with their long and fruitless labour. They have toiled all night—toiled, that is, under the most favourable circumstances—toiled long and earnestly, and have caught nothing. As the second scene of the miracle closes, we see the same disciples embarrassed by a sudden and vast success. The multitude of fishes they have enclosed is so great that it threatens to break their net and they beckon to their partners for help.

We know how constantly these two trials alternate through all the history of the Church. We know how often in her history there has arisen from the fishers of men, worn with toil, disheartened with failure, the cry—"we have toiled all night and have caught nothing;" and we know, too, how often their perseverance and faith have been rewarded by some great and unlooked-for success—a success actually perilous from its very greatness and from the suddenness of its demand upon their strength and skill.

There is another fact too foreshadowed in this miracle which all will admit to have been realised in the history of the Church. It is, that the perils of this latter trial are greater than those of the former; that the Church has often more to fear in the hour of her success than in the hour of her failure. The danger of the night of fruitless toil is obvious. It is, that the disappointed workers should desert their work; that losing all heart and hope they should cease to cast the net. But even in that case, the net itself remains unbroken; it needs but reviving faith to use it again. But in the hour of successful capture it is the net itself that is threatened. The danger is not the delay of the work, but the loss of the fruits of it and the power of renewing it. All who know anything of Church history, or of Church work, know the truth of this. They know that the Church's hour of greatest peril has ever been, not that of her adversity, but that of her prosperity. They are aware how real, how serious, are the dangers of success. They feel how deep is the need for the Church as for the individual, to pray ever the prayer, "In all time of our wealth good Lord deliver us."

So far then, the lessons of this miracle lie upon the surface. It teaches us just those two great lessons of warning and encouragement—of warning against carelessness, of encouragement against despondency—that all Scripture and all experience are ever teaching us. It says to us those two great words, which, in some form or other, Christ is ever saying to His Church, "My grace is sufficient for thee;" and, "What I say unto you I say unto all, watch!"

But there is another lesson in this miracle, not so

apparent, and yet a very important one. It is this. That if the hour of success may be the hour of greatest peril, so on the other hand, the hour of greatest seeming peril may be that of real success.

It is clear that in this narrative the danger arises out of the success of the disciples, is caused by it and is inseparable from it. The contrast between the two trials is, in this respect, very remarkable. The danger of the night was wholly and exclusively a temptation to desert their work. It was one, therefore, which it rested with themselves entirely to avoid; they need not cease to cast the net. But the danger in the other case arises quite independently of their course of action. It did not depend on them whether their net should be in danger of breaking, though it did depend on them whether it should be cast. That is to say, the peril in the latter case is inevitable, is to be reckoned on as sure to come with such success, and, therefore, is to be regarded as an indication of success, as a reason, if for anxiety, yet for thankfulness—a cause for rejoicing, even though they trembled while they rejoiced.

Now, if this be also a fact in the history of the Church —if there be perils and trials which are actually the indications and tests of successful labour—then it is all-important to remember this fact whenever we attempt to estimate the present position and prospects of the Church of Christ, or of any branch of it. We must take care, in so doing, to distinguish between the dangers which are caused by our faults or neglects and those which arise from the very success of our labours; between the dangers that call for repentance and amendment and those that call only for courage and wisdom; between evils which we must cure if we would exist, and evils which we can never cure so long as we exist—which in fact we could not get rid of without losing some greater accompanying good. To confound these together is a very serious error. Not merely because it often leads to needless fear and despondency, but because it often leads to misdirected and wasted effort, to setting ourselves to prevent the inevitable, to alter the unalterable, to change, not the manner of our working, but the essential and unchangeable conditions under which our Master has appointed that we shall work.

It may help us, then, on this occasion—when so many earnest workers for God are gathered together, to pass in review their labour and its results, to take counsel together on its duties and its difficulties and its dangers, to seek to discover their own shortcomings or errors in the doing of it—it may help us to a deeper and a truer estimate of all these things; it may help to deepen our repentance for all that is amiss in ourselves, to strengthen our courage and patience through all that is inevitably trying in our position, if we ponder for a little upon the law which conditions all our work—that its success brings with it inevitable perils of its own—and if we trace the application of this law to some of the difficulties and dangers which at this moment beset us in our great task.

Let us see then what is the danger to which the Church, as here pictured, is exposed. It is the breaking of the net and the threatened escape of the multitude it encloses. What is this net that is in danger of breaking? Clearly it is all that outward enclosure which at any given moment surrounds the included multitude. That is to say, it represents not merely the gospel with which men first were won, nor yet the creeds and the ordinances which enclosed them when won, but the whole of that varied and complex machinery which, from time to time, the Church devises or acquires, by which she seeks to draw men heavenward. All such machinery of organisation and effort as that on which we are about to consult in this our Congress; all that network, too, of influence and association, moral and social; all those subtle and all but invisible yet mighty influences which, like so many meshes, wrap themselves round the whole life of a nation and link it to the life of the Church; all, in one word, that gives the Church a hold in any measure upon the Age. The breaking of any one of these is, so far, a breaking of the net; is so far a danger of the escape of just so many of the multitude as it served to attract or to restrain.

Now there can be no question that the breaking of this net is emphatically the peril of the Church in our day. If we could have any doubt of this ourselves, her enemies at least have none. They are for ever telling us, with shouts of exultation, that the Church is fast losing her hold of the age; that she is fast ceasing to attract or to restrain it. "See," they say, "how the intellect and the free thought of our day are breaking loose from the meshes of your dogmas. See how modern science and criticism are tearing away larger and still larger portions of your creeds. See how the State is withdrawing from its old alliance with you—how the education of the nation is passing out of your control; while, on the other hand, your own internal strifes and party divisions threaten of themselves to tear you to pieces. Your net is breaking at every point, and soon the advancing tide of free thought and life will sweep away its last remaining fragments!" This is what our foes are saying; and, with all allowance for the malignant exaggerations of their hate and their hope, it has in it a measure of truth. There are, indeed, signs that if the net be not broken, it is strained almost to the breaking point. Is there an earnest and thoughtful worker here who, if he were asked—What is the evil you most dread for the Church, what is that thought of fear which lies at this moment deepest in your heart—deep below all the cares or anxieties or sorrows of your own toil—would not reply —"I fear the breaking of the net!" "I dread, not merely the snapping of this or that smaller mesh, the failure of this or that minor organization which might be replaced by another and a better; but the breaking of it altogether—of all things I fear this." Let us look, then, this peril in the face. Let us see whether there be in it no reasons for hope and for courage, as well as for anxiety and for fear.

I. And, first; we observe that the net of the Church is strained and imperilled, simply because it is a net. That is, it is an instrumentality designed for the capture and restraint of unwilling captives. The Gospel of Christ Jesus answers to the deepest wants of human nature. But for that very reason it does not answer to its strongest wishes. What humanity needs is to be saved from itself, its fallen and perverted self; what it craves is to be left to itself. It needs life, and yet will not come to the life-giver. It needs light, and yet loves darkness. It needs the Saviour, and yet is ever praying Him to depart out of its coasts. It needs law, and yet loves lawlessness. It needs discipline, and yet craves indulgence. And therefore it resists and resents every attempt to curb its lawlessness and to restrain its licence. It struggles against each constraining force that would draw it into the presence of the life-giver and the healer. Naturally, then and necessarily this instinctive dislike of the net and of the shore urges ever the enclosed captives to rush against the restraints of faith or discipline that still draw them shoreward and heavenward.

And if the spirit of the age be, as assuredly it is, one of impatient intolerance of all restraint; if it show itself in the State, in Society, in the Family, in an ever increasing lawlessness; if the very idea of obedience, of submission, of reverence of any kind whatever, seems to be fast vanishing away, and in its place there be seen only the idea of the most absolute and uncontrolled self-assertion of each individual; the assertion of his natural right to do and say, in his utter selfishness, only as seems to him best, controlled only by the mere brute force of a larger number of individuals who are determined in their utter selfishness that he shall say and do only what seems to them best; if this utter lawlessness be the characteristic of the age, why should we expect that the Church should escape its influence? The Church which is the oldest, and, therefore, according to modern thought, the most odious of all institutions; the Church which above all other institutions rests not on opinion but on authority; the Church which cannot, dare not, call the voice of the people the voice of God, but which must ever claim that the voice of the people be hushed into silence that they may hear "the word of the Lord;" the Church whose creeds and whose sacraments are not to be reformed again and again in deference to the opinion of the hour; how is it possible that she should not feel, more than any other institution, the rush and the strain of those who, drunk with licence, seek ever, in the name of liberty, to destroy liberty's only safeguard—Law?

It is well for us to remember this fact, that the Church works and must ever work against the grain of human nature. It is well to remember this in an age when popularity is fast becoming the one and only test of success; when it is held sufficient proof that the Church has failed in her mission if her discipline be resisted or her doctrine questioned, if her services fail to "draw" or her sermons fail to interest; when we are assured that the only way to recover our lost ground is to "adapt ourselves to the spirit of the age;" to adapt, that is to say, our faith to its scepticism, our discipline to its licentiousness, our teaching to its fastidious taste and palled and jaded appetites. It may be well for us to remember, aye and to say, that Christ has not sent us into the world merely to be popular, merely to dance to the piping and lament to the mourning of the children in the world's great market place; that if we are, as we are reminded so often, the followers of Him whom "the common people heard gladly," we are also the disciples of Him whose "hard sayings" more than once drove all His hearers away; that we are the followers of Him who, in the hour when in seeming helplessness He was working His mightiest work, was surrounded by the taunting crowd who challenged Him to prove His mission by doing that which would have undone it all, by coming down from the cross and saving Himself. We ought to remember, too, that we might do all we are asked to do and yet not content the world. We might thus only furnish fresh subjects for criticism. We know how of old the world, that said of one teacher who came neither eating nor drinking, "he hath a devil," said of another who came eating and drinking, "behold a gluttonous man and a wine-bibber." Let us take heed; let us take great heed, lest in our fear of the seven times heated furnace of the world's hate or the world's scorn, we bow ourselves down before its idol—popularity, what time we hear the sound of all those musical instruments with which its servants are giving signal for its worship. Let us not be too careful to answer our enemies in this matter. It may be our mission to win them from their idolatry by our faithful refusal to worship with them, by our protest for a higher worship and a purer faith. It may be our destiny, as we pass through the fire unscathed, to bring the world to own that there is no God but our God. Or if not, if still we be but faithful to our charge, if still in sternest faithfulness we utter only what our Master has given us to speak, let us remember that the Church has not always failed in her mission when she has failed to attract and to conciliate; that there is another and a more awful mission that she is accomplishing in the world, when she testifies and condemns; that if the disciples fulfilled their mission, when they dwelt as welcome guests in the home where their sojourn brought the presence of the Son of Peace, they not the less fulfilled it when they shook the dust from their feet as they departed from the house or the city that rejected them.

II. But, in the next place, there is a peril to the net, which arises from the very zeal of those who are drawing it. So long as the net only loosely surrounds the enclosed multitudes and no great effort is made to draw it shorewards, there is no great constraint felt and therefore no great resistance made. But so soon as the hands of the fishermen begin to draw it closely and strongly, so soon as it restrains and constrains as well as contains, then the resistance becomes real as the restraint. There is, in fact, a double strain, that of captor and captive; the strain of those who draw strongly shoreward, and of those who rush strongly seaward. This is a peril, an inevitable peril to the net. Let us be thankful that it is one of our day. Religion is no longer, as it was in days not long past, a decent outward profession of old-fashioned opinions, which troubled no one because it really restrained no one. Whatever school of thought men belong to, they are at least in earnest in their belief. The dogmas of our creeds, the definitions of our articles, the words of our prayers, that men formerly repeated lazily and drowsily together, because they never thought of their meaning, are heard now as voices in their hearts, bidding them turn to the right or to the left. Old words, that in times past had faded out as if written in invisible ink, are revealing themselves anew in the glow and heat of our modern thought. The pillars of cloud are gleaming out as pillars of fire, and we are following them hither and thither. Men are beginning to lay hold of principles and work them to their results. And thus it comes to pass, that now here, now there, some worker, some body of workers, are seizing, now this, now that part of the net, and lifting it into light as they draw it; lifting with it, too, it may be, the incrustations of merely human opinion or practice, that have grown over it; those additions to the creed which every party makes in its turn; those long tangled masses of traditional belief, that hang as dead weight to the net and sorely strain and weary the aching arms of those who draw it. The result of this is a great straining of the net, a sore testing of the strength of every part that is thus drawn upon. It leads, it must lead, to one of two things —the revival of some forgotten truth, or the detection of some unheeded error that this revival has forced into prominence; to a restoration, that is, or to a reformation. Meanwhile the net is in no small peril of being rent to pieces. This is a sore peril, but it is an inevitable one. It is the risk inherent in every revival, whether of doctrine or of practice; it is one that would be ill replaced by the rotting of the net as it hung idly in the waters, unstrained only because it was undrawn.

III. But there is another danger to the Church foreshadowed in this miracle—a great, and yet also an inevitable one. It is that which arises from its catholicity. The net encloses a great multitude, and the greatness of the multitude imperils the net. The Church was designed from the first to enclose no less than the whole world for which Christ died. "Go ye into all the world and preach the Gospel to every creature," is His bidding to the fishers of men. And the multitude they enclose is to be a mixed multitude. Good and bad fish within the net; wheat and tares within the field; clean and unclean within the ark. Spiritual and unspiritual, converted and unconverted, faithful and hypocrite, all are to be admitted within the enclosure of His Church, by one, and one only, portal—Baptism; on one, and only one condition—outward profession of faith in that name into which they are baptised. She may not, she must not, ever narrow this condition. She must not dare to anticipate that separation of the good from the bad which is to be made by Him alone whose fan is in His hand and who has not committed the purging of His garner to another.

But what is the result of this catholicity of the Church? It is that she is ever receiving into her bosom foreign and even hostile elements. A stream of emigrants is ever flowing in upon her, every one of whom becomes a citizen as he touches her shores, and yet a citizen to whom she has still to teach her language and her laws. So has it been from the first. The races, the creeds, the philosophies which the Church encloses within her net, threaten her, each in its turn, with some new schism, as, long after their reception, each strives to break away from her restraint. The Hebrew and the Grecian converts vexed her with their murmurings. The Jew and the Gentile nearly tore her asunder. The Heathen schools of Philosophy, the powers of the Roman State, the wild hordes of Northern barbarians—each in its turn brought within her pale—produced each its own heresy, its own attempt at schism. Each conquest proved thus, in its turn, a real gain and yet a real danger. Ever the larger the multitude the greater the peril of the net. A peril this, but yet one that inevitably attends success. Our real danger respecting it lies in attempting to avoid it by narrowing the conditions of membership, by trying to exclude from the Church all the unspiritual and the unconverted, or all that do not say the shibboleth of our own party or sect; that is, by destroying the catholicity of the Church and reducing it, as of old, to the limits of one race—the spiritual Israel now, as formerly Israel after the flesh. So surely as we do this, we hinder the progress of the Church. The net encloses little or nothing. No great multitude comes within its narrow sweep: no gathering of the nations ever strains its small contracted meshes. It is comparatively safe, because it is comparatively empty.

Such attempts at making the Church less catholic than Christ has made it have an air of spirituality; they really come from slothfulness, or from fear. From slothfulness, when we would fain make of the Church, of our parish, of our party, only a safe and quiet fold wherein the flock, small and select, obey the voice of their favourite pastor, and where the pastor shuns the stormy sea and the weary casting of the net and the aching toil of striving with the struggling captives it encloses. It comes from fear, when the missionary, trembling for the untried strength of his net, dreading the strain upon it of a promiscuous multitude of converts, lays down conditions for their admission other than those which Christ has laid; insisting, for instance, before Baptism, upon proofs of real spiritual conversion, or even of complete conformity to Christian habits of life and thought; insisting, that is, that the sick shall be healed before they enter the hospital intended for their healing.

Let us beware of so doing. Let us, rather, fearlessly and faithfully accept the evil with the good, the peril with the gain. Let us remember that our net cannot be at once full and unstrained; that we cannot have at once the narrow security of the sect whose aim is to exclude and the broad catholic fulness of the Church, whose aim is to include. We cannot have the small sharp neatness of the trim garden that can be weeded and watered in a day, and the stately breadth and height of the forest that crowns the hills and spreads itself far down in the valleys of the open country and is noble and beautiful, because its growth, though not uncultivated nor unpruned, is yet largely natural and free. We must learn to listen undismayed to the reproaches cast upon our Church, that it is divided and distracted by contending parties, or that it is full of merely worldly and unspiritual professors. It must be so, because it is national and catholic. So long as it is the Church of the whole nation, it must feel all the stir and ferment of the national life. Whatever wave of thought or feeling sweeps through the nation must deeply agitate the national Church. The schools of philosophy or of religion, the social and political impulses of the people move the Church, which influences and is influenced by each and all of them. The piety and the virtue of the nation largely find their place in her; largely too its sin and crime. The waifs and strays that no sect will own, all belong to her. Like her Master, she is still a companion of publicans and sinners. Like Him, she seeks to gather round her still the blind and the halt and the lame, that

He may heal them. Others may be select because they are not catholic: she, because she is catholic, must not, dare not, be select.

IV. There is yet another danger foreshadowed in this story. The peril to the net arises not only from the weight of the strain, but from its suddenness. The fabric that could stand the gradual strain of a great weight, snaps with the sudden jerk of a lesser one. This is a peril to which every national church is subject, because it is national. Spread, as she is, all over the nation, bound to supply all its spiritual needs as they arise, the Church is exposed to sudden strains on her resources, by every sudden change in the distribution or even in the habits of the people. The discovery of a coal-bed, or a gold-field, the rush of some new emigration, the invention of some new art or manufacture and the consequent growth of some new hive of human industry, make from time to time fresh and unforeseen demands upon her strength. Suddenly, the net of some quiet country parish is filled with the influx of a great multitude; the village becomes a town, the town a city, almost in a day and the net is strained almost to breaking. Or, again, some hitherto neglected field of labour is discovered; some class hitherto overlooked, some form of evil or sin or suffering that has been burrowing under the surface of society is suddenly laid bare; and the Church, by virtue of her claim to be national, is called on to deal with this and to deal with it at once; and this, too, is especially a trial which increases with success. All workers know how work brings and makes work, how each field of labour that we till brings us still to the verge of another and another; how still the sweep of our net widens and widens and the weight it encloses tries more and more our strength, until we tremble lest it break.

This, again, is a peril of our day; but it too is inevitable, and to be thankfully accepted as a token of success.

Such are some of the dangers arising from the very conditions of our work, perils of success rather than of failure. We are far, indeed, from saying that these are all our dangers, even of this kind, or that there are not many of other kinds. We are far from saying that we have not to grieve and repent for dangers caused by our own sins and our own neglects; far from saying that, as we gather here to ask for God's blessing on our Congress, our hearts should not be full of these; that as we draw nigh to His table, "the remembrance of them" should not be "grievous unto us and the burden intolerable." I would only remind you that if that prayer were to be fully answered, if from this gathering there were to come forth a Pentecost, yet that Pentecost would have perils of its own that we should still have cause to fear the breaking net, still need to beckon to each other for help.

Yes! this—next to our own individual repentance and awakened zeal—this is our great duty, our great safety against the perils of our day—it is to call our partners to our aid. As the net breaks, and wherever it breaks, there should the fishermen gather together. The point of danger should be still the point of union. Wherever the Faith is threatened with heresy, or the Church with schism, or the machinery of the Church's work proves inadequate to some sudden strain, there should the partners assemble to lay upon the net a stronger and a closer grasp; to draw it, with their united strength, ever more strongly and steadily to shore. We beckon, then, to our partners. But who are they? What allies shall the Church call to aid her in her task? In the first place, there is one partner long associated with her in that task, that seems less and less disposed to hear her call. The State was once the active partner of the national Church in her great work. There was a time, when, for a Christian nation, the national recognition of God was held to be its solemn duty and to make national provision for the knowledge of His law and the worship of His name its truest wisdom. This is so no longer. The axiom of all modern statesmanship, more and more plainly avowed, is this, that nations, as nations, have nothing to do with God: that religion is the affair of the individual solely and exclusively, and one in which the State has, and ought to have, no concern whatever; that the Church—like any other voluntary association of individuals—is to be protected so long as it is peaceable, and sternly repressed whenever it grows in any way troublesome. But the idea that Church and Nation are each a divine institution—powers, both of them, "ordained of God," having each their ground in real relations to God and to each other, having therefore their duties to each other, which they may not neglect without peril and without sin,—this is scouted as the merest folly.

I am not asking now whether this view be true or false, whether the modern idea of a godless, creedless, prayerless state be the great truth or the great heresy of the age. I only say that its existence is a fact, and that under its influence the divorce of Church and State seems rapidly accomplishing itself all over Christendom. Men may differ as to whether this divorce between Church and State be desirable or no. All admit it to be probable. Statesmen are questioning whether the State, as they think it ought to be, can continue its union with the Church as it is. Churchmen are questioning how long the Church, as they think it ought to be, can continue its union with the State, as it is likely to be; how long the unbelieving husband may be sanctified by the believing wife, and at what point the infidelity or the cruelty of the husband may compel the wife to accept, nay even to seek, her putting away. To these questions men will give—are giving—very various answers. But all feel that while these are among the questions of our day, it is in vain for the Church to call for fresh aid from the State.

On whom else shall She call? On those other partners, still engaged in the same emprize, but whom the storms and tides of the past have drifted so far away that they are all but beyond the reach of her voice? Oh, if she could but recall these! If, without the loss of one vital truth possessed by each, if only with the lightening of each ship by the casting overboard of its evil freight of error or passion or prejudice, all these partners could come together once more! If for one hour Christendom were one, what in that hour might it not achieve! Shall it ever, can it ever be, that the common peril of the breaking net, the danger of the total loss of faith from the earth, should thus unite those severed Churches and divergent sects? If this ever come, it will come, not by the adopting of each other's errors, nor by the servile copying of each other's defects; nor yet by agreeing to call diversity agreement and palpable schism unity. It will come by the faithful and searching reformation of each communion for itself and by itself; it will come by the turning, not of each to other, but of each and all to the common centre Christ.

Meanwhile it is our duty first to call upon our own partners—upon the members of our own Anglican Communion—to call them, not to union, we are still one, but to co-operation; to co-operation in counsel and in organization, to such united and organized effort as alone can cope with the perils of our day. It is here especially that our Church life needs strengthening and is largely capable of it. The religious revival of the earlier part of this century has filled the Church with individual life. It has even revived and largely strengthened the first unit of ecclesiastical organization—parochial life. But, though this is far from complete, we have hardly made a step beyond it. The higher, the larger forms of organic life, the life of the Diocese, of the Province, of the whole Church, these are but faintly beginning to stir. We are a collection of regiments, but the banding of regiments into divisions, of divisions into one great army, the power of concentrating the whole weight of the Church as that of one man, and throwing it collectively upon the point of need, how far have we attained to this? How far, again, have we utilised all the wealth of materials that the Church possesses in her laity? How far have we organized, and brought to bear systematically upon the vice and the sin and the sorrow of our day, the vigorous business-like aptitude of our practical laymen, or the tender might of Christian woman's love? How far have we aimed at catching and gathering into the one great central reservoir of the Church the half wasted springs of individual benevolence, and pouring them all in well directed channels to every spot that needs them? All this we have scarce begun to do. It is the work, it is the need of our day. It is the felt need that utters itself in all such gatherings for conference and counsel as these. Synods, Convocations, Congresses, all express the deep yearnings of all earnest Churchmen for the completion and the manifestation of the organic life of the Church, as distinguished from the separate life of its individual members. These gatherings are the acknowledgment of a fact, forgotten by those who sneer at all such meetings, as assemblies for talk. They who so speak forget that even if the talk did not result, as it has resulted, in valuable action, even if conference did not bring, as it has brought, more than one practical result, the gathering is in itself a good thing, may be a very blessed thing, in that Church to which He has said, "Where two or three are gathered together in my name there am I in the midst of them."

And if the meeting of a Church Congress anywhere would be a token of this desire for unity, especially so is our meeting here, and now. The fact that the Church Congress, no longer content with giving, as it has given from the first, a welcome place to Irish Churchmen in its assemblies, has resolved that this year the place of its assembling shall be Ireland; the fact that this proposal came, not from Ireland but from England, that our English brethren anticipated the invitation we were hastening to offer and the welcome we were eager to assure them of—this is a significant fact. It is a sign of that ever-growing spirit of brotherhood which every meeting of brethren generates. It is more. It is the declaration, on the part of our English brethren, of their deep and deepening conviction that we are members of a united church; united, not merely nor mainly by the outward bond of a common establishment, but by the inner unity of a common life; joined together in a union which the State never made and which the State can therefore never take away.

This were a significant fact at any time; it is tenfold more so now. Now, when our gathering occurs in so grave a crisis in the history of the united Church—the united Church we say advisedly, for the perils of the crisis are not for us alone—it is indeed a grave and an anxious moment for our common country and our common Church, in which we are assembled. Think what men may of the causes or the merits of the struggle through which we are passing, all must feel that its issues for good or evil must be deep and wide and lasting; that they involve the assertion of more than one great principle which, by the resistless logic of events must work itself out to great and yet unforeseen results. Such moments of great organic change are fraught with peril both to the State and to the Church. We say to the Church as distinguished from the Establishment; for we know full well, what we are so often accused of forgetting, that neither the Establishment nor the Endowment is the Church; that her "life consisteth not in the abundance of the things that she possesseth." This is as true for the Church as it is for the individual. But it is, nevertheless, equally true for the individual as for the Church that the loss of possessions, the sudden and violent change in all outward circumstances and relations, must seriously try and endanger spiritual life. We know that at such a time a man's friends will anxiously watch how he bears himself, how the life that is in him is sustaining him under the shock of such a trial.

It is at such a moment—when we are threatened with such a trial—which involves so much more than the loss of money only—a moment when the anxiety of suspense is even harder to bear than the trial itself may prove, should it come upon us—at such a moment, in the providence of God, you, our English brethren, have come amongst us. You have come—we love to know it—to help us with your sympathy, your counsel, your prayers; come with the not unnatural desire to see and judge us for yourselves; come to watch how we bear ourselves in the presence of a danger that may one day be also yours.

We bid you one and all a hearty and a loving welcome —all the more hearty and the more loving because we believe that you represent the feelings towards us of the large majority of our English brethren. We believe, we know, that it is not in their hearts, any more than it is in yours, to watch in coward and selfish security, from your harbour of present safety the perils and the efforts of your brethren caught in the storm and struggling with the waves; to note with sneering criticism how, as they toil against the tempest, their movements have not all the exact order, nor their voices quite the measured calm their critics can boast of; to scoff at their sea craft; to exult over their breaking net. You have come, if but for a moment, to take your place beside us; to lay your hands in brotherly love upon our net and to understand, as you do so, how, if it be in no peril of breaking from the multitude it encloses, it may be so from the strength of the currents and the violence of the tides with which it contends. You come to learn from us how it is that we have toiled so long and won so little ; come to hear how ours has been no favourable night for toil ; not calm and still and warm, like the eastern night of those first fishermen, but rather like one of our own northern nights, wild and tempestuous, lit but by the lightening flashes of civil and religious strife. You have come to hear that if we have won few, we have lost none; come to see that we have not and will not cease to toil, but still, as our Lord commands us, are ready to labour on, spent yet undismayed.

One thing you will not hear from us. You will hear no unmanly cries of terror nor of rage; no weak entreaties for compassion. Nay, rather you shall hear us tell you, in all brotherly kindness, this, that if we need your help, you, too, need ours—need it as really, if not as much, as in those old days when ours was the fulness, yours the need ; when England sought and found from Ireland missionaries to help her to win her heathen population to the Gospel. Now it is otherwise. Ours is now the weakness, yours the strength ; and, therefore, yours the especial dangers of success ; yours far more than ours the peril of the breaking net. The very smallness of our numbers, the very strength and number of our enemies keep us a compact and homogeneous body. There are perils, therefore, to which you are exposed, from which we are free. There are aspects too of truth which are given to us to bring out, as there are others given to you. We have our share, our important and essential share, in the development of the life of the Church catholic, as you have yours. You cannot but be helped by our spiritual life, hurt by our spiritual weakness. Let us hope and pray that we may each of us more and more understand and realize this fact. Let us hope and pray that as year by year the action of each of these portions of the Church on the other grows closer and stronger, we shall come more readily and closely to the help each of the other and learn to know and love each other better. Let but this spirit animate us; let but our hearts glow with a still deeper and more loving brotherhood, springing from that out of which alone it can spring—from closer union with our common Lord and deeper longing to do His work on earth — and there is no fear that our work shall ever perish. The storm may rage and the black clouds gather and the waves run high, but there shall ever reveal itself more and more distinctly, the form of Him who came of old, walking on the wild waters, to the aid of his imperilled disciples. We shall see Him still, though it were but by the storm-light upon the deep. Amidst the roar of the elements, we shall still hear Him say, "It is I, be not afraid." Nearer and nearer still, through the gloom of the tempest, shall grow the shore where we shall draw our nets to land and hear His welcome, at whose command we first, in fear and yet in faith, launched out into the deep and let down our nets for the draught.

CHRISTIANITY, A GOSPEL FOR THE POOR.

CHRISTIANITY A GOSPEL FOR THE POOR.

St. Paul's Cathedral, 1876.

"The dead are raised up, and the poor have the gospel preached to them. And blessed is he, whosoever shall not be offended in me."
MATTHEW xi. 5, 6.

THESE words are part of a message sent by Christ to one who was in danger of becoming "offended in Him." For this surely, and not the information nor the conversion of his messengers, was the motive for the question which John the Baptist sent his disciples to ask of Christ, "Art thou He that should come, or do we look for another?" John sent this message, as we know, from a prison, and from a prison into which he had been cast for fulfilling his mission as the forerunner of God's kingdom of righteousness on earth. As the herald of that kingdom, he had boldly rebuked vice and commanded repentance; and the result is that he is languishing in chains and waiting for death. As he lies thus, he hears of the triumphs of that kingdom of God to the coming and to the nature of which he had witnessed. He hears of the mighty miracles of the King of Righteousness, whom he had owned and proclaimed in his baptism; and yet he —the prophet of that kingdom—the herald of that King —is left unaided, and seemingly unpitied, to perish. Why is this? Not certainly for want of power. The hand that healed the sick and raised the dead could have opened his prison door with a touch. If it be not, then, for want of power that he is thus neglected, is it for want of will? If so, can He who thus neglects him be the true King of God's kingdom of righteousness on earth? The axe that John beheld, in his prophetic vision of that kingdom, already laid to the root of the overshadowing tyrannies and cruelties of this world, why smites it not in his behalf? Why does it lie, in his case, motionless as if the hand that held it had been smitten with palsy? The fan which he beheld in the hand of his Divine Lord and Master, and which was to winnow with righteous judgment the good from the evil and to gather the good into safety, why does it not deliver him by sweeping away his enemies. Perplexed by this mystery, weary and sick with hope deferred, he sends at last his message, if not of doubt, at least of remonstrance and of indignation: "Art thou He"—Thou who leavest thy servant here to die—"Art thou He that should come, or must we look for another?" Surely this is the true meaning of John's exceeding bitter cry. We feel that it must mean this, because it is the same cry that our own hearts so often have raised since then. What is this question but the utterance of the perplexity and distress of all those who are disappointed with Christ and with Christianity? Who that has ever thought seriously of the facts of his own life, or of the life of Christ on earth, has not asked it at one time or another? Who,—comparing the greatness of the aims of Christianity with the smallness apparently of its results, its lofty claims with its sad and distressing failures, its victories with its seeming defeats—has not been tempted to ask, Is Christianity after all the Divine thing it claims to be? Thus, through age after age, down along all the centuries of human sorrow and suffering, of seemingly unpitied wrong and unredressed woe, the cry has risen up again and again from many an imprisoned soul, bound in the chains of its own doubts and fears, "Art thou He that should come, or do we look for another?" Deeply, therefore, does it concern us to study the answer of Christ to the question of his distressed and all but despairing servant. For the answer, like the question, is assuredly recorded for our learning. Let us listen, then, to what Christ has to say to this question. It may be that in so doing we shall win the blessing which He pronounces upon those who are not "offended in Him."

I. The answer of our Lord to the question of the Baptist is twofold. He bids his disciples tell John of His works and of His word, of His miracles and of His teaching. "Tell John the things ye see and hear." The evidences of Christianity then, as appealed to by Christ Himself, are seen to range themselves from the first under those two heads under which its defenders have ever since classed them—the external and the internal, the miracles which attest it to the intellect, the teaching which attests it to the heart of man as a message from his Maker and Father. "Tell John the things ye see." What were these? Miracles; but not miracles merely, not marvels only to wonder at; not merely barren prodigies, to awaken a stare of admiration or of terror; they were signs—wonders, that is to say, which were deeply significant. And of what were they the signs? Of this: that the supernatural kingdom which they heralded was established by God, for the undoing therein of all evil, and the restoring and completing of all good. And these wonders, which ushered in its coming, were the tokens that there dwelt in it a supernatural power, which in the realm of the physical world showed itself capable of suspending one order of things and of introducing another and a better order, and which therefore might be held to be capable of effecting the like in the realm of the moral and the social. The presence of the supernatural, as it thus attests the coming of the new kingdom of righteousness, assures us that this order of nature in which we live is not necessarily eternal; that there may yet come a state of things in which it shall be as unnatural for man to suffer and sorrow and die as it is now natural, in which it shall be as natural for man to be perfectly holy and perfectly happy as it is now natural—only too natural —for him to be perfectly sinful and perfectly miserable. This is the true significance of the miracles of Christ.

Nevertheless, those who witnessed these must have seen, as we see now more clearly, that this miraculous power was limited in its extent and application within very narrow bounds. All the sick were not healed; all the hungry were not fed; all the dead were not raised; all suffering and sorrowing souls in Christ's day were not comforted nor healed by Him. How then can we take upon ourselves to say that a complete deliverance from these evils shall ever come to pass? How can we venture to affirm that these limitations of His power or of His will may not last for ever. How shall we know that the time is sure to come when all the dead shall be raised, and all sickness, and all sin and sorrow supernaturally banished from this world? We need something more than miracles, we need a revelation accompanying the miracles to assure us of this; and accordingly, to the appeal which Christ makes to His miracles, He adds an appeal to His teaching. "Tell John," tell the world, "the things that ye hear" as well as the things that ye see. Tell him of the word as well as of the works of his Master. And what is that word? It is the everlasting Gospel of the Son of God. "The Gospel is preached," and this is the good news of that Gospel, notwithstanding all that which seems to us now to confute it, God loves the world He has made; that He so loves this world, where sin and sorrow seem to reign instead and in spite of Him, that He has not forgotten us in the prison house of time and sense wherein we languish waiting for death; that He so loves this world that He will yet fully deliver it from all evil and that to assure us of this He has sent His Son to live in it and to die for it, so that he that believeth in Him shall not perish, but have everlasting life. And this is the Word that by the Gospel is preached unto us. And as we tell the things men saw and heard of old—as we tell the old story of wonder and interpret it by the ever new message of love—there comes into our hearts—begotten of faith and fighting against doubt—the assurance of the Almighty love that girdles us round within its infinite embrace and we drink into our souls the deep blessedness of those who are not offended with Christ.

II. But our Lord speaks here of one special characteristic of this Gospel. It is not only a Gospel generally for all men, but it is especially a Gospel for the poor. And what is there in this fact that should be so significant that our Lord gives it a place in the evidences of that Gospel beside His miracles —beside the very raising of the dead? Let us try to understand this one special evidence of the Gospel of Christ, namely, that it is good news for the poor; and let us if we can show these two things respecting it. First; that no other system has any good news for the poor; next, that Christianity has for the poor good news. And let us see, in the first place, why it is difficult to imagine that there should be any Gospel for poverty in this world. What is poverty? Poverty is only another word for human imperfection and weakness. The life of mankind on earth is a life of struggle with nature. That is no discovery of modern science; it is as old as the word recorded in the first chapter of our Bibles: "Replenish the earth and subdue it." It is in proportion as man subdues the earth and by his strength and skill wrings from it its treasures, that progress, civilization, and wealth, and with them, human comfort and happiness, increase and prosper. But all men are not equally fitted for this struggle with nature; all are not equally gifted with the power of acquiring or of keeping their acquisitions. The strong frame, the keen intellect, the resolute will, conquer circumstances in nature; they acquire the earth and subdue it. The weaker fail to do this, and consequently they lack and suffer hunger; and the result is that though there is enough for all, a feast spread for all, the strong force their way to the table where it is spread and the weak are thrust aside. And the strong we call rich; and the weak we call poor. And this is the inevitable law of human society as it is at present constituted. You cannot change this state of things, do what you will, because its source lies deep in the natural inequality of human beings. Social inequality is only another word for physical inequality and that must always exist amongst men. Always must there be in the world the Dives and the Lazarus. They may change places here and there; but they exist and exist continually. It is a law, then, of society that it must always have its poor. This is a state of things that the rich accept with wonderful equanimity. It is quite true, they hasten to assure you, that it is the law of this world that one must gain and another lose—that one must be rich and another poor, and that we can not help this. No! But do you ever stop, you that are rich, to think what those words "poverty" and "loss" mean? Do you ever try to realise what poverty is in itself? I am not speaking of the pangs of physical hunger, but of loss, of degradation, of the waste of life; of the failure of aspirations; of human souls rich in capacities for joy born into a world of weariness and sorrow; of energies, that might make life beautiful and glorious, spent and seemingly wasted in making it barely possible. I speak of ignorance, of sorrow, of weariness, of shame, of vice, of crime. Aye, crime! for it is easy to be virtuous on £10,000 a year. God only knows the temptations that beset the poor. Yes, poverty is loss. Not the poverty of poetry, but the poverty of real life is a terrible reality, a sad and pitiful loss of almost all that constitutes the happiness, the beauty, the graciousness of life. Most deeply true are the words of the preacher, that "the destruction of the poor man is his poverty." And this poverty, as we have said, seems to be an essential element of human society, seems even to grow with the growth and strengthen with the strength of social organization and progress, seems to be the ever-growing Nemesis of wealth, the ever eating and corroding canker of civilization. You cannot cure it by law: the attempt to do so ends and can end only in a universally destructive communism. You can but very imperfectly remedy it by benevolence: nothing is more difficult to bestow usefully and safely, nothing is more dangerous if bestowed unwisely, than charity. Those who have tried most earnestly to heal poverty by gifts are just those who mourn most over their want of success. They tell you that all their efforts are at best but the sewing of a coarse hard patch upon the thin worn robe of poverty, which too often makes the rent it would repair worse than it was before they tried to mend it. Where, then, in this world of ours is there room for a Gospel for the poor?

Let us see what Christianity has to say to this question. Christianity claims to give the poor man, as such, a place and a future in the new kingdom of God, of which I shall presently speak; but to estimate this place and this future rightly let us begin by comparing them with the promises which other systems have to offer in their stead. To do this fairly let us suppose that the dreams of the prophets of infidelity of our day were realized, that the millennium of the nineteenth century, which they are ever foretelling to us, has at last dawned upon us. Let us suppose that humanity has at last risen up, in the glorious dawn of that day of emancipated intellect that is prophesied for us, to proclaim its acceptance of the great infidel Gospel —the good news that there is no God and no future life for men; that man is only a considerably improved brute, and that there is no hereafter for him any more than there is for any other brute. Let us suppose, I say, that mankind has arrived at this stage in its progress towards its prophesied millennium. What, then, have the prophets and heralds of this kingdom of Atheism to say to the poor? What is their Gospel for poverty? Two, and only two utterances are possible as regards poverty when once you have got rid of the supernatural. Speaking only from the ground of the natural, men must say one or other of two things. One is the Gospel, if we may call it so, of the politician; the other is the Gospel of the philosopher. And what is the Gospel of the politician for the poor? It is this. That poverty is not natural, but unnatural and artificial; that it is entirely the result of cruel, cunning laws made by the rich for their own advantage, and that if the masses would only believe this and rise in their might, they would reconstitute society and give to every man enough and not too much for any. This has the sound of good news. It might be a Gospel only for one thing, namely, that it is a lie, a wicked, cruel, and misleading lie, a lie to which all philosophy, all experience, all history supply the denial and the refutation. A lie, because it is based upon a denial of the fundamental facts of human nature itself; a dream and a folly, because it proposes to reconstitute society, and forgets that the only element out of which society as it ought to be can be constituted is just that very human nature which by its necessary workings has produced society as it is. A cruel lie—and for none more cruel than for the poor—for it is in the convulsions of society that the weakest ever suffer most: a false, mad, wicked dream, of "Liberty, Equality, and Fraternity" that gives only liberty of evil, equality in misery, and the fratricidal brotherhood of Cain. There is no Gospel for poverty in communism.

But there is a directly opposite teaching for the poor—the teaching not of the politician, but of the man of science. What has he to say to the poor? Why, that the present state of the poor man is not unnatural; that it is natural, is necessary, is inevitable; that it is the result of that great law, which we are beginning to understand rules all forms of life—the survival of the fittest—growth by natural selection; that the law, which conditions the progress of all the lower forms of animal life, holds good of mankind, and that what we human animals call poverty is nothing else than the working of the beneficent order of nature—why beneficent they do not stop to tell us—by which the weak perish and the strong survive, the individual suffers and the type or race gains. Is this true? We have reason to believe it is not all the truth, but it is a large part of it. Let us grant that it *is* true—horribly, hideously, scientifically true; but it is surely no Gospel. Tell us, if you will, of these great discoveries of modern science. We dispute them not for a moment. Nay, they make for our argument for the Gospel; for the more proof you give us of the terrible suffering inherent in the natural condition of humanity, the more reason do you give for the need of a supernatural deliverer for it. We grant you these discoveries are true; but we only beseech you not to mock our understanding and our hearts by calling them good news. Try your gospel of science on the poor man. Tell him, when you see him looking with eyes of tearless agony upon the wan pinched faces of the little ones that are crying to him for the bread he cannot give them—tell him this : " Your suffering is the result of the working of a great law of nature and of society. It is necessary for the progress of the race that you, the weaker, should give way to the stronger—that the fitter should survive, and that you should perish ; it must be so for the sake of the progress of humanity ; your comfort is that in some remote future mankind will be happier because you are miserable now; and as for the weak impulse of benevolence that tempts me to relieve your poverty, it is, I fear, a scientific mistake, for it can be scientifically demonstrated that society were better without you; but meanwhile accept this teaching as the new Gospel which science has to preach to the poor—meanwhile suffer and die!" Again, I say, we are not questioning the truth of these teachings. We only venture to doubt that they are a Gospel for the poor.

III. Here then, are two utterances : one a seeming Gospel that is a lie ; the other a sad truth which is no Gospel. And if you blot out the supernatural from the world, this is all that you can have to say to the poor. Now let us turn to the Gospel of Christianity and let see what *it* has to say. What is the Gospel that Christ sends us to preach to poverty? What word has it to say to the poor man? It says, in the first place, what is a lie on the lips of the communist—but which, spoken by Christianity is a truth and a blessed one—namely, that the present condition of the poor is not a natural one, is not that in which man was first placed, and is not that to which man is at last to attain. There is another, a better, a truer, a more deeply natural—although it be also a supernatural—order of things. "The things that are seen," with all their inexorable conditions of suffering, with all their dumb, confused strife and misery—these are only phenomena, these are the things that are passing away; but "the things that are not seen," but which are full surely to be seen hereafter, they are eternal. God has another world in which to redress the inequalities of this; God has an eternity in which to console the poor. And what is the picture which our Gospel gives of this consolation of the poor in that other world which Christianity reveals to him? It tells him of "things that eye hath not seen nor ear heard, neither has it entered into the heart of man to conceive" concerning the fulness of the glory and the deep quiet of the rest and peace that await him there. It tells him of a world to come where he "shall hunger no more, neither thirst any more," where "sorrow and sighing shall flee away" and there shall be no more pain, for there "God shall wipe away the tears from all eyes." Does not this sound something more like a poor man's Gospel? Is not this a light from heaven upon the poor man's path? We who preach it know the blessedness of the joyful sound which promises such consolation. We know how it falls upon the gloom of the poor man's home as the glory of the Lord fell long ago upon the weary watchers in the depth of their night; how it gilds the toil of his daily task and lightens, with a tender and gracious beauty, his dying bed. Yes, this is a Gospel for the poor. But is it a truth or only a dream—a vision only such as might visit the fevered sleep of some shipwrecked mariner, picturing for him green fields and sparkling streams which his waking eyes may never see? Not so! for the Gospel of Christianity, though it has its future in prophecy, has its past in history. Deep-rooted in historic fact lie the reasons for the promise of the Christian's future. The city of God that is to come down from heaven has had its foundation-stone laid already upon earth. We believe the things that men saw in the days of Christ—in the historic times of the Cæsars—and what they saw was this: the sick healed, the leper cleansed, the hungry fed, the dead raised up. The Gospel that tells of a world after death, is the same Gospel that tells of men who in this world have been raised up from the dead. The Gospel of the poor man is the Gospel of the resurrection, and they who preach it stand beside an open grave as angels stood to utter it on the dawning of the world's great Easter morning.

Once more. The Gospel of Christianity is more than a Gospel of the resurrection. In its promises of future happiness Christianity resembles somewhat and shares its promises somewhat, with other religions; but it has a distinct peculiarity of its own, and that is, that it promises not only glory after suffering, but as the result and the fruit of suffering in this life. "Made perfect through suffering." This is the law that governs the kingdom of Christ—a law to which even its King was made subject that He might bring many sons to glory, a law which requires that the sin which hinders our happiness should be burnt out by sorrow and that we should bear the cross of chastening in this life in order that we may wear the crown of happiness in the life to come. Thus it is that our Lord tells the rich man that if he would walk heavenward with Him he must be ready to part with his riches and become poor at His bidding; and thus he tells the poor man that weariness, toil, suffering, disappointment, if only carried as a cross, if only lifted as a burden the Saviour has appointed, will bear rich fruit in heaven. And so out of suffering comes joy; out of labour rest; out of sorrow eternal peace; and so the trials of the poor man in this world are made his spiritual wealth in the world to come. Is it no Gospel, then, for the poor to be told, as he labours toil-worn in the great mine of life, that the jewels he is gathering there are not and need not be for others only, but that they shall one day sparkle in the crown of glory that he shall win from the righteous Judge at His appearing? The Gospel for the poor that we have to preach is not only good news because it is the Gospel of the resurrection, but because it is the Gospel of Christ the sufferer as well as the healer and restorer. And thus that other fact which science reveals—the reality of which we fully recognise—the fact of vicarious suffering, acquires its deepest meaning in the kingdom of Christ. It *is* true that joy can only be purchased by sorrow; it *is* true that wealth can only be purchased by poverty and life by death. So true is this, that He who was rich, for our sakes became poor; that by His stripes we are healed and that the chastening of our sins is upon Him, because our life, our eternal life, needed to be purchased by His death. The Gospel of the resurrection is also the Gospel of the cross, and therefore it is the true and only Gospel for the poor.

But, in the last place, Christianity is the Gospel of poverty, even in this world. It has the promise of this life, as well as of that which is to come. Christianity is a Gospel of brotherhood—of real brotherhood, because it reveals a real fatherhood—the only real fatherhood of humanity, the fatherhood of God. All other talk of fraternity is a hollow mockery, an unreal imitation of the true fraternity in Christ. And what does that brotherhood mean as it regards the poor? It means that Christianity gives brother as against brother in the kingdom of Christ rights and privileges that cannot be found elsewhere. It gives the poor man the right to appeal against the tyranny of the many to the over-mastering judgment of the righteous One; it gives him a protest from his neglectful or cruel brother to his Father in heaven. It leaves him no longer the unnoticed, unnumbered unit in the vast heap that men call humanity. It clothes the meanest and poorest amongst those created by the Father and redeemed by the Son, with the majesty of immortality and girds him round with the sanctities of redemption. It gives the poor man the right to use two words of magic power on the hearts of those who believe in the names they utter. It gives him the right to protest against injustice in the name of God; it gives him the right to beseech for pity in the name of Christ. Yes, Christianity, with its Fatherhood in heaven, with its brotherhood on earth—Gospel of the resurrection, Gospel of the cross, Gospel of the true fraternity of man in Christ the Elder Brother—Christianity is the Gospel, and the only Gospel of the poor.

What word of exhortation and of counsel, then, may we carry home with us concerning this Gospel? Let me ask you, in the first place, Do you believe it for yourselves? I have said it is a Gospel for the poor, and for that very reason it is also a Gospel for the rich. For there is at least one hour in the life of every man in which he finds himself absolutely helpless and poor, and that is his last hour. Rich we may live, but we must die paupers. All our possessions we must leave behind. Naked came we into the world, and naked must we leave it. In that last supreme moment to what is the rich man to cling? To the wealth he has accumulated? To the strength he has possessed? To the earth he has subdued? His wealth is passing to others. His strength is gone. The earth that is about to cover him is all that is left him of his possessions. What can help him? In the poverty and helplessness of his dying moments there is for him only the Gospel for the poor—Believe on the Lord Jesus Christ and thou shalt be saved. Believe in Him, then, now, ye rich. Believe now the Gospel for the poor! You cannot tell how many hours it may be before its promises shall be all that will be yours. In the next place, preach that Gospel to your poorer brethren. If the rich and respectable members of our great London congregations only had the love of God deep in their hearts, they would resolve that not one of the great masses of the poor of this city should be left beyond reach of hearing the message of this Gospel. If they would only understand and remember that the Gospel of Christ is not meant to be a Gospel in a book only, but a Gospel preached with living, loving lips, from heart to heart, and if they would only send this Gospel to those who so sorely need it, how marvellous, even in this life, would be the change in the condition of the poor? Preach the Gospel then to these your brethren by the lips of Christ's messengers, who shall bear His message and with it the gifts of love which you send because you believe that message. Manifest this Gospel to them by your demeanour towards them. Is it true—and there are those who say it is true—that never, in the history of England, was the chasm between class and class, the separation between Dives and Lazarus, so wide and deep as it is now? Whether that be so or not, God knows that it is deep and wide enough. Oh, bridge it over; hasten to close up this yawning gulf in our English life by deeds and words of lovingkindness. Remember the brotherhood of the poor to you. Try to make the poor man feel that the Gospel of the poor is not only in the future, but in the present, because it is teaching his Christian brethren to own his brotherhood in Christ. For Christianity cannot live altogether on the past. Its proofs are partly in the past, but its life and main evidences are in the present. It is not enough that men should hear from us only what men saw and heard in the days of John the Baptist; let them also see your deeds of mercy, let them hear your words of love. Thus shall there still be preserved amongst us the living manifestation of the Gospel of Christ Jesus —the Gospel which still is in its promises and which should be in its gifts and in its blessings, Christ's gift, Christ's legacy to the poor.

THE GATHERING OF THE VULTURES.

THE GATHERING OF THE VULTURES.

St. Paul's Cathedral, February 17th, 1878.

"And they answered and said unto Him, 'Where, Lord?' and He said unto them, 'Wheresoever the body is, thither will the eagles be gathered together.'"—Luke xvii. 37.

ADD to this question of the disciples of Christ as to the place where the day of the Son of Man should be revealed, that other question which we know they asked Him as to the time of its revelation; add to the question "where" the question "when shall these things be?" and you have the twofold inquiry which always greets the foreteller of things to come. Naturally, inevitably, these two questions rise to the lips of all men who hear any prophecy which does not answer them by anticipation, for these are prompted by two of the strongest motives in human nature. One is curiosity, the other is self-interest. We know how strong in our nature is the desire for knowledge, and, above all, for knowledge of the future. We know how eagerly, how passionately at times, men long to lift, or, if they cannot lift, to peep through, the curtain that hides to-morrow. And if to this motive of curiosity concerning the future be added that of self-interest; if the undated prophecy contain a promise or a threat in which we are personally concerned, then the desire becomes an intense craving to know the *where* and the *when*; to know whether we stand within the predestined area of time or space wherein the threatened woe or the promised blessing is to come. Inevitably, then, as I have said, do those who hear such prophecies ask these questions, "Where?" and "When?" To the foreteller of the terrible or of the joyful, men say in their hearts, "Lift not at all, or lift altogether, the veil which hides from us the future of which you speak; tell us where, tell us when."

How strong this feeling is, the whole history of superstition and imposture testifies. From the astrologer of old who scanned the heavens to cast the horoscopes of men or of nations, down to the village gipsy who scans the hand of her dupe with a promise to tell his fortune; from the soothsayer of old who claimed to evoke and to question the dead, down to the vulgar spiritrapper and medium of our own day, men have traded on and reaped rich harvests from the passionate desire of humanity to know the future. The strength of this feeling is, however, nowhere more strongly manifested than in the treatment that the prophecies of Scripture have received at the hands of too many of their interpreters. The object of these seems mainly to have been to wring out of prophecy what, happily for us, it never will give—definite answers to these two questions. Whole libraries might be collected out of the learned and elaborate guesses of commentators, whose one idea of the prophets seems to have been that they were the authors of a series of inspired acrostics which were to be solved in course of time by the Church, and who have spent accordingly vast amounts of time and labour in constructing ingenious prophetical almanacks in which the date of the end of the world is fixed with the greatest accuracy in the first edition, to be altered perhaps in the second, postponed in the third and rearranged in the fourth, for the unabated edification of their admiring disciples, and, alas! for the amusement, too, of an incredulous world.

This school of prophetic interpretation, happily now a

diminishing one, is exactly represented in these questions addressed to our Lord by His disciples, and His reply teaches us how such inquiries should always be answered, or in other words, what is the true way of dealing with the prophecies of Scripture. We see that He refuses to answer, in the way at least that they desired, the "when" and the "where" of His disciples. Neither on this nor on any other like occasion will He give the time or the place of the fulfilment of His predictions. On the contrary, He distinctly tells them, what so many of our prophetic interpreters seem to have forgotten, that "it is not for them to know the times or the seasons which the Father hath put in His own power." On this point, in all His own predictions as recorded in the Gospels and in all the inspired writings of His apostles, there is observed a constant and carefully guarded reserve. Most remarkably so in the book which seems at first sight specially designed to inform the Church on these very points. The book of the Revelations, which commences with the call to the apostle to come up into the presence of his Lord in heaven that He "may shew him things to come," is the very one of all others which proves most obstinately perplexing and disappointing to those who seek to extract from it a knowledge of the dates and the places of the events which it foretells. Times and seasons and the signs of these it seems at first to set forth in abundance. But as we study them in order to find our own place in this great prophetic chart, they seem to shift, to melt into one another, to grow confused and indistinct, so that we can never say precisely at any given moment in what predicted era we are living, or how far off or how near any predicted event may be. And well it is for us that this is so. Had it been otherwise—had the predictions of Scripture been precisely dated and the times and places of their fulfilment clearly revealed from the first—they would have altogether failed to produce their true and proper effect upon the Church. For prophecy was given us not to make us knowing, but to make us wise, and wise unto salvation. Its object was to keep the Church in a state of watchful preparedness for her Lord's coming; not the preparedness of dreamy contemplation and expectation, but that of patient, active work; the readiness of the servant who, because his master may come at any time, busies himself in doing his master's work at all times. But, if our Lord had clearly dated the hour and the day of His coming and of the Day of Judgment, then, in the earlier days of the Church there could have been no earnest expectation, in the latter days of the Church there could be no earnest preparation. In the one case men would have thought with a languid interest, if they thought at all, of the far-off day, and in the latter case they would think of it with an all-absorbing interest that would make all other thought and action impossible. And, therefore, that the Church might neither regard His coming with the comparative indifference of a distant, nor with the paralysing awe a near event, our Lord, while He gives us abundant assurance that He will come, keeps back from us in loving wisdom the knowledge of the hour of His coming.

The merely curious student of prophecy, then, it would seem, must look in vain for any satisfaction of his curiosity by our Lord. And yet He does answer, in another and in a very important sense, the question "where and when." He will not tell us this to our hurt, but he does tell it us for our edification. Observe what is the answer that our Lord gives to the disciples' question. He answers them by quoting a proverb founded on a familiar fact. A saying well known in that day was this, "Wheresoever the carcase is, there shall the eagles"—or, as we should render it now, "the vultures"—"be gathered together." The proverb alludes to the fact, well known then as now, that no sooner does the body of some dead creature lie upon the sand of the desert than, far off in the clear sky, are to be seen tiny specks, which, rapidly drawing near, reveal the forms of the keen-sighted vultures swooping down upon their meal of carrion. And so soon and so certainly are these always seen, that the fact had become a proverb to express the certainty with which temptation brings crime and crime brings punishment. Men were in the habit of saying, when they saw some great crime inviting judgment, "See where the carcase lies; soon will the vultures be gathered together to devour it."

Our Lord's answer, then, in fact is this: My judgments shall come upon the earth as comes the vulture upon the dead. They shall come necessarily, inevitably, as it were by a sure and a terrible instinct. They shall come wheresoever and whensoever they are needed. Wheresoever in God's moral world there lies a dead thing that threatens corruption and pollution, there must swiftly come the destroying judgment that shall devour and carry it away. So surely, then, as there is ripeness for it and wherever there is that ripeness, there shall come a day of the Lord. Wherever moral corruption is, there shall gather together the messengers and ministers of destruction.

Now, if this be the meaning of our Lord's words, mark in the next place what they tell us concerning the nature of God's judgments.

I. They tell us, in the first place, that these are not arbitrary; that they are not attached to the offence which provokes them merely by the will of the law-giver; but that they are brought about in obedience to a natural and necessary law, by a law as certainly a part of the natural order of things as is the instinct of the vulture which brings him upon his prey. Not more surely, not more necessarily and naturally, does the dead body bring down the vulture, or the tall tree-top draw the lightning, or the action of gravitation draw the meteor-stone to the earth that it dints and pierces in its fall; not more necessarily, not more inevitably, do these things happen in the world of nature than do the judgments of God fall where they are needed and called for in the world of His divine order and government. And it is this fact which seems at once to reveal to us what is most terrible and what is most hopeful in the judgments of God—most terrible in this, that where there is ripeness for them there is no escape from them; that the wealth of the world cannot buy, nor the litanies of the world beg them off—most hopeful, on the other hand, in this, that they fall only where there is that ripeness. If there be no caprice of forgiveness, neither is there caprice of punishment, in God's kingdom. It needs, then, but that we be removed from out of the range of the judgment to escape it; it needs but that we be living and not dead, and then the destructions that sweep away dead things hurt us not; and the Judge who has thus defined for us the law which thus conditions all His judgments is also the Saviour who has come to deliver us from death and to translate us into His kingdom of life.

But when we know that God's judgments are thus necessary and not arbitrary, we know something more, namely, that as there will be one last and crowning day of judgment upon all that is ripe for it, so, before that, day must there be many lesser and as it were preliminary days of judgment. If this prophecy of Christ's teaches us that the progress of humanity is not to a peaceful millennium but to an awful day of the Lord — that the world is to go on, not from better to better but from worse to worse, until at last, strewed with the carcases of dead faiths, dead churches, dead civilisations, it invites the coming of the Judge, then it tells us more than this—it tells us that, ever and again, as any one section of humanity ripens here or there for destruction, there too upon that dead fragment must come the preliminary and prophetic judgment of God.

In the next place, our Lord shews us where we are to look for the signs of His coming. He bids us look, not into the far distant heaven of prophecy, where we can as yet ill read those signs; not there alone at least, but elsewhere, for surer and clearer signs of His coming. Not into the heavens afar off need we send our gaze. Let us look rather at the dead thing that lies, it may be, at our very feet and see there, in what we cannot mistake, the loud-speaking call for, the sure sign of, a coming day of judgment.

Thus does our Lord teach us to answer the *where* and the *when* concerning His coming and the judgments which are to accompany it. He teaches us in fact this—that all human history is but the record of ripening here and there and of judgment here and there; that it is not so much one long straight line unfolding itself, as a series of parallel circles, ever widening and widening still, each perfecting itself in sin and judgment, until at last the widest circle of human transgression shall have spread itself all out and the great ocean of humanity blacken all over beneath the cloud that broods over it heavy with the wrath of God.

II. This is our Lord's teaching concerning His days of judgment. Can we discern any facts in history which go to prove and to illustrate His teaching? Is it true that we can see, here and there, facts that call His eagles of judgment, and that they come at their calling? Can we see this to be the case as regards individuals? We answer "No," and for these reasons. In the first place; because the life of the individual is, for all other men, so largely a hidden life, its past history so little known, its motives, its temptations so entirely unknown to us, that we may never dare say of any man, not even of the vilest offender, that his moral condition is such as to provoke the judgment of God; still less may we dare to say of any evil that befals him that it is sent as a punishment for his sins. And in the second place; because the day of final judgment for individuals is fixed not in this life but in the next. It will not be until we shall stand, each one of us, in the presence of the Judge, when the secrets of all hearts shall be disclosed, that the true meaning and worth of every man's life shall be revealed. Meanwhile we may not presume to judge our fellow men. We are, indeed, most strictly forbidden to do so; we are warned against the rash and uncharitable judgment which pronounces those on whom some calamity has fallen to have been sinners "above all other men;" we are bidden, in the presence of such calamities, to think not of others' sins but of our own; we are told that we should see in them—even when they wear the aspect of punishment, even when we think that we can trace in them some connection with the past sins of the sufferer—only a warning for ourselves that, "unless we repent, we shall all likewise perish."

But it is otherwise with families, with churches, with nations. For these there is no judgment in the life to come. Can we see it then in this life? Can we see how death—moral death—may invade the Family, the Church, the Nation and bring after it the judgment of destruction? Let us consider. What is the life of the family? What is it that originates and sustains that life if it be not love? The love which makes each find in the other a dearer self, which delights in the surrender of the will, the passion, or the need of each to other, is the life of the family. So long as it lives the family lives — in spite of all calamities and sorrows, in spite of many a sore trial that is not a judgment of destruction but of correction; lives, aye, and its life grows all the stronger and the deeper for the sorrow or the calamity that may come upon it. Who has not known, and has not thanked God for the knowledge, how sorrow deepens love; how, in the darkening night of some sore affliction, loving hands reach out in the gloom and clasp each other with a fonder and a closer grasp; how lips that are white and quivering with agony breathe new vows of affection, deeper, truer, tenderer than they ever breathed when they were wreathed with smiles and tremulous with delight? Not so is the family destroyed; but let love die out of the house, and let there come instead of it the spirit of wilful and lawless selfishness, and the true life of the family is gone. And then what comes? The vultures of judgment; strife at the board, hate beside the hearth, or it may be shame—bitter, nameless shame—in the sanctuary of the home; the family is broken up, and children blush to bear their parents' name, because hard upon the death of love has come the judgment of dissolution and destruction.

Take, again, the history of the Church. The life of the Church is holiness; it is the Spirit of God in the hearts of His people. Rites, ceremonies, sacraments, institutions, are the outward and visible body of the Church, but the spirit of God in the hearts of men, the inner life of holiness, is her soul. While this lives the Church lives, in spite of adverse circumstances; in spite, it may be, of many an error, many an imperfection. She lives on—a maimed it may be, a defective, a feeble life—but still she lives. But let this die out in the Church, and all the orthodoxy of her creed and all the perfection of her organisation will not save her from being a dead thing and a dead thing near to judgment. Men may still go on repeating with parrot-like accuracy the dead phrases of what have become in their hearts dead creeds, formal and frozen shibboleths which, just because they are formal and frozen, they can still preserve in sharpest outline of orthodoxy; but the life is gone out of that Church and she lies as a mummy, though wrapped all round with the swathing bands of the very strictest and most orthodox dogma. The Jewish Church was living when the Jews hung their harps on the willows and could find no voice to sing the songs of Zion amidst the mockery of her enemies; the Jewish Church was dead when multitudes thronged her temple, whose gilded roof rose glittering in the sun, while the feet of those that should carry out the nation to judgment were even then at its doors. As it was then so has it ever been, so must it ever be; when once the life of holiness dies out of any Church, dead orthodoxy will not save her from destruction.

And in the last place, consider the life of the Nation. What is it? It is righteousness. As holiness is the life of the Church, righteousness is the life of the nation. By righteousness I mean fair purpose, honest dealing, true speech, right made might, not might made right, between man and man. Where this is the nation lives with a deep and real life in spite of external circumstances that may seem most hostile to her life; lives, though it be in poverty or in fear, but lives still. Where this is not, where this has ceased to be, the nation is dead; dead, though she seems to be fevered with active life; dead, though business is all alive and brisk, though art is thriving and commerce flourishing and the treasury overflowing and taxes low; dead, though her armies march unresisted to fresh conquests, and her navies sweep over seas where they fear no rival; dead to her very heart's core and waiting ripe for the coming judgments of Almighty God. And these judgments may come in this way or in that; they may come by foreign invasion, tempted by bloated wealth or wasteful and enfeebling luxury; they may come by internal strife; by the warfare of the suffering poor against the selfish rich; they may come by the upheaval of those fires that lie deep below the thin crust of a superficial civilisation, when crime and greed and ambition and maddening want and fierce despair join together in wild revolt against all government and all authority, seeking by some displacement of external institutions that peace and happiness that can only come from the pure hearts and righteous lives of her citizens. But come in some way or other they surely will, for God is not mocked, and that which nations sow in unrighteousness, that and nothing else they shall full surely reap in judgment.

Thus we see that God has his judgments, in time and not hereafter, for the Family, for the Church, for the Nation; and they come as surely, as necessarily, as naturally as any other event that comes by the laws of nature in that physical world of the unchangeableness of whose laws we hear so much, but the laws of which are not one whit more inevitable, not one whit more certain, than are the laws of God's providence and of His moral government of man.

III. But if this be indeed the law and these, so far as we can trace them, be indeed the facts concerning God's judgments in this world—what, in the last place, is our practical and necessary conclusion from these? What else can it be but the old lesson and the old warning, "Judge therefore yourselves, brethren, that ye be not judged of the Lord?" "Search and see if there be any wicked way amongst you, lest the judgment of the Lord come upon you as that wickedness neglected ripens for destruction. And if it be well for us to remember this at all times, surely we have special need to call it to mind in such times as these. At such a moment as this, when God's judgments are abroad in the world and the most careless of men are compelled to study them, we are in special danger of forgetting this most needful truth. What is it that we have been doing for weeks and months in the past? We have been looking on, as the judgments—the great and terrible judgments—of God have moved to and fro upon the stage of human history; we have been watching—who could help watching?—with straining eyes and listening ears, the horrors of the scene. We have gazed with a terrible fascination, and have not been able to turn away our eyes from the horrors of a war, not more horrible perhaps than other wars, but whose horrors have, by modern skill and modern speed of communication, been brought before us with a swift and hideous fidelity. We have watched the rush and the strife of the combatants; we have beheld as it were before our very eyes the corpses thick piled in ghastly heaps upon the battlefield, and heard the shrieks of the wounded, and the groans of the dying, and the wail of the desolate, and the pitiful cries of the starving little ones that die their innocent death of misery for the sins of others. We have watched and listened until sick with horror, we have gladly hailed the news which tells us that such scenes—for the present at least—are at an end. What has been our danger through it all —a danger, it may be, worse than any political or military peril? It has been this, that we have been tempted to look on merely as critical and Pharisaical spectators and judges, awarding the palm to one or another of the combatants according as our inclination or our conscience swayed us; to look down upon this hideous scene as the citizens of Rome might have looked from the seats of their amphitheatre upon the arena below, upon the struggle between wild beast and wilder man; to mark the deadly thrust and the skilful parry, the fierce assault and the obstinate and despairing defence, and to say "Ah, ah, so would we have it; there falls the judgment upon the oppressor; or, here comes the judgment upon the ambitious tyrant." And so we have been awarding and dispensing our judgments among these unhappy combatants and forgetting this—that we see in them not merely Russian or Turk, but sinning and suffering human nature and God its judge, and that the human nature that sins and suffers in these is the same within the heart of every one of us. We do well when the judgments of God are abroad in the world to learn righteousness: but let us learn it in the first place not for others but for ourselves. In the midst of what we must feel to be the enacting of one of God's great judgments amongst men, we do well to look at home and ask, Is there nothing here that might provoke for us the judgments of God? There are other national sins than ambition, there are other national crimes than oppression. Peace has her sins and her crimes, her sorrows and her shames, as well as war. In the fulness of our wealth, in the indulgence of our luxury, in the mad riot of our intemperance, in the fierce restlessness and bitterness of our political strife, is there nothing to make him who loves this England of ours dread for her some coming judgment? Is there nothing in the Family, is there nothing in the Church, is there nothing in the Nation, that may make the heart of the religious patriot tremble? Is our family life so increasingly pure that we may feel that our homes are the abodes of love and of holiness? Is our Church so entirely free from the bitterness of needless strife or from the assaults of a dangerous and sapping scepticism; is she so full of spiritual life that she need dread no judgments from her Master? Is the Nation so full of righteousness; are we so honest in our dealings, so true, so just, so kindly, so forbearing, so thoughtful, class with class, man with man, that we can claim to be regarded as a righteous people? And if not, if the peaceful wealth and prosperity of England be breeding sins and shames, that provoke God's wrath; if there be sores, cancerous eating sores in her that "have not been healed, nor bound up, nor mollified with ointment," let us look to it lest this end for us in national death and after death there should come national judgment.

Yes, there is a worse invasion than that of a foreign army; it is the invasion of domestic luxury and vice. The march of the foreign foe seems to make deep tracks and furrows in a nation's life, and yet, after all, they are but upon the surface. The invader sweeps along destroying and desolating as he advances; but the time comes when the houses he has desolated are rebuilt and the plains he has ravaged, fertilised with his dead, grow green again, and men can scarce believe that the quiet fields they walk in, where their little ones gather flowers, have been in times past blackened with the smoke of combat and torn with the furious struggles of multitudes of armed men. Not so with the invasion of vice. That makes itself a lasting home, and its desolations are not so soon nor so easily repaired. The locusts of war consume the green leaves of a nation's prosperity; but vice is the worm at the root that gnaws out its very life, until it shrivels and withers into barrenness and dust.

Brethren, if this be so with us, or if there be any danger that this should be so, is it not our greatest, our most pressing duty to go forth to war against these evils? Should we not gird ourselves in all haste in the name of our great Lord and Master to wage His great battle against vice and crime, and against the selfishness and the irreligion in which vice and crime have their deep root and source? Let us do this in our own hearts, in our families, in our Church, in our nation; lest, if we do it not, there come upon us first the death, and after it the judgment, that in this life follows upon the moral death of nations; lest, if we do it not, there come a time when men shall write the epitaph of England's empire, and when they who write it in the spirit of merely secular history may assign this or that cause for her political decline, her national decay and death; but when he who would write it in the light of God's Word and Christ's prophecy shall have to say, "Lo here, once more, where the carcase was, were the eagles gathered together."

KNOWLEDGE WITHOUT LOVE.

KNOWLEDGE WITHOUT LOVE.

The "Pride" Sermon preached before the University of Oxford, on Sunday, November 23rd, 1879.

"Knowledge puffeth up, but charity edifieth."—1 Cor. viii. 1.

TAKEN as a general proposition, apart from their context, these words read as a deprecation of knowledge, and as a deprecation of it from the religious point of view. The charity that is here spoken of is clearly not the merely human emotion but the Divine grace of love, that grace by which man attains to loving first his heavenly Father, and then his brother men. And this love is contrasted with knowledge. This love which edifies—that is to say which builds up the whole man and the society, of which each man is a part, to perfection—is contrasted with the knowledge that puffs up and which, therefore, does not edify the individual nor Society. And not only is there here an apparent contrast between knowledge and love, but an apparent opposition; as if knowledge hindered that which love would effect; as if the state of mind which knowledge genders must prevent the edification that love should bring. Now, if this be what St. Paul's words mean, the necessary inference from them would be that knowledge is, in some respects, undesirable for Christian men. For those who hold this Divine grace of love to be of all things the most precious—to be that in them to which everything else should be subordinated and, if needs be, even sacrificed—it would seem to be undesirable to know too much lest they should love too little. And from this it would follow that the religious man should, in the interests of religion, deprecate and dread the advance of knowledge. Is this so? If it is—if there be in very deed such opposition between faith and science as that, in order to be religious, we must be ignorant—then we know what must be the fate of our faith. Sooner or later that which is bound up with ignorance and error must die the death of all things false and erroneous; and therefore if once we come to believe that ignorance is essential to religion, the end of our religion, nearer or remoter as it may be, is as certain as the rising of to-morrow's sun. But that this cannot be so we Christians firmly hold; and that it is not so is apparent from the context in which these words stand; for when we look at that context we find that the knowledge which the Apostle appears here to deprecate is not, primarily at least, secular, but religious. The knowledge of which he is speaking is that which the Corinthian converts from heathenism had learned from his own teaching, namely, that "an idol is nothing in the world," and that "there is none other God but one." But these are truths not of science but of theology. It is theological knowledge, therefore, that the Apostle speaks of as "puffing up," and that he seems to deprecate in comparison with love. If our text then be not a disparagement of secular knowledge as compared with love, is it a disparagement of dogma as compared with religious feeling? Have we here an anticipation, by one of the earliest and greatest teachers of Christianity, of the great modern discovery that religion has nothing to do with theology? Is St. Paul, the great teacher of dogma, here telling his disciples—

whom by the power of the doctrines that he spent his life in preaching he had delivered from the sins and miseries of paganism—is he really telling them this? "All that I have declared unto you concerning the God whom you once 'ignorantly worshipped' and the Christ in whom I have taught you to believe is a matter of indifference, if it be not even injurious to your religious life; my counsel to you is accordingly to forget all such theological teachings. Trouble yourselves no longer with the useless attempt to define or understand dogma. Let it suffice you instead to lose yourselves in a warm haze of agnostic and unreasonable emotion." Surely we can imagine the feeling of almost amused contempt with which the strong common sense, the keenly logical mind of the Apostle would have treated such an interpretation of his words—an interpretation which, with all its great swelling words and its air of profundity, just amounts to this: that we can have effects without causes, emotions without anything to excite them, love without any knowledge of the nature or attributes of the object of our affections. This idea of religion without a basis in the facts or alleged facts of theology would have seemed to the mind of St. Paul as truly inconceivable, as indeed it is, as the idea of Zoology without animals, or of Astronomy without stars.

I. But if the Apostle does not mean in this passage to deprecate absolutely either scientific or religious knowledge as necessarily hurtful to the spiritual life, is there no caution as regards knowledge implied in our text? Assuredly there is. The gift of knowledge, like every other gift that God bestows upon us, is capable of abuse, and the context in which these words stand shows clearly what is the abuse of it respecting which the Apostle seeks to warn us and what is the remedy that he would provide against it. St. Paul is giving his decision here upon a question which had much divided the Church of Corinth. It was one of those difficult problems — partly ecclesiastical, partly social, partly religious—which are sure to arise in that wide region in which religion begins to mix itself up with the affairs of common life. The question was as to the use of meats which, after having been offered to idols, were exposed for sale in the public markets, and we find that the Church of Corinth was divided respecting this matter into two parties—those who scrupled, and those who did not scruple to eat of these idol-offered meats. On the one hand there were those who "eat with conscience of the idol," that is to say, with a scrupulous and troubled conscience, with some lingering remains, possibly, of their old superstitions, fearing, perhaps, the vengeance of those beings whose worship they had forsaken, but in whose existence they had, perhaps, not learned entirely to disbelieve; or who refused to eat from dread of even so far associating themselves with the pollutions of idolatry as to partake of things that had been offered to idols. These must have been the scrupulous, the timid, the morbidly conscientious, in short the weaker portion of the Corinthian Church. And then there was the other party, which must have included all the stronger, wiser, more intelligent, more advanced Christians in that Church, who doubtless were in the habit of saying that "they knew better than to be led away by such weak superstition as this." These strong-minded men, who knew so well "that an idol was nothing and that there was only one God," may have felt it not only their privilege and their right but in some measure even their duty, to eat of things offered to idols, that they might thereby read a lesson from their higher intelligence and more advanced thought to their weaker and more ignorant brethren; they may have even exulted in the thought that they were thereby helping to stamp out a noxious superstition. Some, they would say, through fear and ignorance will "eat only herbs," but we "that are strong" will teach them better "by eating all things." And we can imagine with what confidence these men, the intelligent and rational party amongst the Corinthians, must have appealed to the verdict of the Apostle; how eagerly they must have anticipated the confirmation of their views and their practice by the Great Teacher who had so clearly taught them already that an idol was nothing, and who had so nobly vindicated the privileges of Christian liberty against the restraints and the prejudices of Judaism. With what a feeling of disappointment must they have received the answer of the Apostle? He does not uphold them; he condemns them. He does not sustain their practice; he rebukes them for it, and that, too—strange to say—although he accepts every one of those grounds upon which they rested their vindication of it. He does not dispute; he reasserts that which they had alleged that "an idol is nothing," and that "there is only one God," and he repeats these statements with just that touch of irony that we might expect from a Jew to whom this new truth, of which these Pagan converts to Christianity were making so much, was very old and very familiar, was one of the very first elements of his religion. "We all have," he says, "at least, this much 'knowledge': there is nothing so very new, nor so very striking to me in your discovery of the nothingness of idols; but even when you have known and stated this, you have not quite solved, you have not even correctly stated, the problem you have submitted to me." For this, after all, is not a problem to be solved by the help of knowledge only.

You cannot state it scientifically thus—"Given the fact that an idol is nothing; given the fact that there is only one God; and given also the fact that these meats offered to these mere nothings are publicly exposed in the market place, why may we not eat of them? You cannot quite solve this problem in this way, because there are certain data in it of which you have not yet taken cognisance. There is, for instance, that old, great fact of human nature to be taken into account. These hearts that are stirred with scruples and with difficulties are the hearts of your brother men, and the strange, deep mystery of the human heart has never yet yielded itself patiently and entirely to logic. And there is another fact which you have omitted to take into account, and that is the existence of a Christian brotherhood, with all the widespread duties of sympathy and tenderness and forbearance and self-sacrifice that arise out of it. These men whom you despise, whom you would force to adopt at once your wiser and more knowing practice, they are all your brethren in Christ, and as such have a claim for gentle and tenderly considerate treatment at your hands. And then there is that other fact which you have so lately learned, and of which you as yet know so little in all its bearings and relations, the fact of the incarnation of Jesus Christ, and the lesson that we learn from it of strength condescending to weakness, of power moved by love, of sacrifice of self for others' sake. All these things you have got to take into your account before you can decide this question, and these are things not to be disposed of by knowledge and by logic alone. Into the solution of this practical problem that you have put before me there comes another factor than knowledge; there comes love, which instructs knowledge, by giving it a deeper, clearer insight into human nature and human life, love that teaches you to understand your brother, because it teaches you to place yourself beside him, to step down to his level in order that you may raise him to your own. Without this love which edifies, knowledge only puffs up, and unfits you to judge in this or any other matter between you and your brother."

And now we can see wherein consisted the error of this school of advanced and liberal thought in the Corinthian Church. It lay—not in giving its full value to knowledge nor in bringing it to bear upon practical life and daily conduct—but in bringing it *alone* to bear on these things; it lay in supposing that knowledge was the only and sufficing guide to the conduct of human life. And in so doing the Apostle tells them that they gave proof that they really "knew nothing as they ought to know;" he tells them, that is to say, that their knowledge was practically useless because they were applying it to that respecting which it was an imperfect guide. He tells them that if this knowledge on which they prided themselves was to lead them aright it must be first instructed and enlightened by the Divine grace of love.

II. But let us, in the next place, consider why it is that knowledge alone is thus imperfect in teaching us how to govern ourselves, whether as regards our own life or that of others. The Apostle tells us it is because it "puffeth up," that is to say because it tends, if unsanctified and untempered by love, to generate and foster in us the vice of pride; and if so it generates and fosters in us just those two faults, which most unfit men to judge of the affairs of life. One of these is selfishness and the other is ignorance. Pride is always selfish, and almost always ignorant and unjust. For what is pride? It is the gratification that we feel at the knowledge that we have inferiors. This is the nature of all pride, whether it be of wealth, of health, of strength, of rank, or of knowledge. It is always a selfish delight in the inferiority of others. And inasmuch as every attempt on the part of the inferior to raise himself to a higher level—to lessen the distance between himself and his superior—threatens the loss of this pleasure for the latter, there is always mingled with pride an element of cruelty. We see this most clearly in the pride of race; we see it in the sad history of the wrong and misery that inferior races have suffered at the hands of their superiors, who regarded them as outside the pale of justice or of love. But it is to be seen in all kinds of pride. There is an impatience, an intolerance of the inferior, that manifests itself, now in the calculated cruelty that stamps out resistance and now in the cold, haughty contempt that draws between itself and the object it despises some pale of social exclusion outside which the inferior is told to dwell, and yet through which pass arrows of scorn, that wound and rankle where they strike. Those who are filled with this spirit of scornful and cruel pride—and, as I have said, there is a scornful cruelty in all pride—are manifestly incapable of judging of the relations between themselves and the beings they despise: are utterly incapable, therefore, of deciding wisely for the happiness of others, and, consequently, for their own; for, be it remembered, we cannot injure our brother man—not the very meanest member of this great complex human society of ours, in which we are linked and bound to one another by thousands of known and thousands of unknown cords of sympathy and relationship—without injuring ourselves. The eye may say to the hand, "I have no need of thee," and the head may say to the feet, "I have no need of you," but the neglected and injured member will nevertheless surely, sooner or later, revenge itself; its weakness will enfeeble, its disease will poison the whole body, to the ultimate injury or destruction of the nobler member that despised or wounded it; and thus it comes to pass that pride, by virtue of its cruelty and injustice, unfits us to govern even our own lives wisely and happily for ourselves.

But not only is pride thus selfishly and mischievously unjust, it is short-sightedly ignorant. That which we despise and dislike we cannot understand. Whenever we look down in the pride of rank or knowledge upon any class or any person, be sure of this, that we are profoundly ignorant of that class or that person. Let me give you one illustration of this in passing. Let us take, as an instance of the hard and shallow ignorance that pride brings with it, that which is so commonly regarded as an instance of wonderful knowledge. I mean the knowledge of human nature which we are wont to ascribe to our satirists. If you have studied, as doubtless many of you have, the writings of this or that cruel and bitter dissector of human nature, some satirist of old or of modern days, as you have enjoyed, perhaps, and admired his ruthless and scornful exhibition of all the littleness and infirmity and disease of our nature: as you read, for instance, the savage sarcasm of Swift, or the keen, shrewd knowingness of Rochefoucauld, or the sharp, cruel wit of Voltaire, you are tempted, as you turn over such pages to say, "What knowledge of the world! what marvellous insight! how this man knows human nature." Knows human nature! We might as well say that he knows English history who has studied the records only of our criminal trials, or that he best knows the functions of the human body who has only studied morbid anatomy.

The knowledge which such writers display is after all but a miserable ignorance of all the nobler, better elements of that nature which, because they so despise, they cannot understand. Of that true " human heart by which we live," of its tenderness, its joys, its hopes, its fears; of all those " thoughts that do often lie too deep for tears," and which the loving and reverent contemplation of human life alone can bring us, such men know and can know nothing. Believe me that there is not one of you young men who since he has entered this University has been striving to live a pure, honest, kindly Christian life, striving so to live that when he returns home he may look his mother and his sisters in the face without a feeling of shame, who has not been gaining a deeper and a truer knowledge of human nature than he could find in all the writings of all our satirists put together.

II. And we can now see, further, how it is that love "edifies," as distinguished from the merely scornful "knowledge which puffeth up." Love edifies, that is to say, it builds up perfectly the whole man; because it secures the full harmonious and proportionate development of his whole nature. It does so by casting out that spirit of selfishness in man, which always tends to a diseased and one-sided growth of his nature. Long-continued self-indulgence always ends in this, that the most powerful passion, the fiercest appetite, of a man—by a process of natural evolution and the survival of the strongest within him—comes to dominate his whole being, until he becomes the incarnation of his special vice—a monstrous, unnatural, diseased growth of manhood. We see this in the world's great criminals; we see it in some of the world's greatest heroes and tyrants; we see it perhaps most distinctly in the ideals of the old world worship. The gods whom the heathen worshipped were, each one of them, nothing else than some one single attribute of human nature, not in itself necessarily evil, magnified, deified, untempered, unchecked by any other attribute. Thus amongst the gods of the heathen we see force without justice, which is tyranny; courage without pity, which is ferocity; passion without tenderness, which is lust; knowledge without truthfulness, which is cunning; and so as each one of these gods passes before us we behold the deified and yet the diseased outgrowth of some part of human nature, and as we consider them thus, we learn the deep meaning of the Apostle's saying that the things which the Gentiles sacrificed were "sacrificed unto devils, and not unto God;" for let any one single attribute or quality of any man's nature become his absolute master and the man is as nearly a devil as it is possible for a man in this world and in the flesh to be. And if this be so, if this be the evil and one-sided tendency of indulged self, then we can see how love which casts out self, which is set over against self-indulgence, must ever check this diseased growth and must tend to harmonise and cause to grow together in unity the whole man. We can see, too, how it is that this love must especially check and counteract the vice of pride; for if that vice be the preference of self, in one of its most diseased and exaggerated forms, what can so powerfully check it as love, which is the preference of others to self? Have you never noted, and smiled perhaps as you noted it, the wonderful humility of love; how the loving heart delights to prostrate itself before the object of its worship; how it invests its often unlovely and common-place idol with a thousand imaginary graces and perfections; how happy it is to be allowed to offer homage and sacrifice to a being in every way so much better and nobler than itself! And if the merely human passion of love can thus beautify and idealise its objects, how much more powerful, in this respect, must be the effect of the love which, bringing us first into the presence of this all-perfect Father, teaches us to lay ourselves in the dust at His feet, to love for His sake all souls whom He has created and whom His Son has redeemed; which teaches us, in lowliness of heart—remembering that we have nothing that we have not received from Him and are nothing but what He has made us—to honour in each fellow man the humanity in which Christ became incarnate and for which Christ has died; which bids us recognise in every human brother his lineage and descent from the common Father, his equal share with ourselves in the inheritance of glory which that Father has promised to all His children alike.

And now we can fully see how it is that the Apostle contrasts the pride of knowledge with the edification of love, and why it is that he warns us against the selfishness of unsanctified knowledge—whether it be that of the hard, Pharisaic theologian who, standing far apart in the pride of his orthodoxy from the erring heretic, loses, in his impatient ignorance, a whole flood of light which would otherwise have fallen upon the angles of his own belief, and would have shewn him its deeper and truer meanings as he came to understand why others do not receive it—or whether, on the other hand, it be the shallow conceit of the man who, believing that in science he has a calculus that can explain all things, seeks by its help to solve problems that were never meant for its solution and sneers with supremest scorn at beliefs or practices which have no "scientific basis." Surely we have enough, and more than enough, in our own age of this "knowledge that puffeth up." Shall we ever hear the last of the vauntings that are dinned again and again into our ears concerning the "march of science," the "progress of science," the "triumphs of science," from those who are ever foretelling the time when men shall not only be scientifically learned and wealthy and comfortable; but when they shall be scientifically wise, and moral and happy; who are ever prophesying to us, that when once we all come to know thoroughly the chemical composition of our bodies, we shall all be able to control our bodily appetites, when every one is able to spell correctly the words vice and virtue, we shall all cease to be vicious and become truly virtuous, and that when once we all know the history of morals, we shall all become severely and accurately moral. Meanwhile, we may be allowed some little scepticism of our own upon these points. We may be allowed to doubt whether science after all can solve and settle everything. We may be allowed to question whether we are so much wiser, or so very much happier than our fathers because we are so much more knowing; whether, for instance, the telegraphic wire flashes more infallible wisdom than that which men of old spoke and wrote; whether the sins and the shames and the sorrows of our great cities are beginning to melt away in the beams of the electric light. We may even believe that there are thousands of problems which knowledge cannot solve, old problems over which the heart of humanity has pored and vexed itself in the unscientific ages of the past and with which it will continue to vex itself in the scientific ages yet to come; we may still hold that life and death, and time and eternity, and God and the conscience and the soul are mysteries that are not to be solved by science, nor to be attacked by logic; we may believe that he who holds that science and logic can solve these, will find at last that there are whole regions of existence to which science has not the key; but that love—trusting that it may understand, believing that it may know—love that sees the invisible, that knows the infinite and incomprehensible, brings for these the only true key and gives the only possible entrance. Therefore, because knowledge, unsanctified and untempered with love and the humility which love brings, "puffs up," we desire, not that knowledge be diminished, but that love may be increased. We would not check in the very slightest degree if we could, and we could not if we would, the rising tide of knowledge. We would not—least of all in this place, where men gather together to impart or to acquire learning—indulge in a narrow and ignorant tirade against the progress of science, but we do maintain that knowledge cannot explain all things, that there are many things it cannot understand. And thus—when the man of science warns off, as he has a right to do, the man of faith from intruding his dogmas into the domain of knowledge and bids him keep within that of faith—we, on the other hand, claim the right to warn off, if not with like scorn yet with equal authority, the man of science from his intrusion into the domain of the spiritual. We have the right to say, and we do say, "this territory is not yours; keep within your own limits and you do well, but into the deeper mysteries of human nature, into those profounder truths that are revealed to that in us which is spiritual, to that which trusts and loves, you cannot so much as find your entrance by the power of that magic pass-word of yours, the perpetual 'why' of the sceptical intellect; that will not give you entrance here, because here admission is not, in the first place, for the understanding, but for the heart and soul of man." Between these two, between the knowledge of the understanding and the loving insight of the soul, we thank the God who made us that there is no essential opposition. If there be antagonism, it comes from the ignorance of their respective votaries, it is not in the nature of the things themselves. What we pray therefore and desire above all things for the youth who are studying in this ancient seat of learning is not a return to the old superstitions which once subjected learning to the restraints of religion, but the mingling with all knowledge of that love which religion brings to the aid of learning. There is no true and perfect knowledge, there is not and there cannot be, the edifying and building up of the whole man without this aid. Know all things then that you can know; advance as far as it is possible for each one of you to advance, in the knowledge that enlightens; but, with it all, see that you join love; learn to trust, learn to believe, and then, however far you may advance in human knowledge, you will with it, in proportion, advance in that truer, deeper lore which consists in the knowledge of your own hearts and souls, in the knowledge and the love of God.

THE ETHICS OF FORGIVENESS

THE ETHICS OF FORGIVENESS.

PREACHED BEFORE THE UNIVERSITY OF OXFORD, 1880.

"Forgive us our debts as we forgive our debtors."—MATTHEW vi. 12.

HE who taught us these words of prayer is more than a Teacher. He is more to us even than a Divinely inspired Teacher. We regard Him—in common with the whole Catholic Church throughout the world—as our Divine Redeemer and Mediator. We believe that He has come amongst us not only to tell us that we may approach the Father, but to make that approach possible. We believe that He has come not only to reveal to us the way to God, but to be Himself that way. "I am the way, the truth, and the life. No man cometh unto the Father but by Me;" and, "Whatsoever you shall ask the Father in My name, He will give it you," is the teaching of our Lord, and has ever been the teaching of His Church. She has ever placed Him where He has claimed to place Himself —between the human soul and God. The doctrines of atonement and of intercession are inseparably connected in all her teaching with the great central doctrine of her creeds, the incarnation of our Lord Jesus Christ. Christianity does not call upon us to believe in the stupendous mystery of God becoming man without an adequate reason for it. The publication of a new religion would be no such adequate reason—that might need an inspired teacher, not an incarnate one; it might need a Moses, but it could not need a Christ. The Church, therefore, when she proclaims her belief in the incarnate Christ, expresses her belief in the doctrine that "God is in Christ reconciling the world unto Himself, and not imputing their trespasses unto men. She declares that it was "for us men, and for our salvation," that "the very God of very God" came down from heaven, "and was incarnate, by the Holy Ghost, of the Virgin Mary." Incarnation and Atonement. Inseparably these two ideas are linked together. Take away one, and the other will not long remain. Take away the belief in the divine and eternal Christ, and we lose the true ground of the Atonement. Take away the idea of the Atonement and we lose the only sufficient reason for the Incarnation. The time would then come, and come very soon too—as many of our modern seers are anticipating—when men would no more care to discuss the nature of Christ, than they care now to discuss the nature of Socrates; and in truth it would concern them very little more to do so.

Closely related, however, as these two great Christian dogmas are, they are rejected by modern thought on very different grounds. One of them, the Incarnation, is rejected as impossible; the other, the Atonement, as immoral. Incarnation is a miracle, and modern science, we are told, pronounces miracles to be impossibilities. Of course for those who so think there is an end of the question. It would be absurd to expect them to discuss the moral bearings of an event which they believe, not only never happened—but never could possibly have happened. Not so, however, as regards the doctrine of the Atonement; that is impugned not on scientific but on moral grounds. It rests, we are told, upon a low and unworthy conception of the moral nature of God. To say of Him, that He requires, as the condition of His forgiving our offences against Him, the sufferings and the mediation of Christ, is to represent Him, it is urged, as less merciful and forgiving than we expect an ordinarily good man to be. A good man is, before all things, merciful and compassionate; he forgives fully and freely those who offend against him, and the more fully and freely he does so, the better and the nobler man we hold him to be. How then can we suppose the perfectly good God to be less placable than we feel that we ourselves ought to be? Why should we go out of our way to mar the grand and noble conception of a Loving Father of all men freely forgiving the sins of his penitent children, by adding to it the barbarous and superfluous idea of an apparatus of sacrifice and intercession, which are somehow to induce Him to be merciful? What is this doctrine of atonement and mediation but a survival of the old pagan conception of angry deities, whose grudges against offending mortals could only be satisfied by suffering, or bribed away by gifts? Why, we are asked, if you cannot advance with modern thought, will you not at least go back to the older and better teachings contained in your own Bibles? Why cannot you rise to the sublime ideas of the Hebrew prophets and Psalmists, who, in their protest against the sanguinary ritual of their day, could take their place beside altars, smoking with the blood of innocent victims, and proclaim a God who "desired not sacrifice," else would they give it Him —a God, who could not "eat the flesh of bulls, or drink the blood of goats"—a "merciful and compassionate" Lord, who only bids the wicked "forsake his way and the unrighteous man his thoughts" in order that he may "abundantly pardon him." If Christianity had only caught the true spirit of such teaching as this, it could never, we are told, have retained in its creed the

Pagan old-world notions of sacrifice and atonement that now disfigure it.

Now such an objection as this, resting as it does on moral grounds, is a far more formidable one than any of those that rest on merely scientific grounds.

These, even if now unanswered, need not be regarded as unanswerable. Science has not yet spoken her last word. It is quite conceivable, at least, that some new scientific discovery might place science on the side of miracles. Not so, with the decisions of the conscience; these are final and unanswerable, and the grounds for them lie fully within the ken of all men. Once prove that the God of the Christian is not a perfectly moral being and he ceases for ever to be our God, our supreme good. Most carefully therefore does it behove us to weigh any objection against our creed which appeals, as this does, to the moral sense of mankind.

And in dealing with this objection let us above all things do so honestly. Let us attempt no theological evasion of the difficulty; let us not lie for God; let us not say, for instance, that we cannot argue from the analogy of human forgiveness to the Divine forgiveness, because God's ways are not as our ways, nor His thoughts as our thoughts. That may be true in some respects, but it is not true as regards this. It never can be true when God uses the same word to describe His ways and our ways; for if, in that case, our ways are not like His, then the words which He uses are not so much misleading as utterly unmeaning. They are merely arbitrary and unintelligible symbols. If the words forgiveness, mercy, compassion do not mean, when they are used respecting God, at least as much as they mean when we use them respecting men, they have for us no meaning whatever. Let us be sure then that—when we are told that God loves, that God forgives—we are to understand by those words just what we understand by the words man loves and man forgives. Other and deeper meanings they may have, but at least they have this. Let us then, as I have said, deal honestly with this difficulty; let us see whether, taking it for granted, as we are bound to do, that there is a real analogy between Divine and human forgiveness, we may not find in that very fact good reasons for our belief in the doctrines of Atonement and Mediation. Let us see, in one word, what is the true idea of human forgiveness, by what difficulties, if any, it is beset and what are the laws which really govern it amongst us men as we try to forgive our debtors, and then let us proceed to see how these laws apply to God's forgiveness of our debts to Him.

I. In the first place, then, let us see what is our Lord's teaching concerning the forgiveness of sin, in the words " Forgive us our debts." What does our Lord here teach us respecting sin? He teaches us that it is something that needs forgiveness. That is to say, that it is not merely a disease to be healed, nor an imperfection to be remedied, but an offence, and an offence entailing a penalty, which cleaves to the offender as a debt, until it is paid or remitted, cleaves to the debtor. And He further teaches us that for this debt there is a possibility of remission—the forgiveness of sin being analogous to the remitting of a debt. That is to say, our Lord gives us this as the popular, ordinary, human idea of forgiveness; namely that it is the letting off to a man of the debt he owes; it is the putting of him by the creditor, as far as he can do so, in the position he would have occupied, if he had never contracted that debt. Briefly then our Lord's statement is this: first, in all sin there is guilt; secondly, a debt of penalty for that guilt; thirdly, the possibility of the remission of that debt; and fourthly, a close analogy between the remission of that debt by God to us and our remission of debt to one another. The question then at once arises for us, How far and under what conditions is it possible for us to forgive our human debtors, those who have offended against us? Let us study this question first in its simplest form. Let us suppose an offence committed between two equals, who have no other relation between them than that of their common humanity. Let us suppose that any one of us has been so unfortunate as to have committed some wrong against a fellow man. The instant you do so that man becomes, in spite of you and of himself, your creditor. You are his debtor for two great debts—the debt of penitence, and the debt of reparation. You feel that you ought to be sorry for what you have done and that you ought to make amends for it; and you owe this twofold debt by virtue of a law which either he or you may set in motion, but which neither he nor you can restrain—the law of your own conscience. There is that within you which, when you have injured another, claims from you at once the double penalty of repentance and restitution. There is within your own breast an advocate of the man you have wronged. There is a voice within you crying against you to the throne of God, the judge of all, and if you cannot agree with this your adversary, it gives you over to the tormentors remorse and shame, that abide in your own heart and will not depart from it, until you have paid the uttermost farthing of such debt. Such is the nature of the case as it arises instantly and necessarily between your human creditor and you, his debtor. Now it is quite true that your creditor may remit this debt to you and you hold it to be the noblest charity if he does. He forgives you then, we will suppose, fully, freely, unconditionally, lovingly, nobly if you will—what then? Is all the penalty remitted? Have you escaped all the punishment of your act? He has forgiven you; but have you for that reason forgiven yourself? Nay, is it not the very fulness and freeness of his forgiveness that is heaping coals of fire upon your head, kindled and fanned into a flame by the very breath of his compassion? We know that it is so, and that in all finer and better natures it is ever most keenly so. Already, then, we have discovered this—that there is, even between equals, no complete remission of penalty for sins possible. Behind the figure of the creditor—even of the forgiving creditor—there already begins to rise up and to project itself upon our path the shadow of law—which, because it is law, is pitiless, unforgiving and inevitable. Even in this simplest and most rudimentary case of forgiveness, there is therefore no absolute remission.

Now let us take one step further—let us pass on to the case of social forgiveness. Let us suppose the wrongdoing has had spectators. Let us imagine ourselves spectators of some cruel martyrdom and that we hear the martyr, with his dying breath, breathing out his forgiveness and blessing on his murderers. They are fully forgiven by him. Would any one of us feel disposed to take up that legacy of forgiveness and to repeat the blessings we had just heard the martyr pronounce upon his tormentors? Should we not rather feel our hearts stirred with the deepest and most righteous indignation, calling, in a very passion of justice, for vengeance upon his murderers? Should we not feel that the forgiveness he pronounced, though in him it were the highest expression of charity, were in us the lowest and most exquisite baseness? Should we not feel that we could never know rest nor peace until we had avenged him of his cruel wrong and that this would not, after all, be revenge, but righteous judgment? But why is it that we could not forgive such a wrong upon another? Just for this reason: It is his wrong and not ours. We are not and cannot be, merely spectators of this crime; we are, by the very fact of our being members of a society to which he and we belong, its judges, and we feel that, as such, we have no right to remit its just and righteous penalty.

But there is another reason why we cannot forgive this offence. The instinct of self-preservation is strong in our hearts, as it is strong in the heart of society. Society cannot afford to suffer martyrdom; still less to court or submit to martyrdom. The myriad interests that are entrusted to its guardianship would be sacrificed if it were to allow of crime with impunity. A society founded upon the basis of pure benevolence and universal forgiveness of offences, could not hold together for a single day. Society dare not, cannot forgive its debtors. You see, we have now advanced a step further; we have still the debtor to be paid, and we have still the law and the person or persons who are to enforce it; but you observe to what small dimensions the personal element in this equation has already shrunk. You see how large already looms the idea of law; you see that the debtor and creditor are already becoming, both together, debtors to a great, inexorable law which binds the creditor to punish and the debtor to suffer. In this aspect then we begin to see that human forgiveness is not such an easy thing. The criminal may have little to fear from the anger of his judge who is enforcing the law, but for that very reason he has nothing to hope from his compassion; for law because it is passionless must also be pitiless.

And now let us take one step, and only one step further. Let us suppose the offender to have paid the penalty for his offence; such penalty at least as he can pay and yet live. He has given, we will suppose, in the way of reparation, all that society claimed from him; but is he thereupon freed from all further penalty? Does Society that forgives him give him back what it was compelled to take from him? Can it give him back the happy promise of his now wasted life? Can it bring him back the opportunities, the vanished hopes and joys, of the past? Can it restore to him the honour, love, obedience, that once were his? Can it compel men who shrink from his contact as they would from that of a leper,—to give him the honoured place, as a guest at life's banquet, which he might once have been entitled to? Can it cut off the consequences of his sin, as it continues to injure others by its example or its consequences, and so goes on multiplying and replenishing the earth with its evil progeny, while the birth of every fresh sin that springs from its parentage multiplies guilt against him? Can it do this? Never. And thus we see how, by the very condition of things in which we exist, we reach at last a point at which the personal elements of pity, compassion, justice even, seem to vanish altogether, and man is face to face with a stern, impersonal, mechanical, universal law, certain as death, merciless as the grave, which proclaims that for sin in such a constitution of things there is no possibility of remission. So, then, human forgiveness is not quite so simple; the idea of human remission of all penalty for an offence is not quite so natural and easily intelligible as it appears to us when we first hear these words, "Forgive us our debts, as we forgive our debtors."

II. Let us proceed, in the next place, to apply these

analogies to the doctrine of Divine forgiveness of sin—to the case of the Divine Creditor and the human debtor. God will forgive us, we assume, as easily as we forgive our fellow-men. But we have seen that the idea of the complete forgiveness of a fellow-man is only conceivable on one condition—namely, that we completely isolate the debtor and the creditor from all other relations and regard them only as equals, one of whom has done the other wrong; and yet is it not clear that that is just the very position in which God can never stand towards any one of us? If there be one thing more certain than another, it is that by no ill deed of ours can we wrong or injure God. Our "goodness extendeth not unto Him;" how then can our wrong-doing hurt Him? Can He be supposed to cherish against us a passion of revenge which needs to be appeased? Can He keep a debtor and creditor account of vengeance with us the creatures of His breath? It is impossible. The one relation in which we cannot stand towards Him is that of an equal dealing with an equal for offence and wrong-doing. But as regards our other relations, what is He to us? He is the ruler of all that complex system of society in which wrong produces endless debt. He is the judge of that vast multitude of human beings whom He has created, every one of whom has a claim at his judgment-seat against his fellow who has wronged him. There has been no drop of blood that has ever been shed on this earth, since the blood of righteous Abel, that has not cried for justice to the Lord God of Sabbaoth. There has been no groan of suffering, there has been no complaint of wrong, there has been no cry from wounded and agonized hearts, smarting under the wrongful dealing of fellow-men, that has not echoed in the ears of our righteous Ruler; and if the earthly judges He appoints bear not the sword in vain, how can we suppose that this eternal appeal to Him of suffering humanity for justice shall be in vain? Is it alleged however that God forgives, not of mere compassion, but on condition of penitence, and that he who truly repents has thereby satisfied His requirements and may therefore claim to be forgiven, while he who remains impenitent does so of his own act and choice and therefore deserves his fate? Surely the answer to this is obvious. The refusal of the impenitent to repent is either a sin or a defect: either he will not or he cannot repent. If it is a sin, why not forgive it like any other sin? If it is only an imperfection, why punish it at all? Is it not clear moreover that if God forgives only the penitent He is less compassionate than He bids us to be when He tells us to forgive all our debtors whether penitent or impenitent? And if, on the other hand, penitence is a necessarily antecedent condition of forgiveness, arising out of the nature and constitution of things, then equally so, for aught we can tell, may atonement and mediation be such conditions too. Then there is this further difficulty. God is the author of that very constitution of things, of those inexorable and unalterable laws, under which, as we have seen, forgiveness is scarcely conceivable. Are we to suppose, then, that He will deflect these laws at our bidding? Are we to suppose that those mills of God, which grind so slowly, and yet so surely that nothing escapes them, will cease to revolve at our prayer, after He has once set them in motion? Can we suppose that the great red presses of the vintage of the wrath of God, that are ever crushing out the lees of sin and judgment, will be stayed because some trembling penitent asks that they may be stayed? Where is there room then in the moral constitution of the universe, ruled by a Moral Ruler, for forgiveness of sin? Where then can we find place for the idea of the easily-forgiving God, whom at first we pictured to ourselves? Do you not see that all this magniloquent and windy talk about a merciful and compassionate God, so facile and easy in His forgiveness, is a mere conception of modern Theism; that it is, after all, the poorest and lowest idea we can form of God; that it does not rise above the low thought of the savage, which pictures Him merely as an angry and offended man? Rise but one degree above that, rise up in your thought to the idea of Him as the Judge of all the earth; rise one degree higher to the idea of Him as the Author and Controller of the moral universe, and all this talk about easy, good-natured forgiveness vanishes in your nobler but more awful conception of God, as the cloud-wreath vanishes at the rising of the sun.

III. And now let us see what hope there remains, on the gospel theory, as to the possibility of forgiveness. What does our reason tell us as we contemplate the moral constitution of the world? Does it not tell us that unless the moral laws which surround us can be suspended, or turned aside by some power or other, there is no hope of forgiveness? And what do we call the act that suspends and turns aside some natural law by the introduction of a supernatural law? We call it a miracle; and miracle is a word which modern science forbids religion to speak. But a miracle, nevertheless, is needed in order to the possibility of forgiveness. It needs as much a moral miracle on the part of God to save the sinner from the consequence of his sin, when he transgresses the moral laws of the universe, as it would need a physical miracle to snatch him from a storm or an earthquake. The one is as necessary as the other, and the one is as easy or as difficult to imagine as the other. We thank God then for the fact which Revelation assures us of, that, to accomplish our forgiveness, a miracle has been wrought. What is it that Revelation teaches us concerning the atonement and mediation of Christ but this, that taken together with His incarnation they make the divinest and mightiest of all miracles; that the God who has framed this inexorable moral constitution of things has entered this natural world, where men sin and suffer by the operation of its terrible laws, has taken unto Himself their sinful and suffering humanity and made it, in the person of His Son, a new and perfect humanity? Does it not tell us how that Son has died and risen supernaturally to heaven, and that, in so doing, He has miraculously created for every one who dies and rises with Him, a supernatural kingdom in which they who enter it are no longer under the law of sin and its natural penalty, death, but are under the supernatural law of forgiveness and of everlasting life? Yes, that is what Revelation reveals to us. It reveals to us the miracle of a new world, even the kingdom of the Lord Jesus Christ, into which we may flee and be delivered from the operation of those terrible laws of natural justice and punishment from which otherwise there is no escape. And is this, then, to be regarded as a barbarous addition to the idea of forgiveness? Is this thought of the mediation and atonement of Christ a different system of forgiveness from that described in the story of the Prodigal Son, for instance; or is it not rather the eternal basis and ground which makes that story, with its eternal promise of free forgiveness, possible and true? Picture to yourselves, for one moment, the Hebrew prophet standing, as we supposed him to stand, by the altar of sacrifice and declaring his conviction that sacrifice was worthless and that God would accept the offering of his contrite heart instead—imagine that on the heart of that prophet, thus glowing with love and hope, there had descended some pitiless demonstration of the intellect which had clearly proved to him that there is logically no possibility of his contrite heart being thus accepted of God. Imagine—as this conclusion fell coldly and chillingly upon his heart, quenching all its hopeful aspirations as some driving storm of rain might have quenched the brands upon the altar of his sacrifice—imagine that to such a heart, chilled with terror by the proof that for sin there is no remission, there had come the revelation which Christ has given to us in Himself and in His gospel; that there had come the assurance that the forgiveness, which his intellect so clearly demonstrated to him could not be had without miracle, was to be had by miracle; that there had come to him this revelation of marvel and of mystery, "God so loved the world, that He sent His only begotten Son, that whosoever believeth in Him shall not perish, but have everlasting life;" can we suppose that such a revelation would have been an obstacle and a hindrance, instead of an encouragement and a help to him, in drawing nearer to his Father? True, there might still, there would still have remained for his intellect the question as to the how and the why of this great miracle of forgiveness; but such intellectual difficulties would no more have hindered his approach and need no more hinder our approach, to the mercy-seat of the Father, than the unfathomed depths of the waters that rose right and left for the passage of the ransomed people of God could have hindered their march between their dark walls on to the safe shore beyond.

And now let us gather up the lessons which this great word of our Lord's concerning God's and man's forgiveness has brought before us. We gather them up finally thus:—

To the contemplation of the idea of man's forgiveness there come three different parts of his nature — the conscience, which tells him of a certain and just penalty for sin; the understanding, which tells him either that there is no such thing as sin at all, or that for sin there can be no forgiveness; and the heart that cries, as the human heart will ever cry, "O God, be merciful to me a sinner." And there is one doctrine and one only—there is one revelation and one only that meets and answers and justifies itself as it meets and answers these three utterances from the troubled nature of man. To the conscience which speaks of penalty Revelation answers, "There is a penalty," and deepens the voice of conscience by telling us that this penalty is due for an offence against the Father of our spirits and that it consists in our being cast out of the supernatural kingdom of forgiveness into the natural kingdom of justice and punishment. To the reason which demands a miracle as the essential condition of forgiveness, it speaks of the greatest of miracles, the Incarnation and the Atonement. And then to the heart, the trembling, anxious, yearning human heart, which still refuses to believe that man is a mere victim of necessity, and persists, in spite of all demonstration to the contrary, in believing that there is a compassionate heart in Him who has fashioned us after His image — it gives the answer — "Verily there is forgiveness with Him. Rise up and go to your Father that He may forgive!" And so we clasp our gospel to our heart; so we kneel before the Divine presence of the Son of God and Son of Man, in whom we see incarnated the miraculous might of Divine love and Divine forgiveness; so, spite of all intellectual hindrances that would bar us from our Father's presence, spite of the remorsefulness of our memory, spite of the terrible accusations of our conscience, we can still say—" I WILL arise and go to my Father, and I WILL say to Him, Father, I have sinned against heaven and before Thee." Such is our gospel! a gospel of hope and of joy; and we hold it to be not only more hopeful, but more truly scientific—more in accordance with the facts of man's nature and of his place in God's world—than is that other gospel of fate and of despair that is offered in its stead.

THE HAPPY SERVANTS AND THE UNHAPPY SON.

THE HAPPY SERVANTS AND THE UNHAPPY SON.

PREACHED BEFORE THE UNIVERSITY OF OXFORD, 1881.

"And when he came to himself, he said, How many hired servants of my father's have bread enough and to spare, and I perish with hunger!"
—LUKE xv. 17.

THERE are two tests to which we have the right to submit every religion. There are two questions which we have the right, and which it is our duty, to put to every one who claims to come to us as a teacher from God. And these are, first, "What have you to tell us concerning the nature of God?" and, secondly, "What have you to tell us concerning the nature of man?" We have the right and it is our duty, to put these questions, because religion is the science of the relations between God and man. Every religion, therefore, properly so called, aims at giving us some information concerning these relations and the duties which arise out of them. It follows from this that every religion necessarily and primarily bases itself on certain facts, or alleged facts, in the nature of God and in the nature of man, which must create and condition these relations and duties. What God is or may be to us, and what we are or may be to Him, are questions necessarily arising out of what God is in Himself, and what we are in ourselves. Every religon, therefore, must necessarily have its idea or theory concerning God and its idea or theory concerning man. And we have the right to ask every religious teacher for these theories before we hear him speak of the relations and duties arising out of them; and by the truth or falsehood of these theories all the rest that he has to say must be judged, so far, at least, as this, that if he tell us anything concerning God, or concerning man, which is demonstrably false, which our reason or our conscience rejects, we must reject him. It is not that we may do so, or that we ought to do so, but that we are so constituted—happily so constituted—that we simply cannot accept his teaching. We have the right, then, as I have stated, to say to every teacher of religion: "What have you to tell us respecting these two great questions? Rehearse for us the articles of your belief concerning God and concerning man." And of these two tests it is quite clear which is the simpler and the surer one. Obviously the second. We know the nature of man, or think we do.. Of the Divine nature we are necessarily and naturally in comparative ignorance. We do know something of human life and its conditions, and therefore he who tells us that concerning man's nature which we know to be untrue has lost his claim upon our attention when he goes on to tell us something concerning God. If he has told us earthly things which we simply cannot believe, how can we believe him when he goes on to tell us of heavenly things? Convicted of falsehood, or of absurdity, as regards the visible, he can have no trustworthy message for us concerning the invisible.

Now it is to this test that I propose to submit that religion which we Christians profess. Let us consider in the light of this test—as regards its theory of humanity—the religion of the Bible. There is a theory concerning man's nature and condition on which the whole of this book, and all it professes to teach us, is based. We ask you to consider whether this theory approves itself to you as true; and we propose further to contrast it with certain other theories which we are asked to accept instead of it. And we do so with this desire and hope, that—although on the one hand, if the theory be demonstrably false, we cannot accept it—yet on the other hand, if it seem true to our nature; if there be in its account of us that which commends itself to our very innermost being; if, when the teacher speaks, the very flesh and heart within us cry out, "That is true;" if this revelation, or this professed revelation, thus find us at depths of our nature to which none other can reach, then we may be the more willing to listen to the teacher as he tells us of things that we have not seen—of the Divine nature that we cannot of ourselves comprehend, of the relations between it and us, of the duties, hopes, fears, promises, and helps that link humanity to God. To all these things we shall be the more prepared to give heed, because of the revealing and verifying light that his teaching will have shed upon a nature that we do know and that in some degree we do understand.

I. Let us then define, in the first place, the test to which we propose to submit the Bible theory of humanity. I propose to bring it to the test of one admitted and notorious fact in the nature and condition of man, and to see how it explains that fact and how it proposes to deal with it. The fact is that described in the words of our text—namely, the admitted and notorious one of the exceptional unhappiness of man. Our Lord in this parable of the Prodigal Son confronts Himself with this fact, as every preacher of a gospel, or good news, must do if he is to win the attention of mankind. The hero of this story, the prodigal son, is, as you see, a sufferer, but he is more than that—he is an exceptional sufferer. All the other creatures described in the parable—the lower servants of the Father's house—"have bread and to spare:" he alone suffers hunger. And, more than this, he is a strangely exceptional sufferer; for he who suffers is infinitely superior to those who are happy. They are but the hired servants in the house, and he the son—raised above them all in nearness to the Father and Ruler of the great houschold—he alone is perishing with hunger. Is this a true description then of humanity? Is it true that man is unhappy, and that he is exceptionally so? That man is unhappy we do know; that at least is a fact in all human experience. All our own knowledge, all that we know of the experience of others, all human literature, are full even to triteness of the commonplace of human unhappiness. The poet, the philosopher, the moralist, the satirist treat it in different ways, but they all acknowledge it. The sadness, the sorrowfulness, the weariness, the littleness of life force themselves upon the knowledge of all. Men may laugh at this sad life of ours as they do in one mood, or weep over it as they do in another mood; they may madden over it as they pore upon the mystery of human misery; but the confession of all alike, at some time or other of their life, is one and the same: "Man that is born of woman hath but a short time to live and is full of misery." This, at least, is an accepted and notorious fact in our nature and history: but there is more in it than this. Man is not only unhappy, but he is unquestionably the most unhappy creature in creation. By contrast with him all other creatures may be said to be happy. Nay, are they not actually so? Is not the life of the lower animals one of almost pure physical enjoyment? The mere joy of living, the happiness of existence that we see and envy in the child and which the little one loses as it grows up to boyhood and to manhood—how strongly marked it is in the animal creation! Their lives are unvexed by care, untroubled by anxiety, unhaunted by the fear of death.

> "With Nature never do *they* wage
> A foolish strife; they see
> A happy youth, and their old age
> Is beautiful and free."

In the whole of their joyous existence they have perhaps but the one single pang of terror or of pain that ends it. But man is an exception to all these. How comes it, that as you ascend from one rank to another through all the orders of animal existence, by slow and regular and uniform progression—how is it that when you come to man, the outcome of the ages—man, the perfection of all these existences—each rejoicing in its progress, each in its turn as it grows up and passes away contributing something to the scale of creation, and so passing on into something higher—how is it that when you reach the crown and glory of all creation you come to something infinitely more unhappy than all the rest? Man seems to pay the price of his rank and standing in the great household of the universe by this, that he is capable of an infinity of agonies. He yields for all his greatness a tax of misery from which all other creatures are exempt. This, too, is an admitted fact. And yet this is not all. We might be told, and fairly told, that this, after all, is but the working out of that great law which governs all creation—that the susceptibility to pleasure must always be purchased by a corresponding susceptibility to pain, that you cannot have the high sensibility which gives delight without at the same time being liable to the exquisite suffering that arises from the disturbance of this. And so it may be said that if man is at times the most unhappy, he is also at times the most happy creature in the world, and that a happy man is, at any rate, infinitely happier than a happy brute. This is true; and yet what a strange, what a sad out-look this gives us for that progress of our race of which we hear so much just now! Is it then true that man's infinite progress to perfection must still be infinite progress towards pain? Is it true that in the distant ages, as man advances still further and further to the very glory and perfectness of his being, he must advance still more and more to keener agonies of martyrdom? Is the crown of completeness that science has to offer to humanity so largely and so necessarily a crown of thorns? This is not a happy prospect; this is not altogether a gospel for humanity.

But this is not all; this is not the strangest part of the mystery of human unhappiness. The strangest thing connected with the unhappiness of man is this: that he differs from all other creatures that we know of in this respect, that he is often unhappy directly in proportion to the degree and extent to which he obeys his own nature. Consider this for a moment. All animals that we know of, save man, seem to be subject to this twofold law. Each creature has, on the one hand, its instincts, its desires, its appetites; and, on the other hand, in the climate or element in which it exists there are corresponding objects of gratification for these. Given the concurrence of these two—given the appetite that craves and the object which satisfies that appetite—and the animal is perfectly happy in itself and needs no more. It has "the portion of goods that falleth to it," and it desires nothing further.

Now, rise from the animal to the man; pass, as we are told nature has passed, by slight and imperceptible gradations, from the lowest to the highest stage of animal existence—to the human, in which there is but a slight anatomical difference of structure between the anthropoid creature and the man—and then you come to the strange fact that this law is altogether reversed. You come to a creature who is often eminently unhappy just because he has obeyed the strongest impulses and enjoyed the gratification of the most powerful instincts of his being. He suffers from two different causes, which are mighty factors in the pain of suffering humanity. One is the pain of satiety and the other the pain of remorse. Give man all the portion of goods that can fall to him, or that in his wildest dreams of covetousness and ambition he can desire for himself; give him health, wealth, strength, keen intellect, vivid imagination, gratified ambition; heap these upon him in overflowing abundance until he revel in the fulness of his enjoyment of them all; and if human history and human experience tell us anything they tell us this: that when he has enjoyed these to the very full and just because he has so enjoyed them, there begins to be felt a famine in his pleasures, there comes the weariness of satiety into his heart and soul. The eye is not satisfied with all its seeing, nor the ear with all its hearing; worn, blasèd, exhausted by the pursuit of pleasure, which still something in him compels him to pursue, the man wearies at last of his very life. He finds that, somehow or other, there seems to be still some end of his being, beyond possession and enjoyment, which he cannot attain unto; that, somehow or other, his life does not consist in the abundance of the things that he possesses. How is this? Why is this? How is it that you find an animal—when you come to man—which, the more its instincts are gratified, the more unhappy does it often become?

Mark now the other source of human pain and sorrow. It is remorse. How does it come to pass, that often when man obeys the strongest impulses and instincts of his nature he is not, like other animals, therefore happy, but therefore miserable? How is it that when he does this, he does not, as we are told all other animals before him did, ascend a step in the scale of creation, but that he sinks and knows he has sunk and fallen back towards the brute? What is the reason that when a man has yielded himself to some one or other of the strong inherent instincts or passions of his nature, there so often wakes up in him a feeling of shame and remorse? Why is it that he is haunted by the furies of an accusing conscience? It is a strange fact, when you consider it in the dry light of science, that when an animal, because he is an animal, does that which is natural, he becomes unhappy. Test this by a single instance. Take a case in which you see some stronger human animal dealing with a weaker one. Take the case in which some strong and savage man has just savagely stamped out the life from the weaker creature whom he once vowed to cherish and protect. The strong animal stands beside the weaker, a triumphant illustration of the law of the survival of the fittest. The human herd has just been weeded of one of its weaker elements, as happens in herds of other animals, by a useful violence. Why is it that such deed of violence fills you with indignation, and that you proceed to denounce that man and to charge him with having broken law? "What law?" he may ask you; "the law of society, the law that you have made for your convenience and your protection against my strength,—what other law?" "The law of your nature," you will tell him. "What law, and what nature? My nature! Why what I have done is natural, or else I could not have done it. It was just because my nature moved me to do this that I have done it; why do you tell me then that it is unnatural? You appeal to my conscience. My conscience has proved itself feebler than the passion which has overmastered it. In the name of science, then, in the name of purely materialistic science, which knows of nothing but force, I maintain and plead that this force in me which you call conscience, has not the right to rule, has not the scientific right to command. It has proved itself the weaker element in my nature by the very fact that it has given way. Why, then, am I to mutilate one part of my being at the bidding of another? How do you know that I am not the new type of future humanity, stronger and fiercer than yourself and therefore all the more likely to survive you? True, I am in the minority just now, and so has ever been the type of the new creature, in the first exercise of its new and nascent strength. But what is there in me that you can point out to me, and say, by virtue of that fact in my nature, that I am doing what is unnatural and wrong? You might as well blame the balance because it inclines to the heaviest weight, or the chain because it snaps at its weakest point, as blame me for doing that which I am most inclined to do." Such is the unanswerable plea of the natural man who is obeying some instinct of his nature; and yet although that plea is scientifically unanswerable, there is that within him which is answering him all the while, fitfully and intermittently, it may be, in proportion to the strength of those instincts and passions to which he naturally gives way, but never, perhaps, entirely silenced. There is a voice within him which—pleading weakly at some times, powerfully at others—tells him that what he is doing is evil, unnatural, deadly even to his own nature. The voice of conscience will sting him with remorse and haunt him with shame; will plead as some discrowned and dethroned monarch pleads, although in vain, for his legitimate rule against his revolted subjects. And the man will feel this, and he will know too that it is no use to feel it, that he cannot bring all parts of his nature into subjection to that which claims to rule the rest. He will, in his better moments, confess to you, " I am unhappy because of this contest in my nature between the law which claims to be supreme and yet fails to prove its supremacy, and the appetites that are ever proving their right to rule by the very fact that they dethrone my better nature and rule me. 'Oh, wretched man that I am, who will deliver me from this law in my members' that has subdued and conquered the better law in my mind, and that is bringing me into captivity to what I feel and know to be a law of sin and death?" This is the misery, this is the strange, exceptional misery of man.

II. And now with this fact we confront the teachers of the new gospel for humanity, the gospel of materialism, which weighs and measures and calculates the forces of matter and tells us that these are all. We say, explain to us, if you can, the strange difference between this human animal and all other animals with which you are acquainted. Tell us what is wrong with this machine, which should be the very perfection of all machines; tell us why its movements are so erratic, so incalculable, so violent at times and so self-destructive. Can you account for this strange contest between its constituent elements and forces; can you lay your hand on this or that part of it, and say, here is the evil, and not there? Or can you, at least, however ignorantly, try to amend it: can you put to rights your machine, if you cannot explain it? Can you make it keep temperate time and measure, and do that work in the world which you believe, but which you have no scientific reason for so believing, that it was designed to do? If you cannot do this—and certainly you have never yet attempted to do it—then stand aside while we tell you something about it. Hear what we have to say, we believers in the supernatural, we obsolete theologians: listen for a moment or two to our theory, on which we try to account for these facts: listen to us while we tell you what we at least try to do with this machine.

The Bible theory concerning man is not one of continued and uninterrupted progress, though it is a theory of progress. It is a theory of interrupted progress. The Bible history of man is this, that he is not his true self, that he is a creature not in its proper and true element. What Revelation tells us respecting man is this—that he differs from all other creatures in the universe, not in fine and hardly perceptible degree, but in kind: not by anatomical differences of structure merely, but in this essential respect, that the God who made him—whether it were by an instant act of creation, or by an infinitely protracted creative act of evolution—gave him as He did so that mystery of mysteries, a spiritual nature, with a free and self-determining will. It tells us further that the nature of that spiritual part of man is such that only in communion with and obedience to the Spirit which made it, can it find its true happiness; that the only place where man can be perfectly happy, if he can find it, if he can attain to it, is the Father's home. It tells us that the disease and disorganization of man's nature have come from this, that in the exercise of that mysterious power of free will with which he was gifted, he has wandered away from his Father's home and claimed selfish and solitary possession of the goods the Father lavished on him. It tells us that the origin of all human sin and sorrow has been that man has said, "Give me the portion of goods that falleth to me,"—give me the wealth of the imagination, the treasures of the affection, the strength of the intellect—give me all that distinguishes and glorifies me as man, and let me carry all these away into the far country of selfish possession and enjoyment without God. The Bible reveals to us that all man's misery is the result of this vain effort on his part to do, in this world of God, without the God who made him; that all the immense ennui of life, all that wretchedness of satiety which makes man from time to time, and now more than ever, ask—" Is life worth the living?"—is but the sublime discontent of the soul that was made to rest in God and cannot find its rest in anything less than God: the soul that was made to find its life and sustenance in the infinite and therefore cannot satisfy itself in the finite. This is the Bible explanation of the satiety and of the remorse of man whenever the lower part of his nature conquers the higher.

And one thing more that revelation tells him. It assures him of that of which no scientific or anatomical analysis of his nature, no merely human psychology can ever assure him, that the voice within him which claims a sovereignty over all his being is the voice of a rightful sovereign; that the warnings of his conscience are nothing less than the echoes of the law of God; that the claim of this discrowned and dethroned monarch to rule is a rightful claim, although it lost the power to enforce it when the spirit of man revolted against its Maker and lost thereby its command over its own lower vassals, the appetites which rise in perpetual rebellion and strife against it; that the misery of his soul comes from this revolt of his nature; that it is because he is not a true man nor living in his true element that he is unhappy. It reveals to him more than this. It tells him—what revelation alone can tell him—that there is a remedy for his unhappiness. "Rise up and go to thy Father!" The far country in which thou art dwelling must ever be swept again and again by periodic famine, as the soul in thee, the immortal soul, fails to find its life, its sustenance, there. The swine-husks of sensual pleasure were made for lower animals in creation, they were not made for thee. Come to thyself; return to thy better and saner self; go to thy Father, and there find the harmony and the reunion of all thy being; there gain the power to make thyself a true and perfect man; there become what thou wast made to be, the very crown and perfection of all created beings, because thou shalt have thus regained the lost likeness of the perfect Creator.

Now, we are not ashamed to contrast these two philosophies, theory for theory, idea for idea. We are not afraid to say—we unhesitatingly do say—that ours includes all the facts of the case and gives at least a consistent account and hypothesis for those facts; and that the other does not. But is that all we have to say? Are these but theories against theories? Are we but opposing a dream with a dream when we set the idea of the scientist against the idea of the religionist? Not so. Ours is an historical religion. It bases itself upon one life in the past; it is ever renewing and revealing itself in many lives ever since that one was lived on earth. It bases itself on the life of One who all through His existence, as far as we can know it—and the story of His life, if we accept it as true at all, reveals to us the very innermost workings and thoughts of His soul and heart—was a perfect man whose nature was unstained by impurity, unvexed by sensual or evil impulse, whose life was passed in entire and complete obedience to the will of the Father. His was a soul that never knew the hunger of the exiled and rebellious son, because it was ever "meat and drink to Him to do His Father's will;" He who gives us this picture of human unhappiness, as consisting in the wandering from the Father's home, was Himself the perfectly obedient Son. But that is not all. That life which He lived, that life of perfect obedience,—to which all its sorrow came from without and only came from the fact that all around Him were not, as He, perfectly obedient to His Father's will—that life, He tells us, He can supernaturally give to us. "I am come that ye might have,"—not merely knowledge of your lost condition, which any moralist may give you; not merely statements respecting your nature, which any philosopher may try to give you,—but "life," new life. "I am come that ye might have life, and have it more abundantly." And He who promises us this restored, this undying life, and who promises it to us as a supernatural gift, what attestation does He give us of His claim to bestow it? He gives us not merely the miracle of His own existence, which might be a solitary and exceptional one, but the miracles of His healing and restoring within the domain of the natural life of men. He tells us, "You who might otherwise believe yourselves the slaves of physical law, as you vainly struggle against the tyranny of your passions, behold how, when men bring to me those who suffer from physical disease, I heal them with a touch: you who are vexed with storms in your own souls, see how, with a word, I still the storms of external nature: you who feel yourselves to be tied and bound in sinful habits that wrap you round as grave clothes wrap the dead, behold me as standing by an open grave I call its tenant back to life; and as you thus behold me, learn to trust me when I tell you, 'I have power to still the storm in your hearts, to heal the diseases of your moral nature, to raise you from graves of sin and death.'"

And in the last place we have this fact to allege, that all along the history of the Divine society which He came on earth to found, we have instances of this restoring and healing power. All along the history of Christianity, wherever the word and the name of Christ are preached, we meet with what are nowhere else to be seen, the miracles of regeneration and conversion. We do find that men rise up and go to the house of their Father, and that they declare that they have there received a strength and a blessing which they never knew before. All down the ages,—ringing clear and distinct above all the cries of human strife and sin and misery,—there come to us the litanies of the penitent, the joyful hymns of the reconciled. We hear and we see—thank God that we can see—how drunkards suddenly become sober, outcasts chaste, profligates pure, churls loving and bountiful; and we see that this is attributed, by each and all, to the fact, that they had heard a voice that bid them rise and go to the Father, that they had obeyed it and had been healed. Men may mock at all this; they may tell us that the "Father's house" is all a dream, that the Father has no existence; but the robe and the ring with which the returning prodigals are clothed and adorned are facts they cannot deny. The comely robe of righteousness that is seen to cover some sinful soul, the jewelled gifts of grace that are suddenly seen adorning it, these are facts, patent and visible, and it is not scientific, it is not philosophic, to ignore such facts in the history of human life. We repeat it then, that our theory—the Bible theory—of the fall, the restoration, the deliverance of man,—is the one which best accords with the facts of man's nature, of Christian experience and of human life. And if this be so, may we not respectfully ask of modern science not too hastily to reject a philosophy of humanity so manifestly superior to any it has yet devised, solely because it implies the "unscientific idea of a God?" May we not even express, in our turn, our doubts as to those scientific denials of a God which invariably imply such insufficient and unscientific, ideas of Man? May we not, in spite of these denials, still dare to trust the best instincts of our nature, the deepest longings of our hearts, as they echo within us the invitation of the gospel to try the great experiment as to the being of a God which every man may make for himself who will "arise and go to his Father?" None ever made that experiment and failed to reach the Father's home.

MORALITY AND DOGMA.

MORALITY AND DOGMA.

"By manifestation of the truth, commending ourselves to every man's conscience in the sight of God."—2 Cor. iv. 2.

THE truth of which the Apostle is speaking here, by the manifestation of which he commends himself to the conscience of every man, was not, as we might have supposed at first, moral truth; it was dogmatic truth. We find in the following verses that it was "the glorious Gospel of Jesus Christ;" the "light of the glory of the knowledge of God in the face of Jesus Christ." That is to say, it was not the moral precepts of Christianity, but it was that body of Christian doctrine concerning the person and the life of Jesus into which the Apostles baptized their converts, and which we recite when we repeat the Apostles' Creed. Now, of this teaching, it is alleged, that it commended itself to the conscience of every man. This is certainly a very remarkable—almost a startling—claim on behalf of dogmatic teaching. For it does not, at first sight, appear how the faculty in us which judges of the right and wrong of actions can have anything to do with judging of the truth or falsehood of dogmas; still less does it seem to us clear how this relation between conscience and dogma can be so very close and evident that the preaching of these dogmas commends the preacher to the moral sense of his hearers. And accordingly, the idea of there being any real connection between doctrine concerning the supernatural—between religion, in short—and the human conscience, is utterly discarded by a large school of thinkers amongst us at this moment. Such persons strongly insist that, between dogma and the moral sense there can be no possible relation. "How," they ask, " can it in the least affect our obligations to our fellow men in this world, to be told that it had a Creator? How can it affect our duty to do unto all men as we would they should do unto us, to know that he who gave us this precept rose from the dead and ascended into heaven?" And we are further assured that not only is it absurd to insist upon any relation between the supernatural and the human conscience, but that to do so is, in the last degree, dangerous to morality. For this, we are told, is nothing else than to link the future of human morality with the uncertain future of creeds and dogmas. "Join together," we are warned, "in any degree or measure, religion and morality, and then morality must share the fate of religion. And if religions are about to vanish away," as we are told they are, "and you have made morality in any measure dependent upon religion, ill must it fare with morality in the future." And accordingly these teachers are busy, many of them just now—not indeed with any remarkable success, but with great pains and industry—in constructing what they speak of as a "scientific basis" for morality; finding, that is to say, physical reasons why men should be righteous, which shall stand the test of scientific examination and which shall enable morality to survive in the fast-coming day, when human knowledge shall have enabled men to dispense with Divine faith.

Now, before we accept this new basis for morality, before we give up the old belief—old as humanity and wide-spread as the human race—that there is a deep and close relation between religion and morals, let us, at least, endeavour to ascertain what that relation really is and what it is not. Let us clearly see, if we can, what it is that dogma concerning the supernatural—such dogma as we find in our Creeds—can possibly have to do with the human conscience.

I. And, in the first place, we can see clearly from the words of the Apostle—what it has not to do. Supernatural teaching is not, and cannot be, the sole authority for moral obligation. It is not true, it is perilously untrue, to say that our duty to be moral rests upon any external command whatever. To say that I am bound to be honest and just in all my dealings with my fellow men because an Almighty Being has commanded me, under certain penalties, to be so, is at once immoral and illogical. It is immoral if we rest the obligation solely upon the power of the Being who has commanded us, for that is to make might the only measure of right. It is illogical if we rest it upon His goodness; because that can only be proved to us by the goodness of His words and actions, and, therefore, I must settle whether any particular word of His is good, before I can decide for myself the fact of His goodness which is alleged as the reason why I should obey that word. We do not hesitate, therefore, to condemn, as untrue and unwise, the assertion that morality rests upon external command. The law written upon our hearts is superior to any other, however attested; and any law which contradicts this is self-condemned. The voice that bids me be immoral is a voice that I must resist, though it be a voice that stills the storm, or that wakes the dead. And this, be it observed, is exactly what St. Paul is telling us, in his claim to have satisfied the conscience of his hearers. He does not say to the Corinthians, "Receive us as Divinely-sent messengers who have wrought miracles in proof of our mission, and therefore allow us to dictate moral truth to you;" he says what is the very opposite to this, "Listen to the truths we have to proclaim, judge them, in the first instance, by that supreme moral sense which He who sent us has given you; judge us by the conscience within you; if it reject these doctrines as immoral, reject us, whatever be our claims; if it accept them as moral, then listen to what more we have to say to you about our claim to give you other teachings, or other commands: but, first, and before all things, we commend ourselves to the conscience of every man amongst you in the sight of Him who has sent us to minister to you." Most distinctly, then, here, as elsewhere, does Christianity recognise the absolute supremacy of the Conscience.

II. But if Christianity does thus recognise the supremacy of the moral sense; if the supernatural in the Christian system makes no claim to dictate to us moral truth, then, we may be asked, what is the relation of the supernatural to the conscience? Now, it will help us to answer this question if we observe carefully the form in which the supernatural appears in the Creeds. It is very remarkable. It appears in a form which is strictly historical. The Apostles' Creed is almost entirely a recital of alleged historical facts; the facts of the supernatural—the Creation, the Incarnation, the Resurrection, the Ascension, the Descent of the Holy Spirit—appear in it side by side and, as it were, upon the same level with certain other biographical and merely natural facts in the life and death of Jesus Christ. In the same breath in which we say "conceived by the Holy Ghost" we say "born of the Virgin Mary;" in unbroken following of sentences we say, "crucified under Pontius Pilate, dead and buried," and then go on to say, " rose again the third day from the dead, ascended into heaven, and sitteth on the right hand of God, the Father Almighty." It is all one continuous, historical narrative. It is the supernatural appearing within the sphere of the natural, and appearing as simple historical fact. It all comes to us, you observe, as so much news—good news, we have agreed to call it. It is intelligence, it is information, it is light that the Creed claims to give us. Light! Let us pause on that word. The Creed with its story of natural and supernatural facts comes to us as light—it comes to us from Him who is "the light of the world." What light, then, does the story of the supernatural contained in the Creed shed upon the human conscience? Undoubtedly the human conscience needs light. There is no faculty in human nature that so much depends upon light from without as the conscience. All know the difference between an informed and an ignorant conscience, and all can remember instances in which this supreme judge within us has made terrible and pitiless mistakes because it has judged amiss. For conscience is not the law of our actions. It is their judge, and like every other judge, it decides according to the recognised laws of the day in which it is acting and judging. But I am not now speaking of this kind of light, all important as it is, but of another kind of light thrown upon another far deeper and far darker question, and that is—not as to the law by which the conscience is to judge of any particular case—but as to the authority which it has to judge in any case whatsoever. The question which lies at the very root of all morality is—not whether there is any fixed law of morals nor what that law is—but whether there be such a thing as morality at all; not how the conscience shall judge, but why it claims to judge and what is its right to do so? Such a right, viewed merely in the light of natural science, is at least disputable. We cannot say of any force in nature, except in a metaphorical sense, that it has the right to rule any other force. All that we can say as a matter of fact is, that it does always rule; and, therefore, in a metaphorical way it may be said to have the right to do so, just as when we combine two chemical elements we say that one of these—the stronger—*ought* to dominate the other. That is all. But then when we remember that, as a matter of fact, the conscience does not always rule; when we remember that its voice is often overruled by the clamour of the passions and the appetites—by what theologians call the lower parts, but what men of science can only call the stronger parts, of our nature—when we remember this, we can find no scientific authority, no demonstrable basis for the right of the conscience to rule the man. But not merely is the right of conscience to supreme rule and authority a thing disputable in the light of science, but, if we are to read it in the light of some of the latest scientific utterances, it is a thing demonstrably and absurdly false. What is the last light shed upon our nature by the last discoveries of materialistic philosophy? It is this; that we are machines pure and simple, that what we call will and choice are only sensations which accompany, but in which in no way cause or produce, certain other sensations and actings of our nature—mere secretions of the grey matter of the brain which accompany the automatic movements of that automatic machine which we call man; but of which to predicate the words right or wrong—to say that there is anything moral attaching to them—means no more than when we say that a watch keeps wrong time, or that the compass is guilty of aberration. Nay, it does not even mean so much as this. There is less scientific right, upon the principles of materialism, to say of a man that he goes wrong, than there is to say of a watch that it keeps wrong time. For when we say that a watch keeps wrong time, we mean that it is a machine constructed for the purpose of keeping right time; and when we say that it ought to keep that time but does not, we mean that it fails to accomplish the purpose of its maker. That is to say, we assume respecting it the doctrine of design; we regard a watch or a compass as intended to carry out the will of its maker. But that is the very thing which materialism sternly, contemptuously, forbids us to say of the universe or of humanity. If we say that these had a design or a designer, we provoke the scornful laughter of the modern philosopher, who tells us that this was a fit argument for the unscientific divines of the last century, but that to bring it forward now is an anachronism and an absurdity. Be it so: materialism then forbids us to admit the idea of a final cause or aim in man's whole nature. Then why is it that when the materialist is constructing his scientific basis of morality, he must, if he will not use language perfectly absurd, speak as if he believed there was a design in man's nature? Must we go back to the old exploded idea of a final cause—of a maker and his purpose—before we can find a scientific reason for saying of a man that he has done wrong or that he has done right? Where is the scientific basis for morality here? Curious, certainly, in a scientific point of view, strangely curious it is that this automatic machine should now and then seem to check itself and tremble at its own movements; strange and curious it is— that it should seem, in some way or other, to inflict pain upon itself whenever those movements fail to correspond with the impulses of some internal force; strange it is that the grey matter of the brain should secrete these conscientious sensations. Matter for scientific inquiry, doubtless, this is ; but ground for moral obligation, reason for saying—in the sense in which men do say it, when they talk of morality—this is right or that is wrong, why, that is to go back to the exploded science and the mistaken philosophy of the eighteenth century: the nineteenth century is more advanced.

Such is, so far, the net result of the latest attempt to find a scientific basis for morality. That result is that the conscience in man fails to justify itself to the sceptical understanding. The authority within us yields, like the authority without us, to the perpetual solvent of the perpetual questioning of the purely sceptical part of our nature, which asks why, why, and still why is this? And if you will not allow faith to rise up against scepticism in defence of the authority without, you must be consistent and refuse to allow it the right to rise up against scepticism in defence of the authority within. And thus the sceptical understanding, flushed with the success of its assault upon the outward bulwark of morality—Religion, will inevitably proceed to assail, upon the same grounds and with the same success, the innermost fortress and citadel of morality—the human conscience. And let no one say that this is merely an imaginary assault ; let no one tell us that we are merely conjuring up a chimera of the pulpit in order to scare men back into the moralities of religion. It is not so. In all history nothing is more certain than this, that at those periods at which religion has been most attacked assaults upon morality have inevitably appeared. It was so in Greece ; it was so in Rome ; it is so at this day in England. What else is the meaning of all that literature of Pessimism by which men delight to prove that there is no God, no soul, no hereafter, no reason why we should be moral, no hope of the final triumph of righteousness, nothing but the miserable conflict between appetite and conscience, between morality and desire, which distracts men now and is to go on distracting them for ever and ever? What else is the meaning of modern Nihilism which rages frantically, not only against revealed religion, but against the family, against marriage, against all the sanctities and purities of human life? What else is the meaning of that outbreak of modern Paganism in our own English literature which disgraces and defiles it from time to time, as it oozes out in cynical Nature-worship, in the hymning and praising of the beast in man, insisting still that "whatever is in him, is right"? What is all this but the successful assault of the sceptical understanding on the scientific bases of morality? What is it but the pleading of the sceptical part of our nature which—holding now, as ever, its retaining fee from the passions—makes its assaults upon all things that men hold dear within them, as before it made its assaults upon all things that men held dear without and around them? Such contest and such assault must continue so long as there are passions and appetites in man that rage against whatever resists or restrains them. We do not deny—God forbid that we should—that there are materialists among us who resist these assaults upon their own morality. We do not deny—God forbid that we should—that there are materialists infinitely better than their own unhappy belief; as, on the other hand, there are too many Christians worse and lower than their own nobler faith. But we do say that the materialist who does this is unconsciously, though happily, performing an act of faith. He is unconsciously resolving to believe—in spite of all scientific evidence to the contrary—that he is a moral being. But he deceives himself when, because of this, he imagines that, in spite of general scepticism, morality would continue to survive. There are men here and there who might in that case still be moral; but let the restraints of religion be completely swept away, let the idea of the supernatural vanish—not only from this or that calculating and prudently moral leader of human thought, but from the minds of the multitudes who suffer from the passion, the temptation, the trial, the sorrow of the hour—let these be left with only a scientific basis of morality, and we should soon see the result. In vain would you strive to bind the passions and the desires, the needs and the appetites of mankind, with such bonds of flax, as are your philosophic maxims of morality. The consuming fire of passion in human souls would burn these out full swiftly, and men would be filled with a new sense of licentious freedom from any consciousness of sin. The paradise of materialism would lie open before emancipated humanity. The fiery sword of old terrors which, flaming and turning every way, once deterred men from entering there, would have been snatched by Science from the hands of Superstition; and the multitude would rush in to eat, or strive to eat, of all its fruits, and would make of that paradise what raging lust and unsatisfied desire have made of many another paradise, ere now—a hell upon this earth.

III. And, now that we have seen that the "scientific basis of morality" does not help us much in this matter, let us try whether any light is thrown on it by the manifestation of the supernatural. What is there that an external and miraculously attested revelation can tell us respecting morality which we could not have discovered without its aid? Just those very facts, we answer, which, as we have seen, we never could have found out for ourselves and yet without the knowledge of which we never can decide whether there is or is not such a thing as morality—namely, what and whence we are and what is our true place in nature. Its miracles, breaking in as they do upon the otherwise unvarying uniformity of the natural order of the universe, show us that this is neither eternal nor unchangeable, but that above it, around it, embracing, overruling it all, there lies an older and a higher one which is from everlasting to everlasting. Its teachings reveal to us—that it is to this order that we human beings truly and properly belong—that we are not merely natural but supernatural creatures, for that our Maker created us in His own image and likeness; that it was He who gave to us that part of our nature which, speaking in His name and with His voice, forbids us to sin and punishes us when we do so, and which is therefore ever testifying to us at His bidding, that we are not irresponsible atoms moving helplessly to and fro in some unaccountable system of blind force, which has no design and had no designer, but that we are moral and accountable beings placed in the midst of a great system of moral government—ordered, all of it, and ruled by the supreme will of a Righteous Ruler and Judge.

It is this rift which the supernatural makes in the otherwise impenetrable cloud of the natural that tells us whence comes the light in which we live; for it reveals to us the sun of our system—the Godhead which has created and which is enlightening the world.

IV. And now, to sum up finally the arguments which I have been endeavouring to state as regards the province of the supernatural in the matter of the human conscience: —We do not—when we say that the supernatural helps us to a basis of morality,—we do not allege that it dictates to us moral truth; we do not say that it helps to bribe men into being moral by the promise of heaven or to terrify them by the threat of hell. A man who does right only for the sake of heaven or through the fear of hell, can hardly be called moral. We do not say this; but we do allege that it throws light upon facts in our nature, which justify and which alone can justify, our claim to be moral beings. We do say that — not to overrule nor tyrannise over the conscience—but to restore to it its full and rightful authority, the voice of the supernatural has been heard amongst men. We do say that a miraculous Revelation has been given to man not to create, but to strengthen the ground of morality; to widen and deepen the basis upon which it erects its throne; to give it back its old supremacy; to crown it with a crown which is "the light of the glory of the knowledge of God in Jesus Christ." This, we maintain, is the true office of the supernatural in helping us to find a basis for morality. More, far more, we might have said, had time allowed it, as to the relation not merely of the supernatural, but specially of the Christian idea of the supernatural, to human morality. We cannot now do more than touch just the fringe of this great subject. Let us entreat you to follow it out in thought for yourselves. Think, for instance, how the Christian doctrines of sin, of atonement, of forgiveness and of sanctification, speak to the moral sense of man ; think how it dignifies and deepens our motives for just and righteous dealings with one another, to know that we are dealing with those who, like ourselves, derive their descent from God, who come from God and go to Him. Think again of the purifying effect of the great doctrine of Christian holiness, something far deeper than the precepts of mere morality; that doctrine which bids man be pure in his own secret and innermost thoughts, because every thought of his heart lies bare before the eyes of an All Holy One, who cannot endure to look upon iniquity. Think of the help to morality in the doctrine of the descent of the Holy Spirit of God that He might make men holy, that He might gather them into one Holy Catholic Church, one Communion of Saints, whose one object is to " live righteously, soberly, and godly in this present evil world." Think of the effect of all this upon the human conscience and upon human morality, and then try to realise what would be the effect upon the world of the blotting out of all this. Surely, whether Christian dogma be true or false, it is manifestly absurd to say that it does not touch the very basis and root of all morality, namely, the question whether man is, or is not, a moral being, whether he has, or has not, anything more than an imaginary and superstitious claim of right to judge his own actions. We say then to those who scornfully reject the idea of revelation in its relation to morality, do not at any rate imagine it to be one of pure indifference. Reject, if you will, with a smile, or with a sneer, our old-world dream of the supernatural. Tell us, if you will, that we are but cherishing an expiring relic of ancient superstition, when we believe that there was once a golden age of purity and that there shall be again an abode for mankind, where nothing that defileth or hurteth can enter. But do not mock us with the assurance that, when this fond belief shall have vanished away, the basis of morality shall stand securer than ever. Do not ask us to believe in your prophecy of a millennium of materialistic virtue which cannot even justify itself to the science to which it appeals. Let us, if it must be so, face together, with what grim and desperate courage we may, the coming night of moral darkness, in which men shall grope to and fro in search of some reason for morality, drunken with the wine of their own passions and stumbling over every stumbling-block of temptation; but do not tell us that the shadows of this coming night are streaks of the daybreak. Do not deceive yourselves by mistaking the after-glow of the setting sun of Christianity in your own hearts for the dawn of a morning that may never shine for you. Nevertheless, we do not believe that the darkness of materialism will ever wrap this world, in which Christ has lived and died and risen again, in endless night. We do not believe it, for this reason, that deep within the heart of humanity there lies the one indestructible evidence for Christianity of the conscience which, being light, craves for light and compels man to seek for it as the plant unconsciously seeks for the rays of the sun. That light may be quenched in individual souls. Nay, even here and there on some portion of the earth's surface, wherein, for a time, unbelief may have succeeded in crucifying the Son of Man afresh and putting Him to an open shame— above that modern cross there may be darkness in the heavens for a little space; but, spite of this, the soul of man will continue to crave and seek for light from God; and men shall still believe and rejoice in "the light of the glory of God," because that light, as seen "in the face of Jesus Christ," can never lose its power to "commend itself to the conscience of every man" whom God has made and whom Christ has redeemed.

THE BIBLE HUMAN AND YET DIVINE.

THE BIBLE HUMAN AND YET DIVINE.

PREACHED AT THE JUBILEE OF THE PETERBOROUGH AUXILIARY OF THE BRITISH AND FOREIGN BIBLE SOCIETY, PETERBOROUGH CATHEDRAL, APRIL 18, 1882.

"And the Word was made flesh and dwelt among us (and we beheld His glory, the glory as of the only begotten of the Father), full of grace and truth."—S. JOHN i. 14.

"Is not this the carpenter's son?"—S. MATTHEW xiii. 55.

SUCH were the diverse judgments of the Church and of the World upon the Son of man in the days of His flesh. The Church, beholding Him with the eye of faith, saw His glory in spite of His humiliation; the World, beholding Him only with the eye of sense, could not see His glory because of His humiliation. The disciples, believing in Him, saw Him, "full of grace and truth;" the unbelieving world saw Him full only of presumption and false pretence. The Church loved Him, clung to Him and at last worshipped Him; the world denied, hated, and at last crucified Him. And the reward of the faith of the Church and of the doubt of the world came to each in its due exact and natural way of requital. The Church, believing in spite of difficulty—her faith deepening day by day and year by year, as the disciples went to and fro with their Lord—triumphing over all the difficulties and doubts that were raised by the lowliness of His surroundings as contrasted with the greatness of His claims—the Church that followed Him to His Cross and watched by His grave, was rewarded for her faith by being permitted to see the triumphs of the Resurrection and the Ascension. To the faith that had endured through the night of despondency was given, in the day-dawn of the Resurrection, the joy of certainty. The Church saw at last the glory of the Word to be the "glory of the only begotten of the Father." On the other hand, the World, persevering in its doubt, went on from doubt to denial, and from denial to sin. Clinging fast to their first miserable error as to the carpenter's son—seeing in Him nothing else than the carpenter's son—the Jews at last came to believe that the Cross of Jesus upheld only the body of a blasphemer and that the grave of Jesus hid only the remains of an impostor; and so the world, as represented by the Jews of that day, walked darkly on in its unbelief and hardness of heart to its fitting doom. He whom the Jews would not receive as a Saviour, visited as judge the city that He had wept over as prophet, and the destruction He foretold followed, swiftly and surely, the disbelief he had denounced. Such was the progress of faith and of doubt concerning Christ, each to its own appointed and natural end.

And observe, in the next place, that these two widely different and opposite progresses started from the same point. The diverse conclusions of the Church and of the world were pronounced upon the very same facts. The world and the Church looked upon the same Jesus under the same external surroundings and circumstances. The disciples saw Him in the home of the carpenter, and His "brethren and sisters were with them," as they were with the Jews; while on the other hand, the miracles and the marvellous words of Christ were present to the Jews, as they were to the disciples; so much so that in the passage from which my text is taken we find that the Jews were displeased because of these very miracles and these marvellous words. They asked, "Whence hath this man these mighty works and these words?" How dare a mere carpenter's son assume such majesty and such authority in our midst! And they were offended at Him. It was the same Jesus about whom the world and the Church differed; the same facts—the lowliness and the greatness, the humiliation and the majesty of Christ—were present to both; the King came to both "meek and lowly," and the world rejected, while the Church owned her Lord.

I. This diversity of thought respecting the one and the same Jesus was the necessary result of the fact, that the Church and the world were, though with very different eyes, contemplating the same great mystery— the mystery of the incarnation. That which the Church and that which the world saw in Jesus was nothing else than this: the Word made flesh and dwelling amongst men. Now, if the Incarnation be what we Christians believe it to be, what the Word of God declares it to be, then the Incarnate Word must always have been liable to these differing judgments of men. For what is it that we mean when we speak of the Word being made flesh? We mean, not merely that Deity took to Itself humanity as an outward veil and form, beneath which It should hide Itself and through which it should express Itself; but that the Second Person of the Trinity, the Word, did become really and truly man, did empty Himself of His glory, the glory that He had with the Father before the world was; did take to Himself a real and true humanity, as real and as true, "of reasonable soul and human flesh subsisting," as the humanity of any one of us here present; that He became "bone of our bone, and flesh of our flesh;" that He was very man, in all the reality, in all the limitations, in all the weaknesses of humanity, "sin only excepted"; and yet that He was not more truly man than He was really and truly "very God of very God," begotten of His Father before the world. But if that be so, we can see at once how, if I may use the expression, the very completeness of the Incarnation was that which caused the temptation and the difficulty of those who beheld the Christ. If the Incarnation was what I have attempted to describe—the union of very man with very God—then the literal truth and reality of Christ's human nature must have been so constantly, so manifestly, visible to the eyes of men, in all its lowliness and seeming imperfection, that they must have been always tempted to look upon it as mere humanity and to regard Him as nothing more than man—as, in fact, we know they, for the most part, did. And yet, on the other hand, in spite of all these limitations, in spite of the manifest reality of the humanity of Christ, there must ever have been in Him, not merely in His works of wonder—for those He shared with prophets of old—but in His very self, in His words, in His presence, as it were, the shining out, for the eye of faith, of the hidden Divinity; so that it should be ever possible for the world to say of Him, "This is a man just like other men, one of ourselves; is not this the carpenter's son?" and, on the other hand, it should be ever possible for the Church to say, "This is more than man, this is Christ, the Son of the living God." So that always, when the world, offended at His saying, should go away exclaiming, "Who is this carpenter's son, that He should claim to teach and command us thus?" the disciples, coming to His feet, should say, "Lord, to whom shall we go? Thou hast the words of eternal life." It could not have been otherwise, it must have been thus, because our Lord was the Word made flesh and dwelt amongst men as man; and therefore has it come to pass that, while the Church has ever maintained in all her teaching this great central verity of Christianity —the true and real incarnation of Jesus Christ, God and man, the World has ever seen in Him only man.

And yet it is clear that while the Church thus holds strongly, clings as for her very life, to her belief in the true and real Divinity as well as the true humanity of her Lord, she is exposed to this great danger, that while she asserts His Divinity against the denial of it on the part of the world, she may, while she is asserting it and because she is asserting it, lose sight of the other truth of His real humanity. We are in danger of so dwelling upon the truth that the Christ whom we worship is very God of very God as to lose sight of, nay, almost to keep back, the great and equal truth that He is man truly and really. Those who know anything of Church history know how often the popular belief has fallen into this very mistake, how from the first strange heresies sprang up from time to time in her midst, arising from the desire to magnify the truth of His Divinity and the shrinking from too strong an assertion of His humanity. When we read those wonderfully balanced sentences in the Athanasian Creed which speak of the Incarnation, if we read them with any knowledge of the history of doctrine, we find in them a record, as it were, of the swinging to and fro of the pendulum of popular belief, now swinging too much to one side, now to the other, and needing to be carefully and constantly corrected and restrained by the successive definitions of the Creeds. Or, to take an illustration which may be more familiar to the minds of those who are listening to me, we may remember how great the loss and injury to the Church has been when—holding too exclusively to the idea of our Lord's Divinity and thus removing Him too far from her affection—she has fallen into the error of looking for human sympathy and pity in the tenderness of His mother, in the sympathy of His saints; forgetting the infinite depths of tenderness—tenderness passing the love of woman, sympathy closer than that of a brother—that must have filled the heart of the great High Priest who was "made like unto us in all things," that He might be touched with the feeling of our infirmities. In the worship of the Virgin, in the worship of the saints, we see the evil consequences of a too exclusive and one-sided teaching of the Divinity of our Lord, and forgetfulness of His humanity. The Church has shown her wisdom, her adherence to Christian truth, in this, that she has ever strongly maintained in her authoritative creeds and formularies the great double truth of the Divinity and humanity—that is to say, the truth of the real incarnation—of Jesus Christ.

II. And now you will probably have anticipated the parallel that I am about to draw between this mystery of the Incarnation and the manner in which it has been dealt with at divers times, and that other mystery —theme of to-day's service and to-day's meditations— the mystery of the Holy Spirit of God so dwelling amongst men, that they might "behold His glory" too. The mystery of the inspiration of the written Word is parallel to that of the incarnation of the Word in the person of Christ. In both there is the meeting of the Divine and the human; in both there is the shining out of the Divine through the human; in both there is such an outward display of the human, as that men may deny, if they will, the presence of the Divine. The Bible is God's Word. "Holy men of God spake as they were moved by the Holy Ghost." As truly and as certainly as in Jesus

Christ dwelt the fulness of the Godhead bodily, so truly and so certainly, in the hearts of those who gave us this Book, dwelt the Divine Spirit of God. The Bible is, in a sense in which it is true of no other book, God's Book and God's Word; but equally true is it that the Bible is man's book and man's word. God the Holy Ghost, when He inspired holy men to give us these books, did not speak through their lips as the oracles of old were said to have spoken, through the lips of the subject of their inspiration, as through hollow-sounding masks, but spoke first in the souls of those whom He stirred to give us these inspired words. They are therefore their words as well as His. The hearts of men were first filled with the Spirit before their lips spoke out their utterances, and therefore those utterances were as truly theirs as they were God's. The human nature, the human individuality, the human peculiarities of the writers, remained untouched, because God was speaking through the lips of real men. And so it is that the utterances from their lips come to us steeped in the deepest emotions of the human heart. It was the tender thought, the glowing aspiration, the lofty hope, the trembling fear, the solemn awe, the stern indignation of men moved to the very depths of their nature by the power of God working in them, that shaped the words that live and burn in the pages of Scripture to this very day and that stir our hearts because they first stirred the hearts of those who uttered them. This is as true of the humanity of God's Word written, as it is true of the humanity of God's Word incarnate. There is in each a real, true, and visible humanity. Human souls moved by God's Spirit spoke as men and under the conditions and limitations of their day and their generation. Their thoughts were tinged with the philosophy, their knowledge was limited by the scientific knowledge of their own times; they spoke the history and the science, as truly as they spoke the dialect and grammar of their day; to suppose anything else would be to suppose not a supernatural but an unnatural inspiration. Revelation speaks, for instance, through the mind of Moses tinctured with the learning of the Egyptians, as truly as it speaks from the heart of David the thoughts that filled his soul as he tended his flock beneath the starry skies of Palestine. The burning sarcasm of Isaiah; the tender, melancholy pathos of Jeremiah; the rough speech of "the herdsman's son and the gatherer of sycamore fruit;" the deep and mystic philosophy of John; the clear and sharp, and yet impassioned, logic of Paul; the homely simplicity of James—all these were truly and really their own. As every pipe of the organ you have been listening to expresses the music that it was fashioned to give—so fashioned that it might give that note and not another—and yet all are filled by one and the same breath—so these souls, fashioned by the conditions of humanity and the circumstances of their lives, were made each to give out its own note, and yet were all filled by the breath of the Divine Spirit which has made those human and yet Divine utterances ring with a melody unquenched and unquenchable through the great aisles of the Church of the living Christ; or as the light, shining through the stained windows of our cathedral, casts on the floor below, in varied light and shade, human shapes and human forms, yet all of them filled and gleaming with the light that comes from heaven—so is the Bible which God has given us at once truly human and yet truly Divine—the Word of God, veiling itself under and yet shining through the word of man.

But if the conditions and limitations of humanity, as well as the inbreathings and presence of Divinity are in this word, then we need the exercise of faith to see its Divinity in spite of its human conditions; and, on the other hand, there is ever the temptation to the unbelief of the world to see only its human conditions, and not to see, but to deny, the presence in it of the Divine glory. Now, as of old, the Church and the world look upon a Divine mystery with different eyes—one with the eye of faith, the other with the eye of sense. The world looks upon this Book—it seems to be just now specially giving itself to such contemplation of this Book —in the same critical and contemptuous spirit in which the Jews of old judged the carpenter's son. It delights to show us all that is human in Holy Scripture; delights to dwell with critical skill and learning upon the genesis and history of each book in the Bible; delights to question its received authorship, or its received place in the history of the Canon; delights to show us errors in its history, defects in its science, solecisms in its grammar; delights to show how completely human all over the Bible is, dissects the Bible, vivisects the Bible, and having examined it curiously under the knife of its critical dissection, and having failed to find there a living soul— what dissector ever yet carved out a soul?—turns round to us with a look of scorn, and tells us that it is flesh, flesh only. And when we say, The body that you are thus dividing and dissecting by your critical analysis, is living, has in it a soul, breathed into it by its Creator, they laugh at us and ask, "Wherein does this Book differ from other books written by men who, as it were, are 'with us to this very day?' Have we not Homer, and Milton, and Shakespeare, and Dante, and are there not the Koran, the Vedas, the Shastras, and many another so-called sacred book? Wherein does this Book of yours differ from these? Are they not, too, inspired? Why should we bow down and make obeisance to this Joseph of yours that would set itself above its brethren?" And so the world doubts and then denies, as of old it did respecting the incarnate Word, and then proceeds to scourge and then to crucify and then to close the grave over this Book, as of old it did with Him whom the Book portrays; and burying it in the grave of scornful unbelief and setting on it the great stone of atheistic materialism, it writes thereon its new gospel: "There is nothing Divine in this Book, nothing Divine in human life: let us eat and drink, for to-morrow we die." And so the world walks on blindly to a doom as certain, to a destruction more terrible, than was the judgment on the city of Jerusalem. Yes, the world in its temples of science, in which it denies Christ, may one day shed human blood, as the Jews of old shed it upon the pavement of the temple in which they had mocked their Lord. The destruction, the uprooting of society from its very depths may be the judgment that shall yet come upon a world which denies the presence of the Holy Spirit, as it came of old upon the doomed city that denied the presence of the Lord of Life.

On the other hand, the Church clings to the truth that this Word—intensely human as she knows and owns it to be—is also Divine; and that in it dwells the Spirit of God; that in it are the infallible oracles of God; that it is therefore as truly God's Book as it is man's book. And yet—just as the Church in her early history fell into the error of an excessive assertion of one truth, and thus lost sight of another and equally important truth concerning our Lord's real nature—so may there be the danger, so there has been, so at this moment there is the danger, of the Church—in her horror of the doctrine that this Book is merely man's word and nothing more—falling into the opposite error of maintaining that it is God's Word, and nothing else. The Church, in times past, has so insisted on the true Divinity of the written Word that she had almost forgotten its humanity. Men made of the Bible, not a supernatural book, which it is, but an unnatural book; they forgot the essential condition of all true revelation, the limitation which the Bible itself has put upon itself; that it must, if it is to serve any useful purpose, be progressive; that God, accordingly, spake at "divers times, and in divers manners"—in different degrees, and in different portions of truth—to the fathers "in times past" as He saw that they needed it; that He did not give all truth and all revelation at any one time to all men; that there was in Revelation an advance, a growth, as truly as there was in our Lord Jesus Christ in the days of His flesh, when He increased "in wisdom and stature, and in favour with God and man." The consequence of this error was that men were determined to find the whole Bible, as it were, in every text of the Bible; they were placing ever, for instance, the Old Testament exactly on a line and a level with the New; they were always forgetting the great truth that when Christ came and manifested God to man, there was and must have been a larger light, a fuller revelation, than could possibly have been before He dwelt among men; they were for ever treating the Bible as the Jews treated it, forcing on it strange and cabalistic interpretations, mysticizing, allegorizing it, giving it some meaning which seemed to them more worthy of the Divine Word than the simple truth that lay on the surface of that particular portion they were reading; they were for ever turning rhetoric into logic; vision into history; poetry into hardest and most literal prose—that is to say, they were for ever forgetting that God, in this Revelation, was using human hearts, human thought, human knowledge, human peculiarities of character, in order that in and through them His Word might be conveyed to us.

And what has been the result? Why, that the Church, at times, has trembled at the feeblest criticisms of the world upon this Word. She has shuddered when she has been told that this sentence is not good grammar, that that sentence is not perfectly accurate history, that science questions as to this, that there is some historic doubt as to that; and she has too often attempted to evade the pressure of these criticisms—by wire-drawn explanations, far-fetched harmonizings, ingenious hypotheses, which do more credit to the ability than to the candour of those who have resorted to them—instead of meeting them by the simple straightforward admission that they are, in many cases at any rate, quite valid, but that they only prove to us what we know already, that this Word is truly human, and that in spite of them we hold it to be also truly Divine. If Christians had, in this spirit of courageous faith, accepted the facts of the Bible, they would be less afraid than many of them still are, of every rash presumptuous criticism of the words of the Bible. Let us have the courage to say, once and for all, "The Bible is what God has made it for us and not what we think He ought to have made it for us." The Bible is what it is, just as truly as the world we live in is what it is, and if all the discoveries of men of science concerning the world, its nature, history, construction, can never banish from the heart of the Church the belief that it had a Divine Creator; why should all the discoveries of men of science concerning the human elements of the Bible shake, for one moment, the faith which lies deep in the heart of the Church, that as truly as the world had a Divine Creator, so truly has the Bible had a Divine

Author? In such a state of mind we should be able to encounter with courage and calmness all the criticisms of an unbelieving world. The world says, "This Book is merely human;" and we answer, "It is intensely human and yet we know it is Divine."

III. One word more. How shall we know this? The mystery of Inspiration, with its two aspects of the Divine and human, will ever present a difficulty, as we have seen, to belief on the one hand and to unbelief on the other. How shall we assure our souls that our view of it is the true one? How did the disciples assure themselves during those three years in which they accompanied their Lord? By ever drawing nearer and nearer to their Master's presence, by listening more and more to His words, by throwing their hearts more and more open to the Divine teaching and light that came from Him, there grew in their souls—they could not have told how or why—a deepening conviction that He was not as other men; and so they passed on to the miracle which changed their trembling trust into assured faith by the certain fact of the Resurrection. In the same way, and in no other, can we deepen in our own souls the conviction of the Divinity of God's Word. It must be by familiar knowledge of it; it must be by laying our hearts bare to all its influences, tearing away the wrappings and concealments of pride and prejudice and suffering this Word to work in us the great miracles of resurrection to life and of ascension to dwell in heavenly places with Jesus Christ our Lord. It is as we study the Bible; as we make it the rule of our life, as we have recourse to it in our hours of sorrow and weakness, trial and temptation, that we find in it ever some Word of God that reaches our souls as no merely human word has ever reached or could reach them. It is as we gather from it our consolation in sorrow, our strength in trial, our courage in adversity, our patience in trouble; it is as we gain from it daily light on our path through the world's tangled wilderness of temptation and sin, that it shall become, in the light of its own revealing, the manifestation of God to us. In no other way shall we be able to hold fast by the Bible. Leave its words outside your hearts, and then the "enemy" will only too easily snatch away that Divine seed from the stony ground of merely mental assent on which you have allowed it to rest. But let that Word sink deep into the soil of your hearts; let them close over it as the earth closes over the seed cast upon it; and then—safe hidden there in the very innermost core of your being from the blighting breath of blasting scepticism, from the furtive hand of the tempter—the seed shall germinate and spring up in green leaf and ripening fruit, and you shall know that the power that makes it so to live and grow in you is not less Divine than is the power that quickens into life and fruit the seed which human hands cast into the ground, but of which God gives the increase.

The Society for which I plead to-day is giving you year by year this very evidence, the evidence of souls which have been quickened by the Bible and which have known it therefore to be the very Word of God. As you send out this Book to every nation and race under heaven, what is the fate of this Word as it goes forth? Never to return again void! It will meet, as He met of old, now with denial, contempt, rejection, hatred, and now with the loving disciple who drawing near to the incarnate Word that it reveals to him, finds in Him the life of all his life, the joy and renovation of his soul; and, as he tells you he has found that, he gives you one evidence more that this Book is from God. And so, as we distribute this most precious gift of God, it never fails to come back to us enriched with some fresh evidence of its Divine origin. It goes out from us with our prayers, it comes back to us with the thanks and blessings of human souls and hearts. Marked by the hard hands of the toiler; stained with the tears of the penitent; worn by long use on sick and dying beds; every such stain and wear is, as it were, a fresh clasp of gold, a fresh adornment of pearls to the Book of books, the priceless gift of our Father in Heaven. Infinitely rich then is the return which God gives us for the effort we make in His cause. As we send forth the Book for Him, He gives it back to us with added proof that it has come from Him. My brethren, persevere then in your distribution of this Book; but see, above and before all things, that you make it first your own in your hearts and lives. So will there ever deepen in your hearts the conviction that it is God's gift to you; that it is, in a very true and a very real sense, the Word of God dwelling amongst us and blessing us with all the infinite blessings of that Divine Presence.

LONDON:
PRINTED BY J. S. VIRTUE AND CO., LIMITED,
CITY ROAD.

www.ingramcontent.com/pod-product-compliance
Lightning Source LLC
Chambersburg PA
CBHW021152230426
43667CB00006B/358